OMNIVM LVX CIVIVM

**BOSTON
PUBLIC
LIBRARY**

D1472613

THE BOOK OF
CLASSICAL MUSIC LISTS

THE BOOK OF
CLASSICAL MUSIC LISTS

HERBERT KUPFERBERG

Facts on File Publications
New York, N.Y.

The Book of Classical Music Lists

Copyright © 1985 by Herbert Kupferberg

All rights reserved. No part of this book may be reproduced or utilized in any form or by any means, electronic or mechanical, including photocopying, recording or by any information storage and retrieval systems, without permission in writing from the Publisher.

Library of Congress Cataloging-in-Publication Data
Kupferberg, Herbert.
  The book of classical music lists.

  Includes index.
  1. Music—Miscellanea.   2. Music—Bibliography.
I. Title.
ML63.K88   1985   016.78   85-20613
ISBN 0-8160-1163-X

Printed in the United States of America

10 9 8 7 6 5 4 3 2 1

To my favorite list

Barbara
Frieda
Jeanie
Dr. Joe
Joel
Natalie
Seth

CONTENTS

PREFACE

This book began as a lark and ended as a labor—though, I add quickly, a labor of love. My original idea had been to compile a book of musical lists consisting entirely of trivia and oddities—a category to which music-lovers are addicted no less incurably than baseball fans or moviegoers. More or less for my own satisfaction, I began jotting down such useless but fascinating lists as the names of Johann Sebastian Bach's 20 children, the names of composers with three letters or less, the works that have been named after cities, animals, insects and other unlikely objects, and all the Dons I could find in opera, starting with Don Giovanni and ending with over 100 others (undoubtedly there are at least 100 more that I've missed).

As I continued amassing such arcane but stimulating data, I began to realize that there also were other, more serious lists to be compiled—lists that might actually be of some use to listeners, that could help to systematize or broaden their musical knowledge by conveying information in a logical, understandable form.

I hope that I have not altogether lost sight of my objective of providing musical fun and enjoyment. But in some of the more sober lists, such as Shakespeare's Plays in Music, Women Composers, and Musicians Who Escaped the Nazis (as well as those who unfortunately did not), my aim has been to illuminate some important aspects of music that are worthy of more attention than they generally receive.

I am well aware that many of these lists could have been longer; contemporary composers especially have been somewhat slighted since I have no desire to anticipate the judgment of posterity. For any other omissions I can only plead forgetfulness, ignorance, the exigencies of space, and the brevity of life itself.

For the most part, this book consists of "reading lists"—that is, lists with commentaries and explanations that (I hope) enhance their meaning and usefulness. However, some of the purely statistical lists, such as the complete roster of operas performed at the Metropolitan Opera during its first 101 years and the most popular works in the repertory of the "Big Five" U.S. symphony orchestras, offer information not readily accessible or available elsewhere.

In style I have sought clarity rather than consistency, using, for example, the English name for *The Barber of Seville* but sticking to the

Italian for *La Traviata*. The full names of composers are included in basic lists and in others where they seem appropriate; otherwise, to avoid repetition, only last names are given.

During a break in my researches I chanced to pick up Umberto Eco's novel *The Name of the Rose* and was pleased to come upon this remark: "There is nothing more wonderful than a list, instrument of wondrous hypotyposis." In common, I am sure, with thousands of other readers, I forthwith looked up *hypotyposis* in my dictionary and found the following definition: "Lifelike depiction of a thing or scene."

I hope that, in a small way, this book provides its own hypotyposis, that is, a lifelike depiction of music and its scene.

Herbert Kupferberg
New York, New York

PART I
OVERTURE

TWELVE DEFINITIONS OF MUSIC

What is music, anyhow? People have been offering definitions, descriptions, aphorisms, and witticisms for hundreds of years without arriving at any consensus on the question. Here, in chronological order, are a dozen attempts, mainly by non-musicians, to characterize music:

Music, moody food of us that trade in love.
   (William Shakespeare, *Antony and Cleopatra*, c.1606)

Music, the greatest good that mortals know,
And all of heaven we have below.
   (Joseph Addison, "Song for St. Cecilia's Day," 1694)

It is the only sensual pleasure without vice.
   (Dr. Samuel Johnson, remark, 1776)

Music is the moonlight in the gloomy night of life.
   (Jean Paul Richter, *Titan*, 1803)

Music is the universal language of mankind.
   (Henry Wadsworth Longfellow, *Outre-Mer*, 1834)

Music is well said to be the speech of angels.
   (Thomas Carlyle, *Essays: The Opera*, 1840)

The only cheap and unpunished rapture upon earth.
   (Sydney Smith, letter, 1844)

Music is love in search of a word.
   (Sidney Lanier, *The Symphony*, 1875)

Cathedrals in sound.
   (Alfred Bruneau, speech at a statue of César Franck in Paris, 1904)

Music is, first of all, motion; after that emotion.
   (James Huneker, *Old Fogy*, 1913)

Music, *n.* An art of sound in time which expresses ideas and emotions in significant forms through the elements of rhythm, melody, harmony and color.
   (*The Random House Dictionary of the English Language*, 1967)

I'll play it first and tell you what it is later.
   (Miles Davis, c.1970)

EIGHT CONTRA MUSIC

On the other hand, you can't please everybody. Following are some negative views of music:

Indulged in to excess, music emasculates instead of invigorating the mind, causing a relaxation of the intellectual faculties, and debasing the warrior into an effeminate slave, destitute of all nerve and energy of soul.
  (Plato, *The Republic*, c. 370 B.C.)

Music helps not the toothache.
  (George Herbert, *Jacula Prudentum*, 1651)

Nothing is capable of being well set to music that is not nonsense.
  (Joseph Addison, *The Spectator*, March 21, 1711)

If you love music, hear it; go to operas, concerts, and pay fiddlers to play to you; but I insist on your neither piping nor fiddling yourself. It puts a gentleman in a very frivolous, contemptible light.
  (Lord Chesterfield, letter to his son, April 19, 1749)

That which isn't worth saying is sung.
  (Figaro in Beaumarchais, *The Barber of Seville*, 1775)

I could never understand what a note of music is, or how one should differ from another.
  (Charles Lamb, *A Chapter on Ears*, 1821)

Music sweeps by me like a messenger
Carrying a message that is not for me.
  (George Eliot, *The Spanish Gypsy*, 1868)

A polite form of self-imposed torture, the concert.
  (Henry Miller, *Tropic of Cancer*, 1934)

MUSIC AS A REMEDY

The Anatomy of Melancholy by Robert Burton (1577–1640) is a curious assemblage of information and speculation about the human condition as viewed by an early 17th-century English churchman, scholar, and writer. One of its chapters deals with the uses of music as a cure for depression, care, and sorrow. Five excerpts follow:

Musick is a tonick to the saddened soul, a Roaring Meg* against Melancholy, to rear and revive the languishing soul, affecting not only

---

*Roaring Meg was a powerful cannon of the time.

the ears, but the very arteries, the vital and animal spirits; it erects the mind, and makes it nimble.

It will . . . in the most dull, severe, and sorrowful souls, expel grief with mirth, and if there be any clouds, dust, or dregs of care yet lurking in our thoughts, most powerfully it wipes them all away, and that which is more, it will perform all this in an instant: cheer up the countenance, expel austerity, bring in hilarity, inform our manners, mitigate anger.

It makes a child quiet, the nurse's song; and many times the sound of a trumpet on a sudden, bells ringing, a carman's whistle, a boy singing some Ballad tune early in the street, alters, revives, recreates, a restless patient that cannot sleep in the night.

Your Princes, Emperors, and persons of any quality maintain it in their Courts: no mirth without Musick.

Many men are melancholy by hearing Musick, but it is a pleasing melancholy that it causeth.

WILLIAM BYRD'S EIGHT REASONS FOR SINGING

William Byrd (1543–1623) was the first of the great English composers. The leading musician of the Elizabethan era, he was a renowned organist and in one of the obituaries that followed his death was described as a "Father of Musicke." He also wrote on music, and in the preface to his *Psalmes, Sonnets & Songs,* published in 1588, he set down these reasons "to perswade every one to learne to sing":

1. It is a knowledge easely taught and quickly learned, where there is a good Master and an apt Scoller.
2. The exercise of singing is delightfull to Nature and good to preserve the health of Man.
3. It doth strengthen all parts of the brest, and doth open the pipes.
4. It is a singular good remedie for stamering in the speech.
5. It is the best meanes to procure a perfect pronunciation, and to make a good Orator.
6. It is the onely way to know where Nature hath bestowed the benefit of a good voyce; which guift is so rare as there is not one among a thousand that hath it; and in many that excellent guift is lost because they want Art to express Nature.
7. There is not any Musicke of Instruments whatsoever comparable to that which is made of the voyces of men, where the voyces are good and the same well sorted and ordered.

5

8. The better the voyce is, the meeter it is to honour and serve God therewith; and the voyce of man is chiefely to be employed to that ende.

> Since singing is so good a thing,
> I wish all men would learne to sing.

SCHUMANN'S MAXIMS

In 1848 the composer Robert Schumann published a list of "House Rules and Maxims for Young Musicians." Here are 20 of them that are still applicable today:

You must practice scales and other finger exercises assiduously. There are people, however, who think they may achieve great ends by doing this; for many years, for many hours, they practice mechanical exercises. That makes as much sense as trying to recite the alphabet faster and faster every day. Put your time to better use.

"Silent keyboards" have been invented; practice on them for a while, just to see how worthless they are. Silent people cannot teach us to speak.

Don't be afraid of words like "theory," "thorough-bass" and "counterpoint." They will meet you halfway if you do likewise.

Never strum along! Always play energetically and never fail to finish the piece you have begun.

Dragging and hurrying are equally great faults.

Try to play easy pieces well. It's better than playing difficult ones badly.

You must reach the point where you can hear the music from the printed page.

Always play as though a master were present.

Never play bad compositions, and never listen to them unless you absolutely have to.

Don't be led astray by applause bestowed on great virtuosos. The applause of a great artist is more to be cherished than that of the majority.

If everybody insisted on playing first violin, there would be no orchestras. Respect every musician in his own field.

As you grow older, converse more frequently with scores than with virtuosos.

There's much to be learned from singers, male and female. But don't believe everything they tell you.

Never lose an opportunity to practice on the organ. No instrument takes a swifter revenge on anything unclear in composition and playing.

Sing regularly in choruses, especially the middle voices. This will make you more musical.

Never miss an opportunity of hearing a good opera.

Honor the old, but also welcome the new. Hold no prejudice against unknown names.

Don't judge a work on first hearing; that which pleases the most at first is not always the best. Masters call for study. Many things will only become clear to you with age.

Have an open eye for life and for the other arts and sciences.

Art was not created as a way to riches. Strive to become a true artist; the rest will take care of itself.

ADDENDUM

Some day I must write a supplement to Schumann's Advice to Young Musicians. The title will be Advice to Old Musicians; and the first precept will run, "Don't be in a hurry to contradict G.B.S., as he never commits himself on a musical subject until he knows at least six times as much about it as you do."

George Bernard Shaw, *The World* (London, January 18, 1893)

RICHARD STRAUSS'S TEN GOLDEN RULES FOR THE ALBUM OF A YOUNG CONDUCTOR

Richard Strauss was not only one of the greatest late Romantic composers; he was also a conductor of importance. These Ten Golden Rules for young conductors were published in 1922:

1. Remember that you are making music not to amuse yourself but to please your audience.
2. Don't perspire while conducting—only the audience should get warm.
3. Conduct *Salomé* and *Elektra* as if they were by Mendelssohn: fairy music.

4. Never look encouragingly at the brass, except with a quick glance to give an important cue.
5. But never let the horns and woodwinds out of sight; if you can hear them at all, they're still too loud.
6. If you think the brass is not blowing hard enough, tone them down another shade or two.
7. It isn't enough that you yourself hear every word the soloist sings—you know it by heart anyway. The audience must be able to follow easily. If people don't understand the words they will go to sleep.
8. Always accompany a singer in such a way that he can sing without effort.
9. When you think you have reached the limits of prestissimo, go twice as fast.
10. If you follow these rules carefully you will, with your fine gifts and great accomplishments, always be the darling of your listeners.

PART II

COMPOSERS AND COMPOSITIONS

MUSICAL EPOCHS AND THEIR COMPOSERS

Music is as old as humankind. We have little knowledge of what ancient music, such as that of the Greeks and Romans, sounded like. However, works survive from the medieval era onward. Most of the earliest music preserved to us is liturgical, but secular music gradually began to appear, and both types have coexisted to the present. Following is a listing of the major musical epochs, with representative composers from each, along with some of their achievements:

MEDIEVAL (600 A.D.–1425)

Leonin (mid-12th century).
Magnus Liber Organum

Perotin (late 12th century).
Sederunt Principes

Adam de la Halle (c.1240–1287).
Le Jeu de Robin et Marion

Philippe de Vitry (1291–1361).
Ars Nova (a treatise on a new, free style of composing)

Guillaume de Machaut (c.1300–1377).
Notre Dame Mass (first complete mass by one composer)

RENAISSANCE (1425–1600)

Guillaume Dufay (c.1400–1474).
masses, motets, hymns

Johannes Ockeghem (c.1420–1496).
masses, motets, chansons

Josquin des Prez (c.1440–1521).
Lament on the Death of Ockeghem, Missa L'Homme Armé, masses, motets, chansons, ballades

Roland de Lassus (1532–1594).
masses, magnificats, psalms, chansons, madrigals

Giovanni Pierluigi da Palestrina (c.1525–1594).
100 masses, including the *Pope Marcellus Mass,* motets, hymns, lamentations

BAROQUE (1600–1750)

Giovanni Gabrieli (1557–1612).
canzoni for brass choirs, *Symphoniae Sacrae*, madrigals, organ works

Claudio Monteverdi (1567–1643).
operas, madrigals, masses, motets, vespers

Arcangelo Corelli (1653–1713).
concerti grossi, including "Christmas" Concerto, trio sonatas, violin sonatas

Henry Purcell (1659–1695).
operas, anthems, odes, chamber music, keyboard works

François Couperin (1668–1733).
Over 200 Pièces de Clavecin for keyboard; religious choral works

Antonio Vivaldi (c.1675–1741).
454 concertos, including The Four Seasons, 40 operas, chamber music, choral music

Georg Philipp Telemann (1681–1767).
Musique de Table, chamber music, keyboard music, choral music

Johann Sebastian Bach (1685–1750).
6 Brandenburg concertos, *Well-Tempered Clavier*, "Goldberg" Variations, English Suites, French Suites, *Musical Offering*, *St. Matthew Passion*, Mass in B Minor, manifold instrumental and choral works, including 198 sacred cantatas

George Frideric Handel (1685–1759).
40 operas, 20 oratorios including *Messiah*, anthems, hymns, 12 concerti grossi, numerous works for orchestra including *Water Music* and *Royal Fireworks Music*

CLASSICAL (1750–1825)

Carl Philipp Emanuel Bach (1714–1788).
symphonies, concertos, chamber music, keyboard pieces

Christoph Willibald von Gluck (1714–1787).
many operas, 11 symphonies, ballets, chamber music, songs

Joseph Haydn (1732–1809).
104 symphonies, 84 string quartets, 125 trios, 52 piano sonatas, 25 concertos, 24 operas, 12 masses, 10 oratorios and cantatas

Muzio Clementi (1752–1832).
Gradus ad Parnassum, 106 piano sonatas, symphonies, overtures

Wolfgang Amadeus Mozart (1756–1791).
49 symphonies (41 numbered in sequence), 27 piano concertos, 5 violin concertos, 26 string quartets, 7 string quintets, 31 diverti-

mentos, serenades, cassations, 20 piano sonatas and fantasias, 16 operas, 15 masses, various concertos, choral works, and orchestral pieces, including *Eine Kleine Nachtmusik*

Luigi Cherubini (1760–1842).
Symphony in D, 6 string quartets, 2 requiems, 30 operas

Ludwig van Beethoven (1770–1827).
9 symphonies, 5 piano concertos, 1 violin concerto, 1 triple concerto (piano, violin, cello), 16 string quartets, 10 violin-piano sonatas, 5 cello-piano sonatas, 2 masses, many other works including chamber music, incidental music, overtures, variations, songs, dances, piano pieces

ROMANTIC (1820–1880)

Carl Maria von Weber (1786–1826).
2 symphonies, Konzertstück for piano and orchestra, 8 operas, orchestral pieces including *Invitation to the Dance*, concertos for various instruments and chamber music

Franz Schubert (1797–1828).
8 symphonies, 15 string quartets, 15 piano sonatas, 7 masses, 600 songs including cycles *Die Schöne Müllerin* and *Winterreise*, 15 stage works, incidental music to *Rosamunde* and other orchestral works, piano pieces and chamber music

Hector Berlioz (1803–1869).
Symphonie Fantastique, Harold in Italy, Romeo and Juliet, 3 operas, 3 overtures, *Requiem*, other choral works

Felix Mendelssohn (1809–1847).
5 symphonies, 2 piano concertos, 1 violin concerto, 6 string quartets and other chamber music, 2 oratorios, overtures and other orchestral works including incidental music to *A Midsummer Night's Dream, Songs Without Words* and other piano pieces

Robert Schumann (1810–1856).
4 symphonies, 1 piano concerto, 1 cello concerto, 3 string quartets, other chamber music, piano works including *Carnaval* and *Kinderszenen*, songs including cycles *Frauenliebe und Leben* and *Dichterliebe*, 1 opera

Frédéric Chopin (1810–1849).
virtually all works for piano including: 51 mazurkas, 27 etudes, 24 preludes, 19 nocturnes, 17 waltzes, 10 polonaises, 3 sonatas, 2 concertos

Franz Liszt (1811–1886).
13 symphonic poems, 2 piano concertos, *Faust Symphony, Dante Symphony*, 20 Hungarian Rhapsodies, 2 oratorios, many piano works

Johannes Brahms (1833–1897).
   4 symphonies, 2 piano concertos, 1 violin concerto, 1 double concerto (violin, cello), 2 overtures, *Variations on a Theme by Haydn*, 3 string quartets, 3 piano quartets and other chamber music, 3 piano sonatas and other piano works, including variations, 3 violin sonatas, *A German Requiem*, other choral works, 200 songs

Camille Saint-Saëns (1835–1921).
   3 symphonies, 5 piano concertos, 3 violin concertos, *Danse Macabre, Carnival of the Animals, Samson et Dalila* (opera), Introduction and Rondo Capriccioso

Peter Ilyich Tchaikovsky (1840–1893).
   6 symphonies, 3 piano concertos, 1 violin concerto, 3 ballets, 11 operas, orchestral suites, overtures, overture-fantasias, 3 string quartets and other chamber music, songs

NATIONALIST (1860–1910)

Bedřich Smetana (Czech, 1824–1884).
   Má Vlast (My Country) orchestral cycle, chamber music, 8 operas

Antonin Dvořák (Czech, 1841–1904).
   9 symphonies, 1 piano concerto, 1 violin concerto, 1 cello concerto, 13 string quartets and other chamber music, songs, piano works, Slavonic Dances

Edvard Grieg (Norwegian, 1843–1907).
   Peer Gynt Suites and other orchestral works, piano concerto, chamber music, songs, piano pieces

Nikolai Rimsky-Korsakov (Russian, 1844–1908).
   Scheherazade, Capriccio Espagnol and other orchestral works, 15 operas

Leoš Janáček (Czech, 1854–1928).
   10 operas, symphonic works, choral works, songs

Edward Elgar (British, 1857–1934).
   Enigma Variations, 2 symphonies, choral works, concertos, marches

Jean Sibelius (Finnish, 1865–1957).
   7 symphonies, 1 violin concerto, tone poems, songs

Charles Ives (American, 1874–1954).
   4 symphonies, other orchestral works, chamber music, piano pieces including *Concord* Sonata, songs

POST-ROMANTIC (1880–1910)

César Franck (1822–1890).
   Symphony in D Minor, 4 symphonic poems, chamber music, organ pieces

Anton Bruckner (1824–1890).
9 symphonies, 3 masses, choral works

Gustav Mahler (1860–1911).
9 symphonies (10th unfinished), song cycles, songs

Richard Strauss (1864–1949).
symphonic poems including *Don Juan, Till Eulenspiegel, Thus Spoke Zarathustra*, concertos, songs, chamber music, 14 operas

Sergei Rachmaninov (1873–1943).
4 piano concertos, 3 symphonies, Rhapsody on a Theme by Paganini, many piano pieces

IMPRESSIONIST (1890–1920)

Claude Debussy (1862–1920).
3 Nocturnes and other works for orchestra, piano pieces, chamber music, 1 opera

Maurice Ravel (1875–1937).
works for orchestra including *Boléro* and *La Valse*, 2 piano concertos, ballet music, chamber music, piano pieces, songs

MODERN (1910–   )

Arnold Schoenberg (1874–1951).
Verklärte Nacht, Gurre-lieder, Pierrot Lunaire, violin concerto, *5 Pieces for Orchestra*, chamber music, piano pieces

Béla Bartók (1881–1945).
Concerto for Orchestra, 6 string quartets, 3 piano concertos, stage works, *Mikrokosmos* and other piano pieces

Igor Stravinsky (1882–1971).
Fire Bird, Petrouchka, Rite of Spring and other ballets and stage works, symphonies and concertos and other orchestral works, 2 operas, choral works, chamber music

Anton Webern (1883–1945).
symphony for small orchestra, chamber music, 3 cantatas

Alban Berg (1885–1935).
Three Pieces for Orchestra, violin concerto, chamber music, 2 operas

Sergei Prokofiev (1891–1953).
7 symphonies, 5 piano concertos, 2 violin concertos, 9 piano sonatas, film scores, chamber music, 6 ballets, 7 operas

Aaron Copland (1900–   ).
3 symphonies, ballets including *Appalachian Spring, Billy the Kid, Rodeo; El Salon Mexico, Lincoln Portrait* and other orchestral works; film scores; chamber music

Dmitri Shostakovich (1906–1975).
   15 symphonies, 15 string quartets, other chamber music, piano pieces including 24 preludes and fugues, songs, 2 operas

Benjamin Britten (1913–1976).
   orchestral works including *Young Person's Guide to the Orchestra*, chamber music, songs, choral works, 8 operas

COMPOSERS AND MORTALITY

Composers tend to live rather long lives—except, of course, for those who don't. The musical mortality tables offer distinguished examples of both extremes:

COMPOSERS WHO DIED BEFORE 40

	AGE AT DEATH
Vincenzo Bellini (1801–1835)	33
Georges Bizet (1838–1875)	36
Frédéric Chopin (1810–1849)	39
George Gershwin (1898–1937)	38
Felix Mendelssohn (1809–1847)	38
Wolfgang Amadeus Mozart (1756–1791)	35
Otto Nicolai (1810–1849)	38
Giovanni Battista Pergolesi (1710–1736)	26
Henry Purcell (1659–1695)	36
Franz Schubert (1797–1828)	31
Carl Maria von Weber (1786–1826)	39

COMPOSERS WHO LIVED PAST 80

	AGE AT DEATH
Gustav Charpentier (1860–1956)	95
Luigi Cherubini (1760–1842)	81
Ernst von Dohnanyi (1877–1960)	82
Johann Adolph Hasse (1699–1783)	84
Josquin des Prez (1440–1521)	81
Charles Koechlin (1867–1950)	83
Frank Martin (1890–1974)	84
Pietro Mascagni (1863–1945)	81
Darius Milhaud (1892–1974)	81
Walter Piston (1894–1976)	82
Carl Ruggles (1876–1971)	95
Camille Saint-Saëns (1835–1921)	86

Heinrich Schütz (1585–1672)	87
Jean Sibelius (1865–1957)	91
Richard Strauss (1864–1949)	85
Igor Stravinsky (1882–1971)	88
Georg Philipp Telemann (1681–1767)	86
Edgar Varèse (1883–1965)	81
Giuseppe Verdi (1813–1901)	88
Ralph Vaughan Williams (1872–1958)	85

COMPOSERS' CAUSE OF DEATH

The medical histories of composers of the past continue to fascinate succeeding generations. Medical science, of course, has advanced greatly in recent years, leading in some cases to a re-evaluation of diagnoses made at the time, many of which were vague and generalized. The following are the best recent estimates of the nature of the fatal diseases suffered by some leading composers:

COMPOSER	CAUSE OF DEATH	AGE AT DEATH
Bach	Cerebral accident (stroke) following an unsuccessful operation on his eyes.	65
Bartók	Leukemia	64
Beethoven	Cirrhosis of the liver was the 19th-century diagnosis, with syphilis mentioned as a contributory factor, but some modern investigators believe the cause was lupus erythematosus, a rare disease	56
Berg	Infection from a septic insect bite	50
Berlioz	Cerebral accident	65
Bizet	Angina pectoris complicated by rheumatoid arthritis	36
Brahms	Cancer of the liver	63
Chopin	Pulmonary tuberculosis	39
Debussy	Cancer of the rectum	56
Delius	Syphilis, with symptoms including blindness and paralysis	72
Dvořák	Cerebral accident	63
Elgar	Brain tumor	76
Gershwin	Brain tumor	38
Grieg	Coronary artery disease with angina pectoris	64

COMPOSER	CAUSE OF DEATH	AGE AT DEATH
Haydn	Arteriosclerosis	77
Liszt	Pneumonia	74
Mahler	Subacute bacterial endocarditis complicated by pneumonia	50
Mendelssohn	Cerebral accident	38
Mozart	"Heated miliary fever" was given as the cause of death at the time; the modern diagnosis is Bright's Disease or nephritis. The theory that Mozart was poisoned, by his rival Antonio Salieri or anybody else, is generally discounted today.	36
Prokofiev	Cerebral hemorrhage	61
Puccini	Cancer of the throat	65
Rachmaninov	Malignant melanoma	69
Ravel	Brain disease, possibly a tumor	62
Rimsky-Korsakov	Coronary artery disease with angina pectoris	64
Rossini	Cancer of the rectum	76
Schubert	Typhoid fever complicated by the effects of syphilis	31
Scriabin	Infection of a facial carbuncle	43
Tchaikovsky	Cholera, probably from drinking unboiled water during the epidemic of 1893 in St. Petersburg	53
Wagner	Coronary heart disease with angina pectoris	69
Weber	Pulmonary tuberculosis and ulcerated larynx	39

COMPOSERS WHO DIED UNNATURAL DEATHS

Charles-Henri Valentin Alkan (real name Morhange, 1813–1888). Alkan, a French eccentric, composed almost exclusively for the piano, of which he was a master. His death occurred at the age of 74 in his Paris home. He was reaching for a copy of the Talmud on a high shelf of Jewish religious books when the entire bookcase fell down and crushed him.

Ernest Chausson (1855–1899). Chausson, the composer of the *Poème* for violin and orchestra, a Symphony in B-flat, and other works still in the repertory, died at Limay, in the Seine-et-Oise, at 44, of injuries sustained in a bicycle accident.

Enrique Granados (1867–1916). This Spanish composer was returning from the world premiere of his opera *Goyescas* at the Metropolitan Opera in New York when his ship, the S.S. Sussex, was sunk by a German submarine in the English Channel on March 24, 1916. Granados drowned at the age of 48.

Jean Marie Leclair (1697–1764). A celebrated French violinist and composer of 48 violin sonatas, Leclair was stabbed to death in his own house in Paris. No one was ever apprehended for the crime, and it is suspected that his estranged wife—who also was the publisher and engraver of his music—may have been responsible.

Jean-Baptiste Lully (1632–1687). Lully, born in Florence, Italy, as Giovanni Battista Lulli, adopted a French spelling of his name when he moved to France, where he became Louis XIV's favorite composer. While conducting, he inadvertently struck his foot a hard blow with a pointed cane he used as a baton; gangrene and blood poisoning set in, and he died at 54.

Alessandro Stradella (1644–1682). The composer of many oratorios and operas, Stradella was murdered in Genoa by parties unknown. He had survived a previous assault in Venice by a nobleman whose mistress he had run off with. Friedrich von Flotow, the composer of *Martha*, wrote a successful opera about Stradella in 1844.

Anton von Webern (1883–1945). The influential 12-tone composer was shot and killed by an American military policeman at the age of 61 when, unaware that an evening curfew had been established by the Allied occupying forces, he stepped out of the house of his daughter, with whom he was staying in Mittersill, near Salzburg.

COMPOSERS WHO DIED INSANE

Emmanuel Chabrier (1841–1894). The last three years of this French composer's life were spent in a state of mental and physical collapse, producing melancholia, paralysis, and death.

Gaetano Donizetti (1797–1848). After suffering for years from headaches and depression, he was stricken with paralysis and died in an institution at Bergamo.

Antonio Salieri (1750–1825). "His body suffers all the pains of infirm old age, and his mind has gone," reported a Viennese journal in 1825. Salieri was Mozart's rival and had been accused of poisoning him. Few people believed at the time that he had actually done so, but the rumors preyed on his mind, and he was demented for the last two years of his life.

Robert Schumann (1810–1856). Signs of mental instability first surfaced in his early 20s and recurred a decade later. In 1854 he attempted suicide, and two years later he died in an asylum at Endenich, near Bonn.

Bedřich Smetana (1824–1884). Smetana's growing deafness preyed on his mind, as did the intrigue of his opponents in Bohemian musical circles. He finally broke down and died in an asylum.

Hugo Wolf (1860–1903). Even as his fame as a song-composer grew, Wolf exhibited signs of mental derangement. He attempted suicide by drowning, was committed to an institution, lapsed into total irrationality, and died.

PART-TIME COMPOSERS

Not all composers have made music their principal occupation. A number have busied themselves in other fields of endeavor even while writing music. These part-time composers have ranged from dilettantes like Prince Albert to musicians of greatness like Charles Ives. Here is a list of some of them:

NAME	PRINCIPAL OCCUPATION	MUSIC
Prince Albert of Saxe-Coburg-Gotha (1819–1861)	Consort of Queen Victoria of Great Britain	*Invocazione alla Armonia* for chorus and orchestra; various songs
Mily Balakirev (1837–1910)	Russian railway official	symphonic poem *Tamara*, overtures, symphonies
Alexander Borodin (1833–1897)	Russian chemist and scientist	*Prince Igor* and other operas; *On the Steppes of Central Asia* and other orchestral works
John Alden Carpenter (1876–1951)	American businessman	*Krazy Kat, Skyscrapers* (ballet scores); *Adventures in a Perambulator* (symphonic suite)
César Cui (1853–1918)	Russian military engineer	6 operas, orchestral works, chamber music
Frederick II, the Great (1712–1786)	Emperor of Prussia	25 flute sonatas, 4 flute concertos, other works
Francis Hopkinson (1737–1791)	American writer and statesman, signer of	*Ode to Music,* My Days Have Been So

NAME	PRINCIPAL OCCUPATION	MUSIC
	the Declaration of Independence	Wond'rous Free; *The Temple of Minerva*
Charles Ives (1874–1954)	American insurance company executive	5 symphonies, many orchestral works, piano pieces and songs, nearly all innovative and original
Leopold I of Hapsburg (1640–1705)	Holy Roman Emperor	7 operas, 15 oratorios, 17 ballets, 2 masses, and other works
Modest Mussorgsky (1839–1881)	Russian civil servant	*Boris Godunov* and other operas; *Songs and Dances of Death*; others
François André Philidor (1726–1795)	French chess master	comic operas including *Sancho Pança* and *Tom Jones*; grand operas; church and chamber music
Jean-Jacques Rousseau (1712–1778)	French philosopher	arias and songs; *Le Devin du Village (The Village Soothsayer)*, an opera
Norodom Sihanouk (1922–)	(former) King of Cambodia	military marches and songs; played saxophone and led his own jazz band
Donald Francis Tovey (1875–1940)	British musical analyst and scholar	his compositions (little played today) include chamber works, a cello concerto, and piano music

COMPOSERS IN—AND OUT OF—WEDLOCK

Romantic love is frequently celebrated by composers in their music, and it frequently motivates their personal lives as well. The following list examines the marital state or lack thereof of a number of composers. In deference to the mutability of such matters, the list does not include living composers:

HAPPILY MARRIED COMPOSERS

COMPOSER	WIFE (MAIDEN NAME)	
Bach	Maria Barbara Bach Anna Magdalena Wülken	Bach's first wife, who died after 14 years of marriage, was a cousin; his second, an excellent soprano, helped him with musical tasks such as copying.
Bartók	Marta Ziegler	He dedicated his opera *Bluebeard's Castle* to her.
Bizet	Geneviève Halévy	She was the daughter of Fromental Halévy, composer of the opera *La Juive*.
Dvořák	Anna Cermakova	Her parents opposed the match, but Anna—energetic and practical—turned out to be just what Dvořák needed.
Franck	Felicité Desmousseaux	Her parents, both actors at the Comédie-Française, resisted the marriage but eventually consented.
Grieg	Nina Hagerup	His wife was a singer who specialized in his songs.
Mahler	Alma Maria Schindler	Alma was a composition student when they met. The marriage had its ups and downs, and Mahler consulted Sigmund Freud about his problems in 1910, but eventually their marriage worked out. After Mahler's death, Alma married first Walter Gropius, the architect, and then Franz Werfel, the writer. She also had a love affair with Oskar Kokoschka, the artist.
Mendelssohn	Cécile Jeanrenaud	Daughter of a French Protestant clergyman, she was an ideal mate for the sensitive composer. They had five children.
Mozart	Constanze Weber	Constanze was a cousin of Carl Maria von Weber and a singer of moderate abilities. Somewhat flighty during Mozart's life, she became as-

HAPPILY MARRIED COMPOSERS

COMPOSER	WIFE (MAIDEN NAME)	
		siduous in preserving his memory. She was remarried to a Danish diplomat.
Rossini	Olympie Desguilliers	Rossini's second marriage, at age 54, to a Parisian hostess was a huge success; their home became famous for its lavish entertainments. For his first marriage, see below.
Schumann	Clara Wieck	An ideal marriage, both musically and personally. Clara, a fine pianist, was a splendid interpreter of Robert's works.
Sibelius	Aino Järnefelt	Sibelius's wife was the daughter of a general, and he was just a penniless musician when they married. She kept out of the spotlight, bore him six daughters, and gave him tranquility in which to work.
Stravinsky	Catherine Nossenko Vera de Bosset Sudekeine	Stravinsky's first wife, a cousin who bore him four children, died in 1939. A year later he married Vera, a former Diaghilev dancer.
Verdi	Margherita Barezzi Giuseppina Strepponi	Margherita, daughter of Verdi's earliest sponsor, died of illness tragically young, as did their two children. Giuseppina was a famous soprano whom he married at 45 after many years of friendship.
Wagner	Cosima von Bülow	Cosima, the daughter of Franz Liszt, left her husband, the conductor Hans von Bülow, to become Richard Wagner's second wife. He was 57 at the time; for further particulars of his love life, see below.
Weill	Lotte Lenya	A musically productive marriage, with Lenya the perfect interpreter of his songs.

UNHAPPILY MARRIED COMPOSERS

COMPOSER	WIFE (MAIDEN NAME)	
Berlioz	Harriet Smithson	She was an Irish Shakespearean actress to whom Berlioz took a passion; their marriage was tempestuous and ended in separation.
Debussy	Rosalie Texier Emma Bardac	Debussy dedicated his Nocturnes to Rosalie, his first wife, under the nickname of "Lily-Lilo." However, after five apparently happy years, he abandoned her for the wife of a banker. In despair, Rosalie shot herself but recovered, and a divorce followed. His second marriage, to the wealthy Emma Bardac, lasted to the end of his life, but was marred by the social ostracism that followed his treatment of Rosalie and the loss by his new wife of much of her fortune.
Gounod	Anna Zimmermann	More or less pushed into marriage by his prospective mother-in-law, Gounod never really liked his wife. Instead he found consolation (but apparently not sexually) with an English singer, Georgina Weldon. His unfortunate wife was with him when he died.
Haydn	Maria Anna Keller	Haydn married the daughter of a Viennese hairdresser and wigmaker. He actually preferred her sister, to whom he was giving lessons, but she entered a nunnery. Frau Haydn has come down in history with a reputation as a domineering spendthrift and religious fanatic whom the composer took care to leave at home when he traveled.

UNHAPPILY MARRIED COMPOSERS

COMPOSER	WIFE (MAIDEN NAME)	
Prokofiev	Lina Llubera	Prokofiev's marriage with this Spanish-born singer broke up after 20 years over his friendship with Myra Mendelson, a young political activist.
Puccini	Elvira Gemignani	A tempestuous marriage. Puccini "stole" Elvira from a friend to whom she was wed. After *their* marriage she was insanely jealous of him, not without reason. Elvira accused a servant girl of having an affair with her husband, and the girl committed suicide, leading to a notorious court case. Eventually Puccini and his wife were reconciled.
Rossini	Isabella Colbran	Wife No. 1 was a Spanish soprano, the mistress of an impresario. She sang in his *Semiramide*. They split up after 15 years. For wife No. 2, see above.
Saint-Saëns	Marie Truffot	A puzzling case. She was 19, he 39 when they married; they had two children who died young. They separated after six years but were never divorced; she died in 1950 at age 95. There are indications that Saint-Saëns may have been homosexual.
Wagner	Minna Planer	Minna, an actress Wagner married when he was 23, was his legal wife for 25 years, but they were hardly tranquil. She endured at least two of his love affairs, with Jennie Laussot and Matilda Wesendonck. She left him in 1861, just before he took up with Cosima Liszt, who became his second wife. See above.

BACHELOR COMPOSERS

Beethoven   See list, BEETHOVEN'S "IMMORTAL BELOVED."

Brahms   On congenial terms with several women, he never married any of them. The closest he came was to Clara Schumann, 17 years his senior and the widow of his friend Robert Schumann.

Chopin   His most celebrated liaison was with the novelist George Sand; he died a year after they parted.

Handel   Crusty and blunt, he does not seem a likely prospect for marriage. Yet he was not insensitive to feminine charms; he simply had no time for them.

Liszt   Though he never married (for a time he considered entering the priesthood) Liszt became a romantic hero, with countless female admirers. His principal liaisons were with the Countess d'Agoult, who bore him three children, and the Princess Carolyne Sayn-Wittgenstein, who helped steer him from virtuoso concertizing to serious composition.

Ravel   Not only did Ravel never marry, he seems to have almost completely ignored the female sex, without even a passing liaison. He led a retired life and devoted himself almost totally to his music.

Schubert   A congenial young man with many friends, he might well have married had he lived past the age of 31.

HOMOSEXUAL COMPOSERS

Tchaikovsky   Tormented by his homosexuality, Tchaikovsky tried to keep it locked up within himself. He was involved with several young men; he also tried marriage with a young woman student, but it proved a disaster and was quickly annulled. The important woman in his life was Madame Nadezhda von Meck, his patroness, whom he never actually met.

   Tchaikovsky is the first of the great composers who was a known homosexual. The number of homosexual composers—or at least of those who avow their preference openly—has greatly increased in the 20th century.

WOMEN COMPOSERS

There has been a great upsurge of women composers in recent times, but women have been writing—as well as performing—music for hundreds of years, going back at least to St. Hildegard in the 11th century.* The following list includes some of the women composers active today as well as notable figures of the past:

Violet Archer (1913–   ). Canadian pianist and composer. She studied with Béla Bartók and Paul Hindemith and has written operas, symphonies, concertos, and chamber works.

Agathe Backer-Grondahl (1847–1907). Norwegian composer and pianist, greatly admired by George Bernard Shaw when he was a music critic.

Thekla Badarzewska (1834–1861). Polish writer of salon music. Her claim to fame is "The Maiden's Prayer."

Marion Eugenie Bauer (1887–1955). American composer and writer; composed mainly in small forms.

Amy Cheney (Mrs. H. H. A.) Beach (1867–1944). American composer. Her Gaelic Symphony, premiered by the Boston Symphony Orchestra in 1896, was the first symphonic work by an American woman.

Carrie Jacobs Bond (1862–1946). American song-writer; composer of "A Perfect Day" and "I Love You Truly."

Victoria Bond (1945–   ). American composer. Her works include a setting of Wallace Stevens's "Peter Quince at the Clavier."

Lili Boulanger (1893–1918). French composer. Younger sister of the famous teacher Nadia, she was the first woman to win the Prix de Rome with her cantata *Faust et Hélène* (1913). She died at 24.

Clémentine de Bourges (? –1561). French poetess and composer. Music signed "Clem. de Bourges" has been variously attributed to her and to a male contemporary named Clément de Bourges.

Doris Bright (1863–1951). English pianist and composer. Performed her two piano concertos with orchestras in England and Germany.

Ingeborg (Starck) Bronsart von Schellendorf (1840–1913). Swedish composer of four operas; her husband Hans also was a composer.

Francesca Caccini (1587–1640). Italian singer and composer, daughter of Giulio Caccini, one of the group that "invented" opera around

---

*An argument might be made that the oldest woman composer known to us by name is Miriam, the sister of Moses, who after the Israelite crossing of the Red Sea timbrelled out a song—presumably of her own composition—with the words "The horse and his rider hath he cast into the sea" (Exodus 15:21). George Frideric Handel later set the same text in his oratorio *Israel in Egypt*.

1600. Her *La Liberazione di Ruggiero dall'Isola d'Alcina (The Liberation of Ruggiero from the Island of Alcina)* (1625) is the first opera written by a woman. It was revived as recently as 1982 in Florence.

Cécile Chaminade (1857–1944). French composer and pianist. Despite her numerous attempts at substantial music, her salon pieces, such as the "Scarf Dance," remain her most enduring works.

Veronica Rosalie Cianchettini (1779–1833). Bohemian pianist and composer, resident in London. She was the daughter of Jan Ladislav Dussek, a celebrated keyboard virtuoso. She wrote two piano concertos and several sonatas.

Ruth Porter Crawford-Seeger (1901–1953). American composer and folksong scholar. Her serious compositions, using avant-garde techniques, gained appreciation only after her death. Among them are chamber pieces and settings of Carl Sandburg poems, as well as other vocal works. She was the wife of ethnomusicologist Charles Seeger and stepmother of folksinger Pete Seeger.

Dotie Davies (1859–1938). English composer under the pseudonym of Hope Temple. She was the wife of French operetta composer André Messager. She collaborated with him and also wrote an operetta of her own, *The Wooden Spoon*.

Hilda Dianda (1925–   ). Argentinian composer who studied with Gian Francesco Malipiero in Italy. Her works include several string quartets and other chamber music, much of it ultra-modern.

Lucia Dlogoszewski (1931–   ). American composer; student of Edgar Varèse and strongly influenced by him. Uses a timbre piano and other percussive devices. Among her titles: *Music for the Left Ear in a Small Room*. Many of her works are for the dance.

Sophie Hutchinson Drinker (1888–1968). American composer. Herself an amateur composer, she devoted much time and effort to the advancement of women musicians. She was the wife of musical scholar Henry S. Drinker.

Vivian Fine (1913–   ). American composer. Her varied works include two ballets. She wrote *A Guide to the Life Expectancy of a Rose*, composed to the text of an article on gardening.

Eliza Flower (1803–1846). English composer of hymns and anthems, who wrote the music of "Nearer My God to Thee" to a text by her sister.

Ruth Gipps (1921–   ). English conductor and composer, a student of Ralph Vaughan Williams. She has composed four symphonies, an oratorio entitled *The Cat*, and a piece for double bassoon and chamber orchestra.

Peggy Glanville-Hicks (1912–   ). Australian composer and critic. Her operas include *The Transposed Heads* (1954) and *Nausicaa* (1961).

Catherine Hamilton (1738–1782). English harpsichordist and composer, married to Sir William Hamilton, British ambassador at Naples. Only one of her pieces, a minuet, has survived. She met Wolfgang Amadeus Mozart when he was 14 and, according to Mozart's father, "trembled" when she was requested to play before him. After her death her successor as Lady Hamilton was Emma Lyon, the inamorata of Lord Nelson.

St. Hildegard of Bingen (1098–1179). German composer and mystic. She headed a convent of 18 nuns outside of Bingen near Mainz. She composed plainsong melodies to be sung as part of the morality plays she put on, and also wrote masses and other religious works.

Imogen Holst (1907–1984). English composer. Many of her pieces are for the piano. Most of her musical activities were devoted to propagating the works of her father Gustav Holst, composer of *The Planets.*

Helen Hopekirk (1856–1945). Scottish pianist and composer who settled in Boston. She played her own piano concerto with the Boston Symphony in 1900.

Natalia Janotha (1856–1932). Polish pianist and composer who studied with Clara Schumann and Johannes Brahms. She wrote piano pieces in the manner of Chopin.

Betsy Jolas (1926–   ). French composer of American parentage. Many of her works have French titles, but "O Wall," a "mini-opera," takes its inspiration from the Pyramus and Thisby episode of Shakespeare's *A Midsummer Night's Dream.*

Josephine Lang (1815–1880). German song composer. Felix Mendelssohn admired her Lieder and her manner of singing them.

Margaret Ruthven Lang (1867–1972). American composer. In her life span of 104 years this Bostonian wrote some 200 songs as well as more elaborate instrumental pieces.

Liza (Elizabetha Nina Mary Frederica) Lehmann (1862–1918). English composer and singer. Her song cycle "In a Persian Garden" is her best-known work.

Isabella Leonarda (1620–1704). Italian composer. She was the abbess of a convent at Novara where she composed masses, motets, and other choral music. A modern record label specializing in music by women bears the name Leonarda.

Elizabeth Maconchy (1907–   ). English composer of Irish extraction. Studied with Ralph Vaughan Williams. Her output includes three one-act operas and many works for orchestra, mostly in a contemporary style.

Nina Makarova (1908–   ). Russian composer whose work includes symphony and opera. Married to Aram Khachaturian.

Mana-Zucca (see Augusta Zuckermann).

Fanny Mendelssohn (1805–1847). German pianist and composer; older sister and confidante of Felix Mendelssohn. She composed chamber music and songs of considerable merit. Some of the latter were published under Felix's name since he wished to propagate them but thought it unladylike for her to be identified publicly as their author.

Thea Musgrave (1928–   ). Scottish composer whose operas include *The Voice of Ariadne* (1974), *Mary Queen of Scots* (1977), and *Harriet: The Woman Called Moses* (1985).

Pauline Oliveros (1932–   ). American avant-garde composer. Much of her work involves mixed media, including oscillators, amplifiers, tapes, a cash-register, and a mynah bird.

Maria Theresia von Paradis (1759–1824). Austrian composer and pianist. Blind from her fifth year, she became an expert musician. She used her own system of notation to compose her works, including operas, chamber music, and a funeral cantata for King Louis XVI of France.

Shulamit Ran (1949–   ). Israeli composer who studied in the United States. She wrote several works for piano and orchestra, and chamber music for unusual combinations of instruments and voices.

Louise Reichardt (1779–1826). German singer and composer. The daughter of the well-known composer Johann Friedrich Reichardt, she lost her voice early in life and turned to composition. Many of her songs were published.

Clara (Wieck) Schumann (1819–1896). German pianist and composer. Robert Schumann's talented wife composed a piano concerto and solo piano pieces and songs, some of which have been revived in modern times.

Ethel Smyth (1858–1944). English composer and suffragist. Dame Ethel Smyth studied in Germany and played a leading role in English musical affairs, especially those involving women. Her most renowned work is the opera *The Wreckers*, presented in German in Leipzig in 1906 and in English in London in 1909.

Margaret Sutherland (1897–   ). Australian composer. She has found much of her inspiration in Baroque forms and has composed works of both symphonic and chamber proportions as well as a chamber opera.

Germaine Tailleferre (1892–1983). French composer; a member of "Les Six." Works include chamber music, piano pieces and songs; her Concertino for Harp and Orchestra was played by the Boston Symphony in 1927.

Louise Talma (1906–   ). American composer born in France and a student of Nadia Boulanger. Has written both vocal and instrumental music including an oratorio, an opera, and a cycle of poems by e.e. cummings.

Phyllis Tate (1911–   ). English composer. She has written a saxophone concerto, a television opera, and other music.

Hope Temple (See Doty Davies).

Pauline Viardot-Garcia (1821–1910). French-Spanish singer and composer. A celebrated opera-singer, the daughter of Manuel Garcia and the sister of Maria Malibran, she composed several operas herself including one called *La Dernière Sorcière*.

Slava Vorlova (1894–1973). Czech composer. She had an extensive output, her specialty being works for seldom-heard solo instruments, especially the bass clarinet, for which she wrote several pieces with orchestral accompaniment. She also wrote display pieces for brass and wind instruments and four operas.

Maria Antonia Walpurgis (1724–1780). The Empress of Saxony, she was a trained musician whose output included two operas for which she wrote both words and music. She used the pseudonym of Ermelinda Talea Pastorella Arcada, her name as a member of the Academy of Arcadians.

Yulia Weissberg (1878–1942). Russian composer. She married the son of Rimsky-Korsakov and studied with Max Reger in Germany. She composed operas, including two for children; also children's songs and choruses.

Augusta Zuckermann (1887–1981). American pianist and composer. She adopted the pseudonym of Mana-Zucca (Zuckermann more or less reversed). She wrote many instrumental pieces, but none as popular as her song "I Love Life."

Ellen Taaffe Zwilich (1939–   ). American composer, winner of the Pulitzer Prize in Music in 1983 for her *Three Movements for Orchestra*.

MUSICAL NUMEROLOGY

"THE THREE Bs"

Johann Sebastian Bach   (1685–1750)
Ludwig van Beethoven   (1770–1827)
Johannes Brahms   (1833–1897)

The phrase "The Three Bs" is credited to conductor Hans von Bülow who may have been influenced in coining it by the circumstance that he was a "B" himself.

"THE FIVE"

Mily Balakirev   (1837–1910)
Alexander Borodin   (1833–1887)
César Cui   (1835–1918)
Modeste Moussorgsky   (1839–1881)
Nikolai Rimsky-Korsakov   (1844–1908)

These five composers were grouped together in 1867 by the writer Vladimir Stasov as creators of a Russian school of nationalist music. His original title was "The Mighty Handful."

"THE SIX"

Georges Auric   (1899–1983)
Louis Durey   (1888–1979)
Arthur Honegger   (1892–1955)
Darius Milhaud   (1892–1974)
Francis Poulenc   (1899–1963)
Germaine Tailleferre   (1892–1983)

"Les Six" was a term invented in 1920 by critic Henri Collet after the composers had published together an album of pieces.

TRANSLATED COMPOSERS

Finding English equivalents for the names of celebrated foreign composers is a diverting if not particularly useful pastime, and a favorite sport of music lovers. Critic-composer Eric Salzman (or Saltman), has called the resultant names "joegreenies," in honor of Giuseppe Verdi, the great opera composer who makes the transition especially gracefully. Here are some examples:

John S. Brook	Johann Sebastian Bach
Joseph Green	Giuseppe Verdi
Claude Greenberg	Claudio Monteverdi
John Phillip Branch	Jean-Philippe Rameau
Mike Judge	Michael Praetorius
Joey Fields	Josquin des Prez
Arnold Belmont	Arnold Schoenberg
Carl M. Weaver	Carl Maria von Weber
Dick Garland	Richard Strauss
Gus Painter	Gustav Mahler
Fred Sourcream	Bedřich Smetana

BACH'S CHILDREN

Johann Sebastian Bach (1685–1750) was the most prolific of the great composers. In his 65 years he produced 1,200 musical works and 20 children. You can find his compositions listed in an encyclopedia.

But do you know the names of his 20 children? Here they are, in order of their appearance:

Catherina Dorothea (1708–1774)
Wilhelm Friedemann (1710–1784)
Twins: Maria Sophia and Johann Christoph (1713–1713)
Carl Philipp Emanuel (1714–1788)
Johann Gottfried Bernhard (1715–1739)
Leopold August (1718–1719)
Christiane Sophie Henriette (1723–1726)
Gottfried Heinrich (1724–1763)
Christian Gottlieb (1725–1728)
Elisabeth Juliane Friederike (1726–1759)
Ernst Andreas (1727–1727)
Regine Johanna (1728–1733)
Christiana Benedicta (1730–1730)
Christiana Dorothea (1731–1732)
Johann Christoph Friedrich (1732–1795)
Johann August Abraham (1733–1733)
Johann Christian (1735–1782)
Johanna Carolina (1737–1781)
Regine Susanna (1742–1809)

Of the 20 children, 11 were boys and 9 girls. Five of the former bore the name Johann, one of the latter Johanna. The first 7 children were borne by Bach's first wife Maria Barbara, who died in 1720, the remaining 13 by his second, Anna Magdalena, whom he married in 1721.

Ten of Bach's children died in infancy or soon afterwards, including twins, Johann Christoph and Maria Sophia, both of whom lived only a few days. Of those who survived, Wilhelm Friedemann, Carl Philipp Emanuel, Johann Christoph Friedrich and Johann Christian all became celebrated composers. Gottfried Heinrich, who lived to the age of 39, was mentally defective.

THE WOMEN IN MOZART'S LIFE

In his brief life of less than 36 years Wolfgang Amadeus Mozart (1756–1791) was closely associated with a number of women, in his family and out of it, who to varying degrees had an effect upon his career, his personality, and his music. His exposure to members of the opposite sex extended from Marie Antoinette, the future Queen of France, for whom he played the clavier at the age of six (she was the same age) to a variety of young society women he taught during his years as the leading pianist in Vienna. Of the women in Mozart's life the most memorable were:

Anna Marie Mozart (née Pertl, 1720–1788). Mozart's mother was an earthy woman and a devoted parent, without particular musical gifts (his father, Leopold Mozart, was a well-known violinist and pedagogue). In 1778, Anna Marie Mozart traveled with her son, then 22, on a extended expedition to Paris, where, it was hoped, he would be able to advance his career. However, the trip produced meager results, and for a final crushing blow, Mozart's mother took ill in Paris and died there, leaving him to return home alone. She was buried in the cemetery of St.-Eustache.

Maria Anna Mozart (1751–1829). Mozart's sister was his elder by four years and survived him by nearly 40. Known in the family as "Nannerl," she was an accomplished pianist, and the two children were exhibited together as prodigies by their father throughout Europe. In adulthood, Nannerl Mozart played her brother's music, and the two corresponded after Wolfgang left their Salzburg home to seek his fortune in Vienna, though in late years the letters became less frequent. Nannerl gave piano lessons and in 1784 married Baron Berchthold zu Sonnenburg, a minor member of the nobility. Left a widow, she lost her eyesight and died in very straitened circumstances.

Maria Anna Thekla Mozart (1758–1841). This was Mozart's charming and complaisant cousin, nicknamed the "Bäsle," with whom he indulged in a youthful romance. Its exact dimensions are unknown, but many of his letters to her are extant, and they are characterized not only by warmth but by cheerful vulgarity and grossness.

Aloysia Lange (née Weber, 1760–1839). Aloysia, a cousin of the composer Carl Maria von Weber and one of the leading sopranos of her era, appears to have been the grand passion of Mozart's life. She first met him in Mannheim when he was 22 and she was 17, and he fell in love with her. However, though for a time she returned his affection, she eventually jilted him and married an actor named Josef Lange. This marriage turned out to be a failure, and in later years Aloysia regretfully observed that she had never realized the genius of Mozart and seen him only as "a little man."

Constanze Mozart (née Weber, 1763–1842). Mozart's wife. Having failed with Aloysia, Mozart in 1781 married her younger sister Constanze, who was somewhat less attractive and also less accomplished as a singer. The union had its ups and downs, and Mozart several times expressed annoyance with his wife's free and easy ways in society. However, no actual infidelities by either have been documented. The couple had two surviving children, and Constanze was genuinely distraught over her husband's untimely death. After 10 years of widowhood she married Georg Nikolaus Nissen, a Danish diplomat. The two of them devoted many years to collecting and collating Mozart manuscripts, with Nissen eventually writing a biography of the composer.

Nancy Storace (1766–1817). An English soprano resident in Vienna whom Mozart admired musically and personally. She created the role of Susanna in *The Marriage of Figaro*. Musicologist Alfred Einstein believes Nancy Storace was "the only woman of whom Constanze would really have a right to be jealous . . . . Between Mozart and her there must have been a deep and sympathetic understanding." In 1784 Nancy married a violinist named Fisher who so mistreated her that she returned to England. She and Mozart continued to correspond, but his letters to her have been lost—possibly destroyed by Nancy, Einstein believes.

Magdalena Hofdemel (born 1766). Was she, indeed, one of the women in Mozart's life? She was, at the time of his death, one of his pupils. The day after Mozart died, her husband, Franz, attempted to stab her to death during a quarrel, and then took his own life. Magdalena, who was five months pregnant at the time, survived her wounds. Hofdemel's attack was ascribed at the time to a fit of jealousy and Mozart's name was mentioned in this connection. Beethoven, for one, believed the story, and according to the biographer, Otto Jahn, once displayed reluctance to perform at a soirée in the presence of Magdalena. Jahn, however, also announced that he had been "able to prove the innocence of Mozart in this matter." The date of Magdalena's death is unknown.

BEETHOVEN'S "IMMORTAL BELOVED"

The day after Ludwig van Beethoven's death on March 26, 1827, a letter he had written to an unknown party was found in a locked drawer in his chambers. Dated "July 6 and 7," with no year indicated, it addressed the intended recipient as *Unsterbliche Geliebte*— (Immortal Beloved). The 10-page document was an expression of the deepest love, containing Beethoven's resolve to "live altogether with you or never see you." It was signed "ever yours ever mine ever ours, L."

Beethoven, a lifelong bachelor, had a wide acquaintanceship with the fashionable women of Vienna, and many historians and commentators have speculated about the identity of the Immortal Beloved. The question has never been resolved, nor is it likely to be, unless some new evidence turns up. Here are some of the leading candidates:

Bettina Brentano (1785–1859). She was a young poet who cultivated the friendship of the artistic personalities of her time, among them Goethe and Beethoven. The composer seems to have been fascinated by her charm, and spent hours talking to her. When she married a poet named Arnim, Beethoven sent her a congratulatory sonnet. After the composer's death, Bettina published several letters she said he had written to her.

Josephine Brunswick (1799–1821). Josephine was one of two sisters of the Brunswick (or Brunsvik) family, members of the Hungarian nobility. Both girls took piano lessons from Beethoven in Vienna. Beethoven developed an interest in Josephine after she became a widow, and often joined in musicales at her home. He also wrote several rhapsodic letters to her that she published after his death.

Therese Brunswick (1775–1861). Although Therese Brunswick always insisted it was her younger sister Josephine in whom Beethoven was really interested, several authorities, including Beethoven biographer A. W. Thayer and the French writer Romain Rolland, have argued that Therese herself was the true Immortal Beloved. The most tangible evidence is a portrait of her found in the same drawer as the famous letter.

Maria Erdödy (1779–1837). Countess Erdödy—she was married at 17 to a Hungarian count—was closest to being a femme fatale among Beethoven's lady friends. A handsome woman but a semi-invalid (she suffered from poor circulation), she frequently played music together with the composer. In 1808, he actually occupied a suite in her fashionable apartment, sparking rumors about an affair between them. After five months they quarreled and he moved out, only to resume their friendship some years later. Around 1820 Erdödy was involved in several financial and family scandals and was accused of neglecting her children. At one point she was the subject of a police investigation, though no action against her was taken. Her relationships with a number of her contemporaries, including Beethoven, remain clouded to this day.

Dorothea von Ertmann (1781–1849). This highly respected pianist maintained an unusually long acquaintance with Beethoven—20 years. Her husband was a military man who became a general in the Austrian Army. She knew both Beethoven and his music quite well—so much so that the young composer Felix Mendelssohn called on her some years after Beethoven's death to inquire how the master had played certain pieces. Beethoven biographer George R. Marek considers her to be one of the likeliest candidates for Immortal Beloved by reason of her physical attractiveness, musical gifts, personal charm, and length of friendship with the composer.

Giulietta Guicciardi (1784–1856). The fact that the *Moonlight* Sonata (No. 14 in C-sharp minor) was dedicated to her has always given a special aura to Giulietta Guicciardi. Beethoven took her on as a pupil when he was 30 and she was 17; if there was a romance between them it was of relatively brief duration. She married Wenzel Robert Count Gallenberg in 1803.* A portrait of Guilietta was found among Beethoven's effects after his death. Beethoven's close friend Anton Schindler was among those who believed that she was the Immortal Beloved.

Rahel Vernhagen von Ense (1771–1833). Born Rahel Levin, she was one of the most beautiful and talented of the young Jewish women who held literary and artistic salons in the Berlin homes in the early 1800s. She was married to a Prussian diplomat named Varnhagen von Ense and first met Beethoven on a visit to the spa of Teplitz. He was struck by her charms and played his music for her. One school of thought has it that Rahel, besides being the Immortal Beloved, also was the subject of Beethoven's song cycle *An die Ferne Geliebte (To the Distant Beloved)*.

Magdalene Willmann (1775–1801). Magdalene was a singer who had known Beethoven in his hometown of Bonn. One account, recorded in Thayer's standard Beethoven biography, is that the composer offered her marriage when both were in Vienna, but that she refused him. The principal authority for this story was a niece of Magdalene, who said it was handed down within the family. No independent corroboration exists.

MUSICAL NICKNAMES

A great many musical works have come down to the present with nicknames attached to them. Some, in fact, have almost become better known than the composition's official designation. Everyone knows, for instance, what music is meant by Beethoven's "Moonlight" Sonata; not so many by his Piano Sonata No. 14 in C-sharp minor, Op. 27, No. 2. The following list, arranged by composer, gives some of the more familiar musical nicknames, together with their origin. Nicknames either given or accepted by the composer are indi-

---

*Gallenberg was a minor composer, specializing in ballet music. For one of his scores, see list of SHAKESPEARE'S PLAYS IN MUSIC, *Hamlet*.

cated with an asterisk (*); others were added afterwards, often by parties unknown:

JOSEPH HAYDN

Haydn's compositions undoubtedly were the champion nickname recipients of all time. He even received one himself—"Papa" Haydn, in deference both to his longevity and his status as the "father" of the symphony and string quartet.

SYMPHONIES

*No. 6 in D, "Le Matin"
*No. 7 in C, "Le Midi"
*No. 8 in D, "Le Soir"

Although Haydn himself was responsible for these morning, noon, and night titles, it requires a good imagination to detect the diurnal progression in the music.

No. 22 in E-flat, "The Philosopher"
The nickname reflects the thoughful nature and somber tone of the opening movement.

No. 26 in D Minor, "Lamentation."
There are a few touches of tragedy in the composition, which sometimes is also called the "Christmas" Symphony.

No. 31 in D, "Hornsignal"
The hunting horn resounds at several points.

No. 43 in E-flat, "Mercury"
Perhaps an allusion to its general fleetness of pace.

N. 44 in E Minor, "Trauer"
"Trauer" means mourning and sadness is pervasive in the composition.

*No. 45 in F-sharp Minor, "Farewell"
To convince his employer, Prince Esterhazy, that it was time to leave his country estate and repair to Vienna, Haydn had his musicians depart the stage gradually during the last movement of this symphony, until only two were left to play the final bars. The Prince took the hint.

No. 48 in C, "Maria Theresia"
This composition celebrated a visit by Empress Maria Theresia to the Esterhazy estate.

No. 49 in F Minor, "La Passione"
A dark-hued, intense work, it was believed to have been written for performance during Holy Week.

No. 55 in E-flat, "The Schoolmaster"
The rhythm of the slow movement suggests the wagging finger of a school-master, while the theme itself is somewhat ponderous and pedantic.

*No. 59 in A, "Fire"
Taken from incidental music that Haydn wrote for "The Burning House," a play given at Esterhazy in 1733.

*No. 60 in C, "Il Distratto"
"Distratto" means absent-minded. This, too, was derived from incidental music composed for a play of the same title.

*No. 63 in C, "La Roxalane"
Roxalane was the heroine of a stage play for whom Haydn wrote an aria. The slow movement of this symphony consists of variations on her melody.

*No. 73 in D, "La Chasse"
The sounds of the hunt resound through the Finale.

Nos. 82–87. The six works in this sequence are known collectively as the *Paris* Symphonies because they were commissioned by the Concert de la Loge Olympique in Paris. This also accounts for the three French nicknames that follow:

> No. 82 in C, "L'Ours"
> The "bear" growls in the last movement—or so some early audiences thought.

> No. 83 in G Minor, "La Poule"
> Here the "hen" clucks in the first movement.

> No. 85 in B-flat, "La Reine"
> The Queen referred to is the Queen of France, Marie Antoinette, who is reputed to have had a particular liking for this music.

No. 92 in G, "Oxford"
It was played at Oxford University when Haydn received an honorary degree there in 1791.

Nos. 93–104. The 12 symphonies in this sequence are known as the "Salomon" Symphonies after John Peter Salomon, the British impresario who brought Haydn to London in 1791–1795.

> *No. 94 in G, "Surprise"
> Named after the sudden fortissimo chord in the 16th measure of the slow movement. Haydn always denied he had put it in to wake up his British audiences.

No. 96 in D, "Miracle"
Allegedly because a chandelier fell at an early performance, miraculously injuring no one.

*No. 100 in G, "Military"
From fanfare and percussive effects introduced into the score.

No. 101 in D, "Clock"
From the tick-tock accompaniment of the slow movement.

No. 103 in E-flat, "Drum-roll"
A drum-roll (Paukenwirbel in German) opens the symphony and is repeated later.

No. 104 in D, "London"
Named for the city in which Haydn's last 12 symphonies were first performed. The last movement is based on a London street song.

"Toy" Symphony, unnumbered.
A piece for children with seven added instruments: Penny trumpet in G, Quail-call in F, Cuckoo-playing G and E, Screech owl whistle, Rattle, Drum in G, and Triangle. Some modern authorities contend the true composer was not Haydn, but Leopold Mozart, father of Wolfgang; others favor Anon. The jury is still out and may never come back.

STRING QUARTETS

Op. 1, No. 1 in B-flat, "La Chasse"
A "hunting call" sets the pace.

Op. 3, No. 5 in F, "Serenade"
So named for its lovely Andante cantabile movement, in which the muted violin carries the melody over a pizzicato accompaniment.

Op. 17, No. 5 in F Major, "Recitative"
An operatic-style recitative and aria for violin opens the Adagio movement, written generally in an operatic style.

Op. 20, Nos. 1–6, "Sun" Quartets
This set was so named from an image of the sun emblazoned on a printed edition issued by J. J. Hummel of Berlin and Amsterdam in 1779.

Op. 33, Nos. 1–6, "Russian" Quartets/"Gli Scherzi"
The set is dedicated to a Russian Grand Duke visiting Vienna in 1781. "Gli Scherzi" alludes to the use of a Scherzo movement in each quartet, also to their general light-heartedness:

COMPOSERS AND COMPOSITIONS

Op. 33, No. 2 in E-flat, "The Joke"
The wit is in the last movement, which ends in a state of suspended animation.

Op. 33, No. 3 in C, "The Bird"
Twittering grace notes characterize the opening movement.

Op. 33, No. 5 in G, "How Do You Do?"
W. W. Cobbett, British authority on chamber music, pointed
out that the words exactly fitted the opening theme. This would
have come as news to Haydn, who spoke little English.

Op. 50, 1–6, "Prussian"
They are dedicated to Frederick William II, King of Prussia.

Op. 50, No. 5 in F, "The Dream"
The second movement is like a reverie.

Op. 50, No. 6 in D, "The Frog"
The croaking may be heard in the Finale.

Op. 55, No. 2 in F Minor, "Razor"
An English publisher named Bland, on a visit to Esterhazy, found
Haydn having trouble shaving and promptly gave him two English
razors. In return Haydn handed him this quartet.

Op. 64, No. 5 in D, "The Lark" or "Hornpipe"
The lark flies in the first movement; the hornpipe dances in the
last.

Op. 74, No. 3 in G Minor, "The Rider" or "Horseman"
A rambunctious preface to the first movement, and jerky synco-
pations in the last suggest a bumpy ride.

Op. 76, No. 2 in D Minor, "Quinten-Quartett"
Descending melodic fifths in the first violin part at the very outset
account for the name German Quintetn, or "Fifths." The canonic third
movement has become known as the Witches' (German: *Hexen*) Minuet.

'Op. 76, No. 3 in C, "Emperor" or "Kaiser"
Haydn composed the melody of the second movement as the
Austrian national anthem in honor of Emperor Franz II.

Op. 76, No. 4 in B-flat, "Sunrise"
This music establishes its radiance at the outset with a violin rising
through the string harmonies.

WOLFGANG AMADEUS MOZART

SYMPHONIES

No. 31 in D, "Paris"
It was written for performance in that city in 1778.

No. 35 in D, "Haffner"
Composed for a family of that name in Salzburg.

No. 36 in C, "Linz"
Written for performance in that city in 1783.

No. 38 in D, "Prague"
Written for performance in that city in 1786.

No. 41 in C, "Jupiter"
No one knows who gave it the name or why; but it certainly has stuck. Mozart's biographer Otto Jahn believed it was so called "to indicate its majesty and splendor."

Piano Concerto No. 21 in C, "Elvira Madigan"
From the motion picture of the same name, for which it provided background music—a rare instance of a 20th-century nickname being affixed to a classic work.

Piano Concerto No. 26 in D, "Coronation"
Played during the coronation of King Leopold II of Prussia at Frankfurt in 1788.

String Quartets 14–19, "Haydn Quartets"
The set was dedicated to Mozart's friend Joseph Haydn with the words "I send my six sons to you.":

> String Quartet No. 17 in B-flat, "Hunt"
> The main theme of the first movement suggests a hunting song.
>
> String Quartet No. 19 in C, "Dissonant"
> The dissonances of the first movement seem less harsh to us today than they did to Mozart's contemporaries.

LUDWIG VAN BEETHOVEN

SYMPHONIES

*Symphony No. 3 in E-flat, "Eroica"
Composed with Napoleon in mind, the symphony eventually emerged with the inscription: "To celebrate the memory of a great man."

*Symphony No. 6 in F, "Pastoral"
The most programmatic of Beethoven's symphonies, it clearly depicts the sounds and sensations of the countryside, from birdcalls to a thunderstorm.

Symphony No. 9 in D Minor, "Choral"
The name comes from the vocal contingent in the Finale. The program at its premiere in Vienna on May 7, 1824, described it as a "Grand Symphony with Solo and Chorus Voices entering the Finale on Schiller's Ode to Joy."

PIANO SONATAS

*No. 8 in C Minor, "Pathétique"
Beethoven himself gave this highly charged, romantic music its name.

No. 12 in A-flat, "Funeral March"
The second movement is marked "Funeral March on the Death of a Hero."

No. 14 in C-sharp minor, "Moonlight"
A fanciful name, donor unknown—but one of the most familiar in music. Beethoven's own designation is "Sonata quasi una Fantasia."

No. 15 in D, "Pastoral"
The music suggests a bucolic mood.

*No. 17 in D, "Tempest"
Beethoven himself related this stormy music to Shakespeare's play of the same title.

*No. 19 in C, "Waldstein"
Dedicated to a patron, Count Waldstein.

No. 23 in F Minor, "Appassionata"
The title was added by a publisher, but the music bears it out.

*No. 26 in E-flat, "Les Adieux"
A going-away gift to the Archduke Rudolf, who was leaving Vienna.

*No. 29 in A, "Hammerklavier"
Composed for a newly designed and powerful piano, the Hammerklavier.

Sonata No. 5 in F for Violin and Piano, "Spring"
The sunny, springlike opening sets a mood that is sustained throughout.

Sonata No. 9 in A, "Kreutzer"
Beethoven dedicated this work to the violinist Rodolphe Kreutzer—but he never played it.

Trio No. 4 in D for Piano, Violin and Cello, "Ghost"
A spooky second movement provides the name.

*Trio No. 9 in B-flat for Piano, Violin and Cello, "Archduke"
Beethoven dedicated it to his friend, Archduke Rudolf.

*String Quartets Nos. 7 in F, 8 in E Minor, 9 in C, Op. 59, "Rasumovsky"
These three quartets were dedicated to another royal patron, Count Rasumovsky.

String Quartet No. 10 in E-flat, "Harp"
Plucked strings in the first movement convey a harp-like quality.

*Rondo a Capriccio in G for Piano, Op. 129, "Rage Over a Lost Penny, Vented in a Caprice"
The manuscript of this curious little piece was purchased at an auction sale after Beethoven's death. The title was inscribed upon it. The circumstances of its composition are unknown.

*Duo in E-flat for Viola and Cello, "Eyeglass"
"Duet with two Eyeglass obbligato" was Beethoven's description of this piece for himself and a cellist friend, both of whom wore glasses.

FRANZ SCHUBERT

*Symphony No. 4 in C Minor, "Tragic"
The serious tone is unmistakable; Schubert appended the title himself.

Symphony No. 8 in B Minor, "Unfinished"
For reasons unknown, Schubert completed only the first two movements.

Symphony No. 9 in C Major, "The Great"
The nickname, of obscure origin, distinguishes this work (also sometimes designated No. 7) from an earlier work in the same key. It also aptly characterizes the quality of the music.

String Quartet No. 12 in C Minor, "Quartettsatz"
This is a one-movement work, "Satz" being German for "movement."

*String Quartet No. 14 in D Minor, "Death and the Maiden"
The second movement uses Schubert's song of the same name.

*Quintet for Piano and Strings in A, "The Trout"
For his fourth-movement theme and variations, Schubert used his song "The Trout."

Sonata in A Minor for Cello and Piano, "Arpeggione"
Named for the arpeggione, a now-obsolete instrument for which it was originally written.

FELIX MENDELSSOHN

*Symphony No. 2 in B-flat, "Lobgesang"
The word means "Hymn of Praise," referring to the work's choral Finale, which is twice as long as its first three instrumental movements combined.

Symphony No. 3 in A Minor, "Scotch" or "Scottish"
Composed after a walking trip through Scotland that also produced the *Hebrides* or *Fingal's Cave Overture.*

*Symphony No. 4 in A, "Italian"
The fruits of an extended stay in Italy, the last movement is an Italian dance, the saltarello.

*Symphony No. 5, "Reformation"
In 1830 Mendelssohn composed this work to celebrate the tercentenary of the Augsburg Confession, the statement of beliefs and doctrines of the Lutheran Church. But the celebration was called off, and the work not played until later.

ROBERT SCHUMANN

*Symphony No. 1 in B-flat, "Spring"
"Within the last few days," Schumann wrote to a friend in 1841, "I have completed . . . a whole symphony—and moreover, a Spring symphony!" Later he referred to the "vernal ardor" of his impulse in writing it.

Symphony No. 3 in E-flat, "Rhenish"
Schumann left no doubt of his intention to depict village life along the Rhine, but does not appear to have affixed the title himself.

FRÉDÉRIC CHOPIN

Etude in G-flat, Op. 10, No. 5, "Black Key"
The right hand has figurations on the black keys alone.

Etude in C Minor, Op. 10, No. 12, "Revolutionary"
According to one story, in 1831 Chopin wrote this brilliantly powerful work upon learning that Warsaw had fallen to the Russians.

Etude in A Minor, Op. 25, No. 11, "Winter Wind"
A quiet introduction is followed by whistling, wintry blasts.

Prelude in D-flat, Op. 28, No. 15, "Raindrop"
The sound is unmistakable; the only question is whether Chopin was really inspired by rain pattering down outside his window.

*Piano Sonata No. 2 in B-flat Minor, "Funeral March"
Chopin marked his third movement "Marche Funèbre."

Waltz in D-flat, Op. 64, No. 1, "Minute Waltz"
It takes a minute to play, though some insist on doing it faster.

FRANZ LISZT

Piano Concerto No. 1 in E-flat, "Triangle"
Critic Eduard Hanslick gave it the nickname in tribute to the prominent part for triangle.

BEDŘICH SMETANA

*String Quartet No. 1 in E Minor, "From My Life"
Smetana's autobiography in music (an abrupt intrusion of a piercing high note represents the advent of his deafness).

ANTONIN DVOŘÁK

String Quartet in F, "American"
Written during Dvořák's stay in Spillville, Iowa, and based on Negro themes.

'Symphony No. 9 in E Minor, "From the New World"
Also written in the U.S. It used to be considered No. 5.

PETER ILYICH TCHAIKOVSKY

*Symphony No. 1 in G Minor, "Winter Daydreams"
Tchaikovsky applied the subtitle to the opening movement.

Symphony No. 2 in C Minor, "Little Russian"
The composer used folksongs from the Ukraine (Little Russia), but a critic added the name.

Symphony No. 3 in D, "Polish"
The Finale is "in tempo polacca."

*Symphony No. 6 in B Minor, "Pathétique"
When his brother Modest suggested the name, Tchaikovsky eagerly accepted it.

CAMILLE SAINT-SAËNS

Symphony No. 3 in C Minor, "Organ"
Both an organ and a piano are added instruments in this symphony.

ANTON BRUCKNER

*Symphony No. 4 in E-flat, "Romantic"
In his early sketches Bruckner indicated several poetical and pictorial associations, which he later withdrew. However, he apparently gave the subtitle his sanction.

GUSTAV MAHLER

*Symphony No. 1, "The Titan"

An early concert program, apparently with the approval of Mahler, described it as the "Titan" Symphony after the romance by Jean-Paul Richter.

Symphony No. 2 in C Minor, "Resurrection"

While Mahler appears not to have used the title himself, he acknowledged the music's inspirational and religious nature.

*Symphony No. 8 in E-flat, "Symphony of a Thousand"

The number approximates the total of the participants in this vast orchestral-choral work.

DIMITRI SHOSTAKOVICH

*Symphony No. 7, "Leningrad"

Composed to celebrate Soviet resistance to the Nazi siege of Leningrad in 1941, this symphony enjoyed a wartime vogue.

*Symphony No. 13, "Babi Yar"

A commemoration, vocal and instrumental, of the Nazi massacre of the Jews of Kiev in 1941, with words by the poet Yevgeny Yevtushenko. It probably is played more in the United States than in Russia.

MUSICAL GEOGRAPHY

Whether to seek new horizons, find new audiences, or escape old creditors, musicians tend to be a restless lot much given to travel. Their wanderings often are reflected in the place names affixed to their compositions. Following is a sampling from the musical atlas:

COUNTRIES, REGIONS, ETC.

L'Africaine (opera)	Meyerbeer
Afro-American Symphony	Still
Alpine Symphony	R. Strauss
America: An Epic Rhapsody	Bloch
American Quartet (No. 12 in F, Op. 96)	Dvořák
American Festival Overture	Schuman
Variations on America	Ives
Sinfonia Antarctica (Symphony No. 7)	Vaughan Williams
Appalachia	Delius
Appalachian Spring	Copland
From Bohemia's Meadows and Forests	Smetana

47

Bachianas Brasilerias	Villa Lobos
Saudados do Brasil	Milhaud
Cuban Overture	Gershwin
Israel in Egypt (oratorio)	Handel
Moses in Egypt (opera)	Rossini
Thamos, King of Egypt (Incidental music)	Mozart
English Suites	Bach
Finlandia	Sibelius
Suite Française	Milhaud
Suite Française	Poulenc
Symphony on a French Mountain Air	d'Indy
French Suites	Bach
A German Requiem	Brahms
Grand Canyon Suite	Grofé
Hebrides Overture	Mendelssohn
Die Fliegende Hollander (The Flying Dutchman, opera)	Wagner
Hungarian Rhapsodies	Liszt
Les Indes Galantes (opera)	Rameau
The Indian Queen (opera)	Purcell
Israel Symphony	Bloch
Il Turco in Italia (opera)	Rossini
Italian Concerto in F	Bach
Italian Symphony (No. 4 in A, Op. 90)	Mendelssohn
Aus Italien	Richard Strauss
Capriccio Italien	Tchaikovsky
Italienisches Liederbuch	Wolf
Japanese Suite	Holst
Latin American Symphonette	Gould
El Salón México	Copland
Postcard from Morocco (opera)	Argento
Three Places in New England	Ives
Norwegian Dances	Grieg
Ocean Symphony (Symphony No. 2)	Rubinstein
Polish Symphony (No. 3 in D, Op. 29)	Tchaikovsky
Suite Provençale	Milhaud
Romanian Rhapsodies	Enesco
Little Russian Symphony (No. 2 in C Minor)	Tchaikovsky
Russian Easter Overture	Rimsky-Korsakov
Scotch Symphony (No. 3 in A Minor)	Mendelssohn
Scottish Fantasy (for violin and orchestra)	Bruch
Sicilian Vespers (opera)	Verdi
Symphonie Espagnole	Lalo
L'Heure Espagnole (opera)	Ravel
Capriccio Espagnol	Rimsky-Korsakov

España	Chabrier
Iberia	Debussy
Swedish Rhapsody	Alfvén
Rondo alla Turca (From Piano Sonata No. 11 in A, K. 331)	Mozart
Turkish March from Ruins of Athens	Beethoven
Utopia Limited (operetta)	Gilbert and Sullivan

CITIES AND TOWNS

The Italian Girl in Algiers (opera)	Rossini
L'Arlesienne Suites	Bizet
The Barber of Bagdad (opera)	Cornelius
Berliner Symphonie	Kurt Weill
Concord Sonata	Ives
Siege of Corinth (opera)	Rossini
Dumbarton Oaks Concerto	Stravinsky
Souvenir de Florence	Tchaikovsky
Threnody for the Victims of Hiroshima	Penderecki
Jerusalem (choral song)	Parry
Jerusalem the Gold (song)	Shemer
Leningrad Symphony (No. 7, Op. 60)	Shostakovich
Linz Symphony (No. 36 in C, K. 425)	Mozart
London Symphony (No. 104 in D)	Haydn
A London Symphony (No. 2)	Vaughan Williams
Lady Macbeth of Mzensk (opera)	Shostakovich
Oxford Symphony (No. 92 in G)	Haydn
Paris, Song of a Great City	Delius
Paris Symphony (No. 31 in D, K. 297)	Mozart
An American in Paris	Gershwin
La Vie Parisienne	Offenbach
The Pirates of Penzance	Gilbert and Sullivan
Prague Symphony (No. 38 in D)	Mozart
Roma	Bizet
Roman Carnival Overture	Berlioz
The Fountains of Rome	Respighi
The Pines of Rome	Respighi
The Barber of Seville	Rossini
Trouble in Tahiti (opera)	Bernstein
Les Deux Aveugles de Tolède (opera)	Méhul
Les Troyens (opera)	Berlioz
Regata Veneziana	Rossini
A Night in Venice (operetta)	J. Strauss
Tales from the Vienna Woods	J. Strauss
Warsaw Concerto	Addinsell
A Survivor from Warsaw	Schoenberg

MUSICAL ASTRONOMY

Mr. Broucek's Flight to the Moon (opera)	Janáček
Clair de Lune	Debussy
"Jupiter" Symphony (No. 41 in C)	Mozart
Lost in the Stars (show)	Weill
The Man in the Moon (opera)	Haydn
"Mercury" Symphony (No. 43 in E-flat)	Haydn
Der Mond (opera)	Orff
Il Mondo della Luna (opera)	Galuppi
"Moonlight" Sonata (No. 14 in C-sharp minor)	Beethoven
Pierrot Lunaire	Schoenberg
The Planets	Holst
Silver Apples of the Moon	Subotnick
Sirius	Stockhausen
The "Sun" Quartets, Opus 20	Haydn
Sun-Treader	Ruggles
Venusberg music from Tannhäuser	Wagner

FISH, FOWL, AND FLESH IN MUSIC

Many musicians show evidence of having been animal lovers in their compositions no less than in their persons. Mozart's letters often wind up with salutations to the family dog, Bimperl; Olivier Messiaen, among many others, was fascinated by birds and their songs. Here are some examples of musical works relating (more or less) to the animal kingdom. Listings are alphabetical according to the name of the creature in the title:

FISH

Poissons d'Or (Goldfish)	Debussy
Albert Herring (opera)	Britten
Porgy and Bess (opera)	Gershwin
Die Forellen (The Trout, song)	Schubert
Trout Quintet in A (Op. 114)	Schubert

BIRDS

Gli Ucelli (The Birds)	Respighi
Catalogue d'Oiseaux (Catalogue of Birds)	Messiaen
L'Oiseau Blue (The Bluebird, opera)	Wolff
Le Coq d'Or (The Golden Cockerel, opera)	Rimsky-Korsakov
On Hearing the First Cuckoo in Spring	Delius

Curlew River (opera)	Britten
The Wings of the Dove (opera)	Moore
The Wood Dove (symphonic poem)	Dvořák
The Ugly Duckling	Prokofiev
The Firebird	Stravinsky
Mother Goose Suite	Ravel
Symphony No. 83 in G, La Poule (The Hen)	Haydn
The Lark Ascending	Vaughan Williams
Lark Quartet in D (Op. 64 No. 5)	Haydn
Hark, Hark the Lark (song)	Schubert
The Thieving Magpie (opera)	Rossini
Le Rossignol (The Nightingale, opera)	Stravinsky
Peacock Variations	Kodály
The White Peacock	Griffes
Les Deux Pigeons (The Two Pigeons, ballet)	Messager
La Rondine (The Swallow, opera)	Puccini
The Swan	Saint-Saëns
Swan Lake	Tchaikovsky
The Silver Swan (madrigal)	Gibbons
The Swan of Tuonela	Sibelius

BEASTS

Carnival of the Animals	Saint-Saëns
Die Fledermaus (The Bat, operetta)	J. Strauss
Symphony No. 82 in C, "The Bear"	Haydn
Cat's Fugue (Sonata in G Minor)	D. Scarlatti
Three Cat Poems	Searle
The Ballad of Baby Doe (opera)	Moore
Limp Preludes for a Dog	Satie
Donkey Serenade	Friml
Babar le Petit Eléphant	Poulenc
Renard (The Fox, opera)	Stravinsky
The Jumping Frog of Calaveras County (opera)	Foss
The Bronze Horse (opera)	Auber
Captain Jinks of the Horse Marines (opera)	Beeson
Rejoice in the Lamb	Britten
Of Mice and Men (opera)	Floyd
Le Boeuf sur le Toit (The Ox on the Roof)	Milhaud
Sheep May Safely Graze (Cantata No. 208)	Bach
The Cunning Little Vixen (opera)	Janáček
And God Created Great Whales	Hovhannes
Vox Balaenae (Voice of Whales)	Crumb

INSECTS

Where the Bee Sucks (song)	Arne
The Flight of the Bumblebee	Rimsky-Korsakov
Madama Butterfly (opera)	Puccini
Le Papillon (The Butterfly, ballet)	Offenbach
Il Grillo del Focolare (The Cricket on the Hearth, opera)	Zandonai
The Firefly	Friml
Song of the Flea	Mussorgsky
The Gold Bug (operetta)	Herbert
The Spider's Feast	Roussel
The Wasps	Vaughan Williams

MUSICAL BESTIARIES

Ever since Joseph Haydn in his oratorio employed the lowest notes of the stringed instruments to depict great whales—and possibly even before—composers have been imaginatively portraying animals in music. The most comprehensive bestiary of all is Camille Saint-Saëns's *Carnival of the Animals*, in which specific instruments or instrumental combinations are selected to portray various creatures:

Introduction and Royal March of the Lion	Two pianos and strings
Hens and Roosters	Two pianos, clarinet, and strings
Wild Asses	Two pianos an octave apart
Tortoises	Strings and one piano in a ponderously slow version of tunes from Offenbach's *Orpheus in the Underworld*
The Elephant	Double-bass solo based on Berlioz's sylphs in *The Damnation of Faust* and Mendelssohn's fairies in *A Midsummer Night's Dream*
Kangaroos	Two pianos playing alternately
Aquarium	Celesta, flute, muted strings, two pianos
Persons with Long Ears	Two violins
The Cuckoo in the Heart of the Woods	Clarinet and pianos
The Aviary	Flute, strings, and pianos
Pianists	Pianists, at familiar exercises
Fossils	Xylophone, clarinet, strings, and piano—among the works parodied is Saint-Saëns's own *Danse Macabre*

| The Swan | Cello, two pianos |
| Finale | Full orchestra |

In Serge Prokofiev's *Peter and the Wolf*, the various participants are depicted by the instruments, as follows:

Bird	Flute
Duck	Oboe
Cat	Clarinet in the low register
Grandfather	Bassoon
Wolf	3 French horns
Peter	String quartet

An operatic bestiary is Leoš Janáček's *The Cunning Little Vixen* (1924). The principal animal characters are:

The Vixen	Soprano
The Fox, her mate	Soprano (or Tenor)
The Badger	Bass
The Dog	Mezzo-soprano

Other creatures with singing roles include the Cricket, Frog, Grasshopper, Hens, Owl, Woodpecker, and others. Human characters include a Forester, his Wife, a Schoolmaster, a Pastor, and a Poacher.

THE TEN MOST BORING COMPOSITIONS

Musical audiences frequently are asked to select their favorite works, but rarely asked to list those they like least. In a poll especially taken for this book in 1984, readers of *Keynote* magazine, published by WNCN, a New York FM radio station, were invited to name the 10 compositions they consider most boring. The following list is based on their responses. For comparative purposes, the result of a similar survey taken 30 years earlier, among readers of the music pages of the *New York Herald Tribune* in 1954, is also given:

MUSICAL BORES: 1984

1. Vivaldi: *The Four Seasons*
2. Ravel: *Boléro*
3. Pachelbel: *Kanon in D*
4. Orff: *Carmina Burana*

5. Glass: *various works**
6. Tchaikovsky: *Symphony No. 5 in E Minor*
7. Dvořák: *Symphony No. 9 in E Minor,* "New World"
8. Liszt: *Les Preludes*
9. Bruckner: *Symphony No. 9 in D Minor*
10. Ives: *Three Places in New England*

MUSICAL BORES: 1954

1. Rimsky-Korsakov: *Scheherazade*
2. Franck: *Symphony in D Minor*
3. Ravel: *Boléro*
4. Wagner: *Parsifal*
5. Beethoven: *Missa Solemnis*
6. Brahms: *Requiem*
7. Dvořák: *Symphony No. 9 in E Minor,* "New World"
8. Beethoven: *Symphony No. 9 in D Minor,* "Choral"
9. Wagner: *Tristan und Isolde*
10. Tchaikovsky: *Symphony No. 5 in E Minor*

---

*No single work by Philip Glass emerged as a clear "winner." However, his music was cited on so many lists as to merit his inclusion in the No. 5 spot.

PART III

FORMS AND INSTRUMENTS

MUSICAL FORMS

SONG FORMS

Music, particularly from the Classical era on, is largely based on individual themes or melodies. These can be designated by letters of the alphabet: A for the first theme, B for the second, etc.:

> TWO PART (or BINARY) FORM is indicated A–B
> THREE PART (or TERNARY) FORM is indicated A–B–A

In vocal music, three-part song form has its equivalent in the *da capo* ("from the beginning") aria, in which the first part is repeated after a contrasting middle section.

RONDO FORM

An elaboration of song form, with the first theme recurring and subsidiary themes introduced at will. Two examples:

> A–B–A–C–A–B–A
> A–B–A–C–A–D–A–B–A

SONATA-ALLEGRO FORM

The basic form of the Classical symphony, quartet, and sonata, almost always used in the first movement:

> Introduction (optional)
> Exposition
>   Theme A (tonic key)
>   Bridge, or transition
>   Theme B (dominant key)
>   Coda, or conclusion
> Development
> Recapitulation
>   Theme A (tonic key)
>   Theme B (tonic key)
>   Coda

SYMPHONIC STRUCTURE

The typical Classical symphony consists of four movements structured as follows:

First movement: Sonata-Allegro form (see above)
Second movement: Three Part Song Form
            Theme and Variations
            Sonata-Allegro or other forms
Third movement: Minuet and Trio
            Scherzo and Trio (These are actually types of Three Part Song Form)
Fourth movement: Rondo
            Theme and Variations
            Sonata-Allegro or other forms

ANCIENT (AND NOT SO ANCIENT) DANCES

Some of the oldest musical forms are derived from dances. In the Baroque era a number of these were combined by composers to form the Suite. A typical Suite by Johann Sebastian Bach would consist of an Allemande, a Courante, a Sarabande, a Gigue, and one or two other dances. While some Suites were light in character, others became a vehicle for music of great depth and expressiveness. Many ancient dance forms, such as the Minuet and Pavane, have survived into modern times, while others such as the Waltz have been added along the way. Following are some dance forms still encountered:

Allemande: Cheerful, moderately paced in 4/4 rhythm, of German origin.
Bolero: Spanish dance in triple rhythm, said to have been invented in Cadiz around 1780. Maurice Ravel made it famous.
Bourrée: Brisk, in 4/4 meter with a single upbeat, from the Auvergne section of France.
Chaconne: A slow and dignified dance transformed by Baroque composers into continuous variations in triple meter. The Chaconne of Bach's Violin Partita No. 2 in D Minor, carries the form to its ultimate. See also *Passacaglia.*
Courante: Moderate to lively in pace, with shifting rhythms. The name means "running."
Fandango: Spanish, in fast triple time. Mozart wrote one in Act III of *The Marriage of Figaro.*

Galliard: Gay, rollicking, in triple time. Of French or Italian ancestry.

Galop: Mid-19th century dance with lively rhythm, executed with hopping movements. Offenbach wrote a Galop Infernal for *Orpheus in the Underworld.*

Gavotte: Of French origin, in 4/4 time, usually starting on the third beat of the bar.

Gigue: Better known as the jig, of English or Irish origin. Particularly suited to violins.

Habanera: A Cuban dance named after the city of Havana and quickly adopted by Spain. In moderate 2/4 meter. Where would *Carmen* be without it?

Hornpipe: Snappy English sailor's dance in 4/4 time.

Jota: From Aragon in northeast Spain. In rapid triple time. Used by Liszt, Saint-Saëns, de Falla, and others.

Ländler: Rustic, waltz-like, of Austrian origin. Mozart, Beethoven, and Schubert wrote many. Later gave way to the Waltz.

Loure: A slower and graver Gigue.

Mazurka: The Polish national dance, raised to high art by Chopin.

Minuet: In 3/4 time, it gained such popularity in the 17th century that it superseded many older dances and became adopted by Classical composers as the third movement of their symphonies and quartets.

Passacaglia: Slow and stately, it resembles the Chaconne almost to the point of indistinguishability. Bach composed a great Passacaglia for organ (in C Minor), Brahms did the same for orchestra (the Finale of his Symphony No. 4 in E Minor).

Passepied: Gay, spirited, and French in 3/8 or 6/8 meter. The English spelled it "paspy."

Pavane: Slow, stately, of Spanish origin, gives the effect of a solemn procession. Ravel composed a *Pavane for a Dead Princess* in both piano and orchestral versions.

Polka: A Bohemian dance in duple meter adopted by composers of many other lands.

Polonaise: Stately, festive, thought to have originated at the Polish court in the 17th century. Many composers have used it, but none like Chopin.

Rigaudon: Lively 4/4 dance of French Provençal origin, sometimes used in the Baroque Suite. Oscar Wilde envisioned a "rigadoon" and a saraband danced by ghosts in "The Ballad of Reading Gaol."

Saltarello: Mendelssohn's "Italian" Symphony (No. 4 in A Major) climaxes in this fast 6/8 dance whose rhythm reflects its Italian name derived from the word *saltare,* "to jump."

Saraband: Dignified, in slow triple meter, first popular in 17th-century Spain. Cervantes denounced it as lascivious, but he may have been referring to an earlier Oriental version.

Seguidilla: Andalusian national dance in fast triple meter.

Tango: A syncopated, slightly faster version of the Habanera, originating in Argentina around 1900. Composers using it include Stravinsky in *L'Histoire du Soldat.*

Tarantella: Neapolitan dance in fast 6/8 time. Name may be associated with the city of Taranto or with its alleged efficacy as a cure for the bite of the tarantula spider.

Waltz: Perhaps the most popular and widespread of all dances. It developed around 1800 from the Ländler, and found its apogee in the Vienna of Johann Strauss. Among countless others who have incorporated it into their music are Beethoven, Weber, Berlioz, Chopin, Brahms, and Ravel.

THE MASS

The Roman Catholic church service known as the Mass has been adapted by composers into a powerful and beautiful musical form. Following are the basic sections of the Mass. The names are derived from the Latin word or words that open each section:

> *Kyrie*
> *Gloria*
>   "Qui tollis"
>   "Quoniam"
>   "Cum sancto spirito"
>   (other subdivisions possible)
> *Credo*
>   "Et incarnatus"
>   "Et resurrexit"
>   "Amen"
>   (other subdivisions possible)
> *Sanctus*
> *Benedictus*
> *Agnus Dei*
>   Dona nobis

REQUIEM MASS

The Requiem Mass omits the *Gloria* and *Credo* and adds:

> *Requiem Aeternam*
> *Lux Aeterna*
> *Dies Irae*

CHAMBER MUSIC FORMS

Chamber music is a broad term covering a multitude of musical combinations. Even though the instruments involved are far fewer than those making up a symphony orchestra, composers have reserved some of their finest concepts for these small but intricate combinations. Here are some of the forms of chamber music and the instruments that make them up:

Sonata (for one instrument). Generally this is the piano, although there also are solo sonatas for violin, cello and, more rarely, other instruments. Beethoven's 32 piano sonatas represent one of his most colossal achievements. Similarly, Bach's six sonatas and partitas for unaccompanied violin have never been surpassed.

Sonata (for two instruments). The most common combination is violin and piano—Beethoven wrote 10 such sonatas. Sonatas have also been composed for many other instruments in partnership with the piano.

String Trio. Violin, viola, cello. Relatively few successful works have been written in this form. One of the most beautiful is Mozart's six-movement *Divertimento in E-flat* (K. 563).

Piano Trio. Violin, cello, and piano. Many fine piano trios have been composed. Beethoven's *"Archduke" Trio, in B-flat* (Op. 97) is a splendid example.

String Quartet. 1st violin, 2nd violin, viola, cello. The classic chamber music ensemble, perfectly balanced in the range and weight of the four instruments. Countless masterpieces have been composed for string quartet by geniuses from Haydn to Bartók.

String Quintet. The string quartet with an added viola or cello. Mozart preferred the former, Schubert the latter.

Piano Quintet. The string quartet plus piano. Robert Schumann wrote a particularly beautiful one in E-flat, Op. 44. Sometimes the string quartet combines with another solo instrument as in the Clarinet Quintets of Mozart and Brahms.

Sextet. Two each of violins, violas, and cellos.

Septet. The combination can vary, but it usually encompasses both stringed and wind instruments. Beethoven's Septet in E-flat is for violin, viola, French horn, clarinet, bassoon, cello, and double-bass.

Octet. Again, variety is permitted. Perhaps the most usual form is a double string quartet, as in Felix Mendelssohn's Octet, composed when he was 16.

Nonet. Among the few that exist is one by Ludwig Spohr (1785–1859), including both strings and winds. Aaron Copland has written a Nonet for Strings.

Decemet. The only progenitor of this 10-toned monster appears to be one Franz Xavier Gebel (1787–1843) who composed much other chamber music, all of it unplayed today. Gebel's "decemet" actually is a double string quintet.

STRING QUARTET NAMES

Finding a name for a string quartet is never a simple task, and one that has grown more complicated in recent years with the tremendous proliferation of such ensembles, especially in the United States. Following are some of the names adopted by string quartets, past and present. Quartets named for their members are not included:

QUARTETS NAMED FOR CITIES

Bamberg Quartet
Budapest String Quartet
Chester String Quartet
Cleveland Quartet
Concord String Quartet
Copenhagen Quartet
Cremona Quartet
Hollywood String Quartet
Lenox Quartet
Lexington Quartet
Louisville Quartet
Manhattan String Quartet
Mannheim String Quartet
Milano Quartet

New Budapest String Quartet
New York Quartet
New Zurich String Quartet
Orlando String Quartet
Philadelphia String Quartet
Portland String Quartet
Prague String Quartet
Quartetto Beethoven di Roma
Shanghai String Quartet
Tel Aviv Quartet
Tokyo String Quartet
Varsovia String Quartet
Zagreb String Quartet

QUARTETS NAMED FOR COMPOSERS

Allegri String Quartet
Amadeus String Quartet*
Arriaga String Quartet
Bartók Quartet
Alban Berg Quartet
Boccherini String Quartet
Borodin Quartet
Composers String Quartet
Enesco Quartet
Gabrieli String Quartet
Glinka Quartet

Haydn String Quartet
Janáček Quartet
Joachim String Quartet
Kodály Quartet
Mendelssohn String Quartet
Mozart Quartet
Paganini Quartet
Prokofiev Quartet
Quartetto Beethoven di Roma
Smetana Quartet

*Amadeus was Mozart's middle name.

QUARTETS NAMED GEOGRAPHICALLY

Berkshire Quartet
Colorado String Quartet
Flonzaley Quartet*
Illinois Quartet
Iowa Quartet
Laurentian String Quartet
Manhattan String Quartet

Moravian Quartet
New World String Quartet
Oklahoma Quartet
Queens String Quartet
Ridge String Quartet
Sequoia String Quartet
Valley String Quartet

QUARTETS NAMED NATIONALLY

American String Quartet
American Art Quartet
Austrian Quartet
Brazilian Quartet
Bulgarian Quartet

Finnish Quartet
Hungarian Quartet
Netherlands Quartet
New Hungarian Quartet
Quartetto Italiano

QUARTETS NAMED AFTER FAMOUS PEOPLE

Audubon Quartet
Emerson String Quartet
Guarneri String Quartet
Medici String Quartet
Muir String Quartet

Razumovsky Quartet
Salomon String Quartet
Stradivari Quartet
Vermeer String Quartet

QUARTETS NAMED AFTER INSTITUTIONS

Eastman Quartet
Interlochen Arts Quartet
Juilliard String Quartet
Mozarteum String Quartet

Quartetto della Scala
Smithson String Quartet†
Stanford Quartet
WQXR String Quartet

NOTES OF THE SCALE IN FIVE LANGUAGES

The musical scale consists of seven notes that look the same and sound the same everywhere. But their names differ in various coun-

---

*The Flonzaley Quartet, which flourished in the early years of the 20th century, took its name from words in the Vaudois dialect of Switzerland meaning "little river."

†The name derives from Smithsonian.

tries. Here are the seven notes in five modern languages (for Latin see below):

ENGLISH	GERMAN	FRENCH	ITALIAN	SPANISH
C	C	ut	do	do
D	D	ré	re	re
E	E	mi	mi	mi
F	F	fa	fa	fa
G	G	sol	sol	sol
A	A	la	la	la
B	H*	si	si	si

The syllables ut–re–mi–fa–sol–la–si that represent the notes in several languages were first used by Guido d'Arezzo, an 11th-century monk and musical theorist. He used the first syllables of a Latin hymn to St. John the Baptist:

Ut queant laxis
Resonare fibris,
Mira gestorum
Famili tuorum
Solve polluti
Labii reatum
Sancte Johannes!

Or, in a free translation by Dorothy Waage: "Keep my lips pure, that as thy servant I may sing praises of thy wondrous deeds, St. John."

*H in German indicates B-flat.

SEVEN ANCIENT GREEK MODES

	COMPASS OF NOTES
Dorian	D to D
Phrygian	E to E
Lydian	F to F
Mixolydian	G to G
Hypodorian (Aeolian)	A to A
Hypophrygian (Locrian)	B to B
Hypolydian (Ionian)	C to C

The Greeks named their musical modes, or scales, after geographic areas, including their confederacies on the western coast of Asia Minor and the nearby islands. Their three primary modes were

NOTE VALUES IN SEVEN LANGUAGES

The time values, or duration, of the notes are indicated by the same symbols everywhere. But, once again, the names vary from language to language. Here are the note values in seven languages:

SYMBOL	AMERICAN	ENGLISH	GERMAN	FRENCH	ITALIAN	SPANISH	LATIN
⊔	double whole-note	breve	Doppel-taktnote	carrée	breve	breve	brevis
o	whole-note	semibreve	Ganze	ronde	semibreve	redonda	semi-brevis
♩	half-note	minim	Halbe	blanche	bianca	bianca	minima
♩	quarter-note	crotchet	Viertel	noire	nera	negra	semi-minima
♪	eighth-note	quaver	Achtel	croche	croma	corchea	fusa
♬	sixteenth-note	semiquaver	Sechzehntel	double-croche	semi-croma	semi-corchea	semi-fusa
♬	thirty-second note	demisemi-quaver	Zweiundreis-sigstel	triple-croche	semi-biscroma	fusa	fusella
♬	sixty-fourth note	hemidemisemi-quaver	Vierundsech-zigstel	quadruple-croche	semi-biscroma	semi-fusa	fusel-lala

the Dorian, the Phrygian, and the Lydian. The names were carried over into medieval usage. For better or worse, no one knows what Greek music actually sounded like. Today only two basic modes exist—major and minor.

MUSICAL KEYS

Whether listeners fully realize it or not, the key in which a composition is written gives it a "feel" of its own. Attempts are occasionally made to express this in verbal terms, and some have even sought to find coloristic equivalents.

André Grétry, one of the masters of opera-comique and a prolific composer and writer on music, listed psychological characterizations of 14 music keys in his *Memoires*, published in 1797.

The relation between color and key has interested a number of composers; one of them, the British musician Arthur Bliss, even wrote a *Colour Symphony*, each movement devoted to a different hue. The Russians have seemed especially interested in the question, with both Nikolai Rimsky-Korsakov and Alexander Scriabin striving to codify the relationship.

GRÉTRY'S CHARACTERIZATION OF FOURTEEN MUSICAL KEYS (PSYCHOLOGICAL)

C Major	Fine and outspoken
C Minor	Pathetic
D Major	Brilliant
D Minor	Melancholy
E-flat major	Noble and sad or gloomy
E Major	Bright
E Minor	Slightly melancholy
F Major	Moderately sad
G Major	Warlike
G Minor	Very sad
A Major	Brilliant
A Minor	Graceful
B-flat major	Noble, but less great than C Major
B Major	Brilliant and playful

COLOR EQUIVALENTS OF ELEVEN KEYS

KEY	RIMSKY-KORSAKOV'S LIST	SCRIABIN'S LIST
C Major	White	Red
G Major	Brownish-gold	Orange-rose
D Major	Yellow	Yellow
A Major	Rosy	Green
E Major	Sapphire blue	Bluish-white
B Major	Dark blue	Bluish-white
F-sharp major	Grayish-green	Bright blue
D-flat major	Dusky	Violet
A-flat major	Grayish-violet	Purple-violet
E-flat major	Bluish-gray	Steely
E major	Green	Red

TEMPOS

These indications of musical speed are usually designated by their Italian names. They came into use in the early 17th century; consequently the correct tempo of many previous works is unknown. These are the most commonly encountered tempos, from the slowest to the fastest:

Largo	Extremely slow, broad
Larghetto	Slightly less slow
Adagio	Slow
Andante	Moderately slow (comes from the Italian word for walk)
Andantino	Less slow than andante
Allegretto	Somewhat lively
Allegro	Lively, fast (comes from the Italian word for cheerful)
Presto	Very fast
Prestissimo	As fast as possible—or faster

MUSICAL INSTRUMENTS, PRO AND CON

VIOLIN

Sharp violins proclaim
Their jealous pangs, and desperation,
Fury, frantic indignation,
Depth of pain, and height of passion.
    (John Dryden, "A Song for St. Cecilia's Day," 1687)

A squeak's heard in the orchestra,
  The leader draws across
The intestines of the agile cat
  The tail of the noble hoss.
    (G. T. Lanigan, "The Amateur Orlando," 1875)

VIOLA

The viola is a philosopher, sad, helpful, always ready to come to the aid of others, but reluctant to call attention to himself.
  (Albert Lavignac, c. 1900)

The Viola is not merely "a big Violin." It is a Viola.
  (Cecil Forsyth, *Orchestration*, 1914)

CELLO

I hear the violoncello,
('tis the young man's heart's complaint).
  (Walt Whitman, "Song of Myself," 1855)

I am not fond of the violoncello: ordinarily I had just as soon hear a bee buzzing in a stone jug.
  (George Bernard Shaw, *The World* (London), July 9, 1890)

DOUBLE-BASS

The first string that the Musician usually touches is the Bass, when he intends to put all in tune. God also plays upon this string first, when he sets the soul in tune for himself.
  (John Bunyan, *The Pilgrim's Progress*, 1678)

A dangerous rogue-elephant.
  (Charles Villiers Stanford, *Musical Composition*, 1911)

FLUTE

The flute is not an instrument with a good moral effect. It is too exciting.
  (Aristotle, *Politics*, 322 B.C.)

The music of the flute is enervating to the mind.
  (Ovid, *Remedia Amoris*, 10 B.C.)

OBOE

A boxen hautboy, loud and sweet of sound,
All varnished and with brazen ringlets round,
I to the victor give.
  (Ambrose Philips, "Pastorals," 1709)

An ill wind that nobody blows good.
(Anonymous)

CLARINET

Ah, if only we had some clarinets, too! You cannot imagine the effect of a symphony with flutes, oboes and clarinets!
(Wolfgang Amadeus Mozart, letter to his father, December 3, 1778)

Clarionet, n.: An instrument of torture operated by a person with cotton in his ears.
(Ambrose Bierce, *The Devil's Dictionary*, 1911)

BASSOON

The bassoon is an acoustical phenomenon of great complexity.
(Bernard Hague, *The Tonal Spectra of Wind Instruments*)

A clarinet with a cold in its chest.
(Samuel Butler, *Notebooks*, 1912)

FRENCH HORN

At the beginning of the (nineteenth) century . . . the horn tone, which soars over all barriers with which the classic style surrounded it, became the symbol of the modern orchestra, which it saturated with its glorious sonority.
(Paul Henry Lang, *Music in Western Civilization*, 1941)

All are not hunters that blow the horn.
(Medieval Latin proverb)

TRUMPET

If the trumpet give an uncertain sound, who shall prepare himself to the battle?
(The First Epistle of Paul to the Corinthians)

He's blowing loudly on a small pipe.
(Sophocles, "Fragment," c. 450 B.C.)

TROMBONE

Directed by the will of a master, the trombones can chant like a choir of priests, threaten, utter gloomy sighs, a mournful lament, or a bright hymn of glory.
(Hector Berlioz, *Traité d'Instrumentation*, 1844)

The structure of the trombone hasn't changed in 400 years.
(Leopold Stokowski, n.d.)

TUBA

The Tuba is not often asked to perform feats of technical dexterity . . . . However, the very best players have a surprising facility and certainty of technique.
(Cecil Forsyth, *Orchestration*, 1914)

People never write pretty melodies for tubas. It just isn't done.
(George Kleinsinger and Paul Tripp, *Tubby the Tuba*, 1945)

TIMPANI

The drum is in hands that will know how to beat it well enough.
(Miguel de Cervantes, *Don Quixote*, 1605)

The noisy drum hath nothing in it but mere air.
(Thomas Fuller, *Gnomologia*, 1732)

PIANO

'Tis wonderful how soon a piano gets into a log-hut on the frontier.
(Ralph Waldo Emerson, "Society and Solitude," *Civilization*, 1870)

Please do not shoot the pianist. He is doing his best.
(Oscar Wilde, *Impressions of America, Leadville*, 1883. Wilde said he saw this sign posted in a saloon.)

AN INSTRUMENTAL ROSTER

While some instruments flourish on their own, most find their fulfillment in the orchestra, where they contribute to a beautiful community of sound. Following is a basic roster of orchestral instruments:

STRINGS

Violin. Its four strings are tuned G, D, A, and E, and its expressive and emotional range is enormous. An instrument called the "fiddle" existed in medieval times, but the present-day violin actually seems to have come into being some time during the 16th century. The great violin-makers, who centered around Cremona in Italy, began creating instruments in the 17th century. Nicola Amati (1596–1684), Antonio Stradivari (1644–1737), and Giuseppe Guarneri del Gésu (1698–1744) fashioned instruments that have never been equalled. The violin became—and remains—the fundamental instrument of the orchestra.

Viola. Tuned a fifth lower than the violin—C, G, D, A—it is larger in size and deeper in tone, but otherwise identical. Early viola players in orchestras tended to be failed violinists, but composers like Mozart gave the instrument a more important role, and today there are viola virtuosos. The German term for viola is *Bratsche,* the French, *alto.*

Cello. The full name is violoncello, not violincello, since the instrument derives from the obsolete violone. Its strings are tuned C, G, D, A, but an octave lower than the viola. Like the violin, the cello seems to have originated in the 16th century. Among its precursors was a six-stringed instrument called the viola da gamba.

Double-bass (Italian: *contrabasso*). The strings are tuned E, A, D, G, and the instrument is notated an octave higher than it sounds. Also known familiarly as the "bull-fiddle" or the "doghouse," this largest and deepest-voiced of the strings dates from the mid-16th century.

HARP

The orchestra's most visible instrument and one of its most beautiful. It only came into the orchestra during the 19th century, after its pedal mechanism was perfected by Sebastian Érard. The pedals vastly increased the range of its 47 strings.

WINDS

Flute. An instrument of great antiquity, found in almost every civilization, and made of all materials from bone and bamboo to metal and plastic. Has long existed both in end-blown and side-blown models. The standard European instrument is the cross-flute (side-blown), and dates from the 12th century. In 1813 Theobold Boehm invented a system of mechanical keys and stoppers that made the flute as controllable and precise as a fine watch. The piccolo (Italian for "little") is a small flute.

Oboe. The French call it hautbois, or "high wood." A double-reed woodwind that developed from an obsolete instrument called the shawm, it became widespread in orchestral use in the early 18th century.

Clarinet. The last of the basic woodwinds to enter the orchestra, gaining acceptance toward the end of the 18th century. It has a single reed mouthpiece and is descended from the now-obsolete chalumeau—a term still used to describe the clarinet's deepest register.

Bassoon. Lowest of the winds; double-reed. Came into the orchestra about the same time as (and in partnership with) the oboe, during the early 18th century. The Germans call it the *Fagott*, the Italians *fagotto*—supposedly because it resembles a bundle of sticks, or faggot.

BRASS

Horn. Often called French horn, supposedly because it's a descendant of the ancient French hunting horn. The composer Jean Baptiste Lully is credited with introducing it into the orchestra in 1664. The most customary keys for horns are F and B-flat. Valves vastly increased the flexibility of the "natural" horn in the 18th century (French: *cor*; Italian: *corno*).

Trumpet. An instrument that goes back to Biblical days and earlier; one was found in King Tut's tomb. European models date from the 14th century. The "natural" (i.e., valveless) trumpet gave way to the valved model in the early 19th century. The cornet closely resembles the trumpet, but is shorter, easier to play, and has a less brilliant but mellower tone.

Trombone. This brass instrument with a telescopic slide dates from around 1400, with an earlier version known in England as the sackbut. Its debut into the symphony orchestra seems to have been in the Finale of Beethoven's Fifth Symphony in Vienna in 1808. Known in German as *Posaune*.

Tuba. A massive valved instrument, the bass of the brass section. It entered the orchestra in the late 19th century. Unwieldly in size and occasionally unpredictable in sound.

PERCUSSION INSTRUMENTS

Timpani. Hollow hemispheres of copper covered with a head of tight parchment, they are the basic orchestral drum. However, many other percussive orchestral instruments exist, usually gathered under the heading of "Battery." Here are some of them:

Bells. Long steel tubes suspended from a wooden frame.

Castanets. Clicking devices of Spanish origin.

Celesta. A dreamy-sounding bell instrument operated by a keyboard.

Cymbals. Large round metallic plates that can be clashed together or suspended and tapped lightly.

Drums. Snare (or side) drum, tenor drum, and bass drum make occasional orchestral appearances.

Glockenspiel. Steel plates that produce chimes when struck by a wooden hammer.

Gong. A heavy, hanging plate; also known as the tam-tam.

Triangle. A steel bar shaped into a triangular form that gives a ringing tone when struck.

Woodblocks. Hollow blocks struck together.

Xylophone. Wooden slabs struck by mallets.

ORCHESTRAL SIZE AND MAKEUP

Orchestras have varied in size through history, and they continue to do so today. The following list illustrates their growth through various epochs:

Les Vingt-Quatre Violins du Roi (The 24 Violins of the King). The official band of King Louis XIV in 17th-century France, usually under the direction of Jean-Baptiste Lully. Its 24 "violins" actually consisted of six violins, six basses (the equivalent of today's cellos), and 12 "violas"—actually instruments tuned to take the various inner parts.

Salomon's Orchestra for Haydn (1792). When Joseph Haydn went to London to conduct his newly composed symphonies, the impresario Johann Peter Salomon provided him with an orchestra of 40— 8 first violins, 8 second violins, 4 violas, 3 cellos, 4 basses, 2 flutes, 2 oboes, 2 clarinets, 2 bassoons, 2 trumpets, 2 French horns, 1 timpani.

The Orchestra of the Late Romantic Period (1900). The Vienna Philharmonic, which performed many works by Richard Strauss, Gustav Mahler, and other early 20th-century figures, numbered 104, including 17 first violins, 16 second violins, 11 violas, 10 cellos, 10 basses, 4 flutes, 4 oboes, 4 clarinets, 4 bassoons, 8 horns, 4 trumpets, 5 trombones, 1 tuba, 2 timpani, 3 percussion, 1 harp. It was probably the largest orchestra of its time.

The Modern Orchestra. Today's orchestras vary in size from 90 to 105 performers—sometimes less, rarely more. The 1984 Philadelphia Orchestra, one of America's most notable ensembles, totalled 105: 17 first violins, 16 second violins, 12 violas, 12 cellos, 9 basses, 4 flutes (including piccolo), 4 oboes (including English horn), 4 clarinets (including bass clarinet), 4 bassoons (including contra-bassoon), 6 horns, 4 trumpets, 4 trombones (including bass trombone), 1 tuba, 2 timpani, 2 battery (percussion), 2 keyboard (celesta, piano or organ), 2 harps. Extra players are added when needed.

Hector Berlioz's Ideal Orchestra. Hector Berlioz, one of the first great orchestrators, projected in 1858 an ideal orchestra which, he argued, would be "the most complete, richest, most majestic, most powerful, and at the same time the softest and smoothest" in existence. It consisted of 119 instruments, differing from today's orchestras mainly in a larger complement of strings. Berlioz also devised a scheme—though he acknowledged it was unlikely ever to exist—for an orchestra of 467 pieces, including 120 violins, 12 bassoons, 30 harps, and 12 pairs of "ancient cymbals in different keys."

The Largest Orchestra? The largest orchestra ever assembled allegedly numbered 987 and played under the direction of Johann

Strauss, Jr., at a World Peace Jubilee in Boston on June 17, 1872. However, doubt has been cast upon its exact size.

MUSICAL INSTRUMENTS IN THE BIBLE

The words, but not the music, of many Biblical songs have survived, the most notable being the Psalms of David. Similarly, we know the names of several of the musical instruments of the Old Testament, but their exact appearance for the most part is either unknown or a matter of dispute. Psalm 150, for example, alludes to "stringed instruments and organs" without going into particulars. According to Genesis 4:21, "the father of all such as handle the harp and organ" was Jubal, son of Lamech and Adah. Here are some of the instruments his descendants played:

Trumpet. While leading the Israelites in their Exodus from Egypt, Moses ordered his metalsmiths to fashion two long silver trumpets that could perform a variety of uses; signaling, summoning assemblies, sounding the alarm, and initiating celebrations (Numbers 10: 1–10).

Shofar. A more humble type of trumpet, this was made from a ram's horn, though playing it demanded a degree of skill. This was the instrument that brought down the walls of Jericho when carried around the city by seven priests for seven days. It is the only Biblical instrument still in use in its ancient form, being sounded in the synagogue on the Jewish High Holy Days (Joshua 6:4).

Pipe. A simple shepherd's instrument, probably single-reed and apparently widely used. "The people piped with pipes" when King Solomon was annointed by Zadok the Priest (I Kings 1:40).

Kinnor. A plucked string instrument translated variously as harp, lyre, or cythara, and mentioned on a number of occasions. The frame was made of wood, occasionally trimmed with amber, and the strings made either of twisted grass or sheep gut. This was the instrument the Israelites hung on the willows by the rivers of Babylon during the Second Exile. Evidently there were a number of types, some quite elaborate, for one Psalm mentions in a single verse the harp, the psaltery, and "an instrument of ten strings" (Psalm 137:2, Psalm 33:2).

Timbrel, or Tabret. A hand drum that resembled a tambourine. Moses' sister Miriam played one to celebrate the crossing of the Red Sea (Exodus 15:20).

Cymbal. "Praise him upon the loud cymbals; praise him upon the high-sounding cymbals" (Psalm 150:5).

ONCE-POPULAR INSTRUMENTS YOU'LL RARELY HEAR

Just as Nature tried out the dinosaurs and gave up on them, so have musicians produced a number of instruments that enjoyed a vogue for a time but have since virtually disappeared from sight—and sound. These are only a few of the dozens that haven't made it over the centuries:

Arpeggione. A short-lived Viennese instrument of the 1820s. Somewhat resembling a guitar, it was the size of a cello, had six strings, and was played with a bow. Franz Schubert immortalized it with a beautiful *Sonata in A Minor,* now played on the cello.

Baryton. An early 18th-century phenomenon, one of the precursors of the cello. It had separate strings designed for bowing and plucking, and would be totally forgotten had not Joseph Haydn composed 175 pieces for it. They're now played—when they're played at all—on the cello.

Basset horn. A kind of enlarged clarinet with a particularly doleful sound. Mozart used it in his Requiem (1791), but it went out of business about a century later. George Bernard Shaw adopted its Italian name, *Corno di Bassetto,* as a pseudonym when he was a music critic in London.

Glass harmonica. Tuned glass bowls suspended in water and rotated by a treadle. The player rubbed the edges to produce sounds. Benjamin Franklin devised a type he called the "Armonica." Mozart composed several pieces for the instrument.

Ophicléide. A U-shaped keyed metal tube invented in Paris in the early 19th century. It flourished for a time in military bands, but eventually gave way to the tuba. The ophicléide came in several sizes, the largest and deepest being called the *ophicléide monstre.*

Serpent. A late 16th-century bass woodwind taking its name from its snakelike shape. Keys were subsequently added to it, and it was used in military bands, especially French. But it died out in the 19th century like the ophicléide, unable to compete with the tuba.

Theorbo. A 14-stringed lute developed in 16th-century Venice that retained its popularity for nearly 200 years. Now encountered mainly as an historical curiosity.

Trumpet marine. An elongated stringed instrument played with a bow, used by street musicians centuries ago. Samuel Pepys mentioned it favorably in his *Diary* in 1667. It was sometimes called the Nun's Fiddle. The origins of both names are obscure.

Virginal. A keyboard instrument said by some to have been named for Elizabeth I, the Virgin Queen of England, although this is disputed by some scholars. With 32 metal plucked strings, it was shaped rectangularly like a clavichord, but sounded like a harpsichord. It is still played occasionally by specialists in old music.

TEN FAVORITE INSTRUMENTS OF AMATEUR MUSICIANS

The American Music Conference of Wilmette, Illinois, periodically surveys the use of musical instruments by amateurs in the United States. The last such survey was taken in 1978–1979, and Conference officials believe that the figures and percentages largely held good in 1984–1985, with the possible exception of a decline in the number of organ players.

	NUMBER OF PLAYERS	MALE	FEMALE	MEDIAN AGE
Piano	18,188,000	21%	79%	28
Guitar	15,140,000	65%	35%	23
Organ	6,196,000	29%	71%	31
Clarinet	2,948,000	31%	69%	19
Drums	2,748,000	94%	6%	19
Flute	2,548,000	17%	83%	19
Trumpet	2,299,000	86%	14%	19
Violin	1,799,000	32%	68%	27
Harmonica	1,549,000	86%	14%	25
Saxophone	1,549,000	82%	18%	22

PART IV
OPERA

OPERATIC SCHOOLS AND COMPOSERS

Opera was invented around the year 1600 by a group of Florentine noblemen called "the Camerata." From Italy it spread first to France, later to Germany and other European countries. Operas are usually classified according to the language in which they were written. Several composers have written successful operas both in Italian and in French, but the only composer to have written masterpieces in Italian and in German was Mozart. This list groups operatic composers and their works according to the national school to which they belonged:

THE ITALIAN LINE

Giulio Caccini (c.1550–1618)

Jacopo Peri (1561–1633)

Ottavio Rinuccini (1563–1621). Peri and Caccini were the first operatic composers, Rinuccini the first librettist. Their operas dealt with mythological subjects, a favorite heroine being Eurydice.

Claudio Monteverdi (1567–1643). The first true genius of opera. He composed *Orfeo, Arianne, L'incoronazione di Poppea.*

Alessandro Scarlatti (1660–1725). His output consisted of 115 operas, fewer than half of which survive.

Pietro Metastasio (1698–1782). Librettist whose texts helped stabilize the operatic form and were used by composers from Scarlatti to Mozart.

Baldassare Galuppi (1706–1785). The "father of opera buffa"; composed 112 operas.

Giovanni Battista Pergolesi (1710–1736). His one comic masterpiece is *La Serva Padrona.*

Giovanni Paisiello (1749–1801). Composed the first, but not the last, *Barber of Seville.*

Domenico Cimarosa (1749–1801). *The Secret Marriage* is the only survivor among his 75 operas.

Gioacchino Rossini (1792–1868). A supreme comic genius, as in *The Barber of Seville* and *La Cenerentola,* he also produced dramatic works like *Otello* and *William Tell.* Composed 40 operas in his first 37 years, lived 38 years more without writing another.

Gaetano Donizetti (1797–1848)

Vincenzo Bellini (1801–1835). Two masters of the bel canto or "beautiful song" type. Bellini composed *Norma* and *I Puritani;* Donizetti's 70 operas include *Lucia di Lammermoor* and three comedies, *The Elixir of Love, Don Pasquale,* and *The Daughter of the Regiment.*

Giuseppe Verdi (1813–1901). Italy's master composer. (See separate list WAGNER AND VERDI).

Amilcare Ponchielli (1834–1886). His *La Gioconda* includes a famous ballet, "The Dance of the Hours."

Alfredo Catalani (1854–1893). Like other late 19th-century Italian operatic composers aside from Verdi and Puccini, he achieved only one real success, *La Wally.*

Ruggero Leoncavallo (1857–1919). His *Pagliacci* is a model of *verismo* (real-life) opera.

Giacomo Puccini (1858–1924). Verdi's successor and the last dominant Italian operatic master. His three most celebrated works are *La Bohème, Tosca,* and *Madama Butterfly,* but many others hold the stage including *Manon Lescaut, Gianni Schicchi,* and *Turandot.*

Pietro Mascagni (1863–1945). *Cavalleria Rusticana* is *Pagliacci*'s partner on many a veristic double-bill.

Francesco Cilea (1866–1950). *Adriana Lecouvreur.*

Umberto Giordano (1867–1948). *Andrea Chénier, Fedora.*

Italo Montemezzi (1875–1952). *L'Amore dei Tre Re.*

Riccardo Zandonai (1883–1944). *Francesca da Rimini.* All of the post-Puccini Italian composers listed above produced only one, or at the most two, successful operas.

Luigi Dallapiccola (1904–1975). His most powerful opera, *Il Prigioniero,* was first heard on radio.

Luigi Nono (1924–   ). Most of his work has a leftist political orientation; his best-known is the opera *Intolleranza.*

THE MOZART LINE

The operas of Wolfgang Amadeus Mozart (1756–1791) merit a classification of their own, since they belong to no national school and comprise both comedy and drama—sometimes both at once. Following is a complete list in order of composition. Unfinished works are marked with an asterisk (*):

Apollo and Hyacinth, intermezzo (1767)
Bastien and Bastienne, operetta in 1 act (1768)
La Finta Semplice, opera buffa (1768)
Mitridate, Rè di Ponto, opera seria (1770)
Ascanio in Alba, seranata teatrale (1771)
Il Sogno di Scipione, serenata drammatica (1772)

Lucio Silla, dramma per musica (1772)
La Finta Gardiniera, opera buffa (1774–1775)
Il Re Pastore, dramma per musica (1775)
*Zaide, operetta (1779–1780)
*Thamos, King of Egypt, heroic drama (1773–1779)
Idomeneo, Rè di Creta, opera seria (1780–1781)
The Abduction from the Seraglio, comic opera (1781–1782)
*L'Oca del Cairo, opera buffa (1783)
*Lo Sposo Deluso, opera buffa (1783)
The Impresario, 1-act comedy with music (1786)
The Marriage of Figaro, opera buffa (1785–1786)
Don Giovanni, dramma giocoso (1787)
Così Fan Tutte, opera buffa (1789–1790)
The Magic Flute, German opera (1791)
La Clemenza di Tito, opera seria (1791)

THE FRENCH LINE

Jean-Baptiste Lully (1632–1687). A transplanted Italian whose stately works include *Alceste*, *Amadis de Gaul*, and *Acis et Galatée*.

Jean Philippe Rameau (1683–1764). The first native French operatic master. He created *Les Indes Galantes*, *Castor et Pollux*, *Hippolyte et Aricie*.

Christoph Willibald von Gluck (1714–1787). His "reforms" ushered in a new operatic age. His *Orpheus and Eurydice*, written both in Italian and French versions, is the oldest opera still in active repertory.

Giacomo Meyerbeer (1791–1864). Another transplant, this one German, who strongly influenced French opera, creating the "grand opera" tradition in Paris with works like *Robert le Diable*, *Le Prophète*, and *Les Huguenots*.

Hector Berlioz (1803–1869). Underrated in his own time, he won recognition years later for such powerful and massive operas as *Les Troyens*, which opened the Metropolitan Opera's centennial season in September 1984.

Ambroise Thomas (1811–1890). His *Mignon* receives occasional revivals.

Charles Gounod (1818–1875). His *Faust* was once the world's most popular opera but has faded somewhat. Other works that are revived periodically are *Roméo et Juliette* and *Mireille*.

Jacques Offenbach (1819–1880). Another German transplant who created a new genre of light opera in works like *Orpheus in the Underworld* and *La Belle Hélène* and who also composed the dramatic fantasy *The Tales of Hoffmann*.

Leo Délibes (1836–1891). Known for his ballets, he wrote one durable opera, *Lakmé*.

Georges Bizet (1838–1875). *Carmen*, "the perfect opera," remains the pinnacle of French style and is performed in all languages and many versions.

Jules Massenet (1842–1912). *Manon, Werther*, and *Le Jongleur de Nôtre-Dame* are the best-known among his more than 20 operas.

Claude Debussy (1862–1918). His *Pelléas et Mélisande* is a unique masterpiece.

Gustav Charpentier (1860–1956). In *Louise* he composed one of the first operas about working people.

Maurice Ravel (1875–1937). *L'Heure Espagnole* and *L'Enfant et les Sortilèges* are distinctive short works with the composer's characteristic flair.

Francis Poulenc (1899–1963). His operas range from the powerfully somber *Les Dialogues des Carmelites* to the satiric and zany *Les Mamelles de Tirésias*.

THE GERMAN LINE

Heinrich Schütz (1585–1672). Composer of the first German opera, *Dafne*, set to a translation of Rinuccini's libretto for a work by Peri (see above). It was performed at a royal wedding in Saxony in 1627.

Ludwig van Beethoven (1770–1827). His lone opera *Fidelio* is the earliest work in German (aside from Mozart's) in the standard repertory.

Carl Maria von Weber (1786–1883). A pioneer of German romanticism, he wrote *Der Freischütz, Euryanthe, Oberon*.

Albert Lortzing (1801–1851). *Zar und Zimmermann* (Czar and Carpenter), about Peter the Great, is popular in Germany but rarely heard elsewhere.

Otto Nicolai (1810–1849). Achieved his greatest success, *The Merry Wives of Windsor*, two months before his death from a stroke.

Friedrich von Flotöw (1812–1883). Of his more than a dozen operas only *Martha* is widely performed.

Richard Wagner (1813–1883). The supreme German operatic master. See separate list WAGNER AND VERDI.

Peter Cornelius (1824–1874). An associate of Liszt and Wagner whose best-known opera is *The Barber of Bagdad*.

Johann Strauss, Jr. (1825–1899). The "Waltz King's" durable operettas include *Die Fledermaus, The Gypsy Baron*, and *A Night in Venice*.

Englebert Humperdinck (1854–1921). Wrote the all-time children's favorite *Hansel and Gretel*. His name was (mis)appropriated by a British rock singer born Arnold George Dorsey.

Richard Strauss (1864–1949). Wagner's successor as the towering figure in German opera, with *Der Rosenkavalier, Elektra, Salome, Die Frau ohne Schatten, Ariadne auf Naxos, Arabella,* and others less frequently revived.

Franz Lehár (1870–1948). Carried on the Viennese operetta tradition in *The Merry Widow, The Count of Luxemburg, The Land of Smiles,* and others.

Arnold Schoenberg (1874–1951). 12-tone composer who emigrated from Nazi Germany to the United States in 1933, dropping the umlaut in the original spelling of "Schönberg" in the process. Left his one opera, *Moses und Aron,* unfinished.

Alban Berg (1885–1935). Pupil of Schoenberg who produced two modern masterpieces, *Wozzeck* and *Lulu.*

Erich Korngold (1897–1957). Born in Brno, Czechoslovakia, studied in Vienna, spent much of his life composing soundtracks in Hollywood. His most successful opera, *Die Tode Stadt,* was written at age 23.

Kurt Weill (1900–1950). Another who successfully made the move from Europe to the United States. In Berlin he wrote *The Rise and Fall of the City of Mahagonny* and *The Threepenny Opera;* on Broadway *Knickerbocker Holiday* (with the famous "September Song") and *Street Scene.* His *Down in the Valley,* an opera in an American idiom, is frequently performed.

OTHER NATIONAL SCHOOLS OF OPERA

Although Italian, French, and German opera predominate in the international repertory, composers of other nations have created high quality works that are performed in their own lands and sometimes abroad:

RUSSIAN

Mikhail Glinka (1804–1857). Sometimes called "the father of Russian music," he composed the first national Russian opera, *A Life for the Tsar,* nowadays performed in the Soviet Union under the title *Ivan Susanin.*

Alexander Borodin (1833–1877). His *Prince Igor* is particularly well-known for its fiery "Polovetsian Dances."

Modest Mussorgsky (1839–1881). *Boris Godunov* is generally accounted the supreme Russian opera; it is often presented in a Rimsky-Korsakov revision, but many prefer the original.

Peter Ilyich Tchaikovsky (1804–1893). Best known among his 11 operas are *Eugene Onegin, The Queen of Spades, Joan of Arc,* and *Iolanthe.*

Nikolai Rimsky-Korsakov (1844–1908). His adeptness in musical color and melody are shown in *Le Coq d'Or, Sadko,* and *The Snow Maiden.*

Sergei Prokofiev (1891–1953). Wrote his most famous opera, *The Love for Three Oranges,* for the Chicago Opera Company; after his return to the Soviet Union he composed *Semyon Kotko* and *War and Peace.* Underwent considerable Soviet censure for "formalism."

Dmitri Shostakovich (1906–1975). Another victim of Soviet censure, he composed two operas, *The Nose* and *Lady Macbeth of Mzensk* (sometimes given as *Katerina Izmailova*), the latter of which incurred the personal ire of Joseph Stalin.

CZECH

Bedřich Smetana (1824–1884). *The Bartered Bride* has become the Czech national opera and also entered the international repertory.

Antonin Dvořák (1841–1904). *Rusalka,* an opera about a water nymph, has a celebrated soprano aria "O lovely moon."

Leoš Janáček (1854–1928). Both his *Jenufa* and *The Makropoulos Case* undergo periodic revivals.

HUNGARIAN

Béla Bartók (1881–1945). The one-act *Bluebeard's Castle* is his only opera.

Zoltán Kodály (1882–1967). *Háry János,* his most notable opera, is best known abroad through an orchestral suite.

ROMANIAN

George Enesco (1881–1955). His *Oedipe,* presented in Paris in 1937, is a modernistic interpretation of the Oedipus legend.

SPANISH

Felipe Pedrell (1841–1922). His call for the creation of a national lyric drama helped create Spanish opera, but of his own 10 works few are known outside of Spain.

Enrique Granados (1867–1916). His *Goyescas* is put together from previously written piano pieces.

Manuel de Falla (1876–1946). *La Vida Breve* is a *verismo* drama with a strong Spanish flavor.

BRITISH

Henry Purcell (c.1660–1695). Of his six operas, *Dido and Aeneas* has the distinction of being the oldest opera in English that is still regularly performed.

George Frideric Handel (1685–1759). Handel wrote operas in his native Germany and in Italy before settling in England, where he produced his greatest works in the form, such as *Rinaldo, Il Pastor Fido, Rodelinda,* and *Julius Caesar.* After the success of John Gay's *The Beggar's Opera* (see below) he turned to oratorio.

John Gay (1685–1732). Gay was the librettist for *The Beggar's Opera,* which used English folk tunes arranged by John Christopher Pepusch to satirize the Italian-style opera of Handel and others. It was produced by John Rich, and its success was said to have made "Rich gay and Gay rich."

Michael Balfe (1808–1870). Born in Dublin, he spent much of his life in London, where he produced his most famous work, *The Bohemian Girl.*

Arthur Sullivan (1842–1900). His collaboration with W. S. Gilbert resulted in the immortal Gilbert and Sullivan light operettas, yet he failed in his most ambitious grand opera project, a setting of Sir Walter Scott's *Ivanhoe.* See GILBERT AND/OR SULLIVAN.

Frederick Delius (1862–1934). An eccentric composer who lived mainly in France, his most notable operas, which undergo occasional revival, being *A Village Romeo and Juliet* and *Koanga.*

Ralph Vaughan Williams (1872–1958). British to the core, he captured a folk-like flavor in *Hugh the Drover, Sir John in Love,* and several other operas.

Benjamin Britten (1913–1976). The greatest native-born British opera composer since Purcell, with *Peter Grimes, The Turn of the Screw, Albert Herring, Billy Budd* and others that have entered the international repertory.

AMERICAN

Francis Hopkinson (1737–1791). The only musician to sign the Declaration of Independence also was the composer in 1781 of an "oratorical entertainment" entitled *The Temple of Minerva* admired, among others, by George Washington.

James Hewitt (1770–1827). He composed a ballad opera entitled *Tammany,* under the auspices of the Tammany Society of New York in 1794; only one number, "The Death Song of the Cherokee Indians," survives.

William Henry Fry (1813–1864). His *Leonora* (1845), cast in the mold of Bellini and Donizetti, was the first grand opera composed in the United States.

George F. Bristow (1825–1898). Bristow, supervisor of music in New York City's public schools, composed *Rip Van Winkle* (1855), the first American opera based on a native theme.

Walter Damrosch (1862–1950). Better known as a conductor and proselytizer than a composer, he wrote *The Scarlet Letter* in 1896.

Scott Joplin (1868–1917). Only recently has the "King of Ragtime's" *Treemonisha* (1911) been rediscovered and reappraised.

Frederick S. Converse (1871–1940). His *The Pipe of Desire* was the first American opera given at the Metropolitan Opera House (1910).

Igor Stravinsky (1882–1971). Stravinsky's operas *Renard, Mavra,* and *Le Rossignol* were composed in Paris after his departure from Russia, but his most imposing opera, *The Rake's Progress,* was written in California in 1951 after he had become a U.S. citizen.

Louis Gruenberg (1884–1964). His *Emperor Jones* (1933) was based on Eugene O'Neill's play about a Pullman porter who becomes ruler of a West Indies island.

Deems Taylor (1885–1966). Two operas, *The King's Henchman* (1927) and *Peter Ibbetson* (1931), achieved Metropolitan productions.

Douglas Moore (1893–1969). *The Devil and Daniel Webster* (1939) and *The Ballad of Baby Doe* (1956) capture an American folk idiom; he wrote 7 other operas.

Howard Hanson (1896–1981). A romantic composer whose *Merry Mount* was commissioned by the Metropolitan Opera (1934).

Virgil Thomson (1896–   ). His *Four Saints in Three Acts* (1934) and *The Mother of Us All* (1947)—the latter an evocation of the era of Susan B. Anthony—have texts by Gertrude Stein. He also composed *Lord Byron* (1972).

George Gershwin (1898–1937). His much-revived *Porgy and Bess* (1937) finally made it to the Metropolitan Opera in 1985.

Samuel Barber (1910–1981). Had two operas performed at the Metropolitan Opera—*Vanessa* in 1958 and *Antony and Cleopatra* at the opening of the company's new home in Lincoln Center in 1966.

Gian Carlo Menotti (1911–   ). Italian by birth and citizenship, Menotti is American in residence and outlook. Many of his works have reached the opera house after premiering elsewhere—*The Old Maid and the Thief* (1939) on radio, *Amahl and the Night Visitors* (1951) on television, *The Medium* (1946) at Columbia University, *The Saint of Bleecker Street* (1954) and *The Consul* (1950)—possibly his masterpiece—in the Broadway theater.

WAGNER AND VERDI

Richard Wagner and Giuseppe Verdi, the greatest masters of German and Italian opera respectively, were born in the same year. Wagner composed 13 operas; Verdi, who lived 18 years longer, 26 (not counting revisions). Verdi took an interest in Wagner's music and expressed sorrow on his death; Wagner totally ignored his Italian rival. Following is a comparative chronology of the premieres of their operas:

YEAR	WAGNER	VERDI
1813	(born May 22)	(born Oct. 10)
1834	*Die Feen* (not produced until 1888)	
1836	*Das Liebesverbot*	
1839		*Oberto, Conte di San Bonifacio*
1840		*Un Giorno di Regno*
1842	*Rienzi*	*Nabucco*
1843	*The Flying Dutchman*	*I Lombardi*
1844		*Ernani* *I Due Foscari*
1845	*Tannhäuser*	*Giovanna d'Arco* *Alzira*
1846		*Attila*
1847		*Macbeth* *I Masnadieri*
1848		*Il Corsaro*
1849		*La Battaglia di Legnano* *Luisa Miller*
1850	*Lohengrin*	*Stiffelio*
1851		*Rigoletto*
1853		*Il Trovatore* *La Traviata*
1855		*The Sicilian Vespers*
1857		*Simon Boccanegra*
1859		*A Masked Ball*
1862		*La Forza del Destino*
1865	*Tristan und Isolde*	
1867		*Don Carlo*
1868	*Die Meistersinger*	
1869	*Das Rheingold*	
1870	*Die Walküre*	
1871		*Aida*
1876	*Siegfried Götterdämerung*	
1882	*Parsifal*	
1883	(died Feb. 13)	
1887		*Otello*
1893		*Falstaff*
1901		(died Jan. 27)

OPERAS THAT WERE NEVER WRITTEN

Unfinished projects bestrew the history of music, and never more so than in opera, where composers were forever considering ideas and tossing them aside—sometimes after doing considerable work on them. These are some fascinating operas that never were—but might have been:

As You Like It, by Claude Debussy. After the success of *Pelléas et Mélisande* Debussy began seeking another likely operatic subject. He seized on the idea of Shakespeare's *As You Like It,* which would have been called in French *Comme Il Vous Plaira.* But though he kept it in mind to the end of his life, and actually received sketches for a libretto from the French poet Paul-Jean Toulet, the work never materialized.

Conchita, by Giacomo Puccini. This Carmen-like story of a Spanish dance hall femme fatale was rejected by Puccini when preferred to him. Based on Pierre Louÿs's *La Femme et le Pantin* (The Woman and the Puppet), it had the elements of sensuality and violence that Puccini used in some of his other operas. Later the younger composer Riccardo Zandonai took up the subject and made it his first success.

Jesus of Nazareth, by Richard Wagner. In 1848, when Wagner was 35 years old, he sketched out for himself a religious musical drama, *Jesus of Nazareth.* He returned to the idea several times, but finally decided that the saga of Siegfried and the Ring of the Nibelung was more adaptable to the kind of musical treatment he could provide.

King Lear, by Giuseppe Verdi. For years Verdi weighed the idea of writing a King Lear opera; indeed, he even worked out the vocal assignments: Lear was to be a baritone, Cordelia a dramatic (rather than a lyric) soprano, the Fool a contralto. Some authorities believe Verdi actually made sketches of some of the music, but if he did they have never been found.

The Ring of the Nibelungs, by Felix Mendelssohn. Mendelssohn, who composed only one opera, the youthful *Wedding of Camacho,* considered a number of subjects for another. Among them was the Nibelungen legends. He discussed the possibility with his sister Fanny, who wrote to him in 1840, "I am heartily glad you are entering into the idea of the Nibelungen with such zest . . . . The conclusion strikes me as the greatest difficulty, for who would finish an opera with all that horrible carnage?" The answer: Richard Wagner.

Romeo and Juliet, by Peter Ilyich Tchaikovsky. Through much of his life Tchaikovsky harbored a desire to compose a Romeo and Juliet opera, and got so far as writing a soprano-tenor duet found in his papers after his death. One deterrent to his carrying out the project may have been the success of Gounod's *Roméo et Juliette*, a work he adored.

Le Tonnelier de Nuremberg, by Georges Bizet. The distance between *Carmen* and *Die Meistersinger von Nürnberg* may seem enormous, yet Bizet did consider the latter subject, as set forth in E. T. A. Hoffmann's tale "The Cooper of Nuremberg." "The singing contest will be a very original and undoubtedly effective scene," he wrote in 1859 to his mother, who was unimpressed. Wagner already had the same idea, and produced his version 12 years later.

PUSHKIN AND OPERA

One hesitates to think where Russian opera would be without Alexander Sergeyevich Pushkin (1799–1837). His plays, poems, and novels have provided inspiration—not to mention libretti—for composers from Mussorgsky to Stravinsky. Following is a list of operas based on Pushkin:

Boris Assafiev: *The Bronze Horseman; A Feast in Time of Plague*
César Cui: *The Captive in the Caucasus; A Feast in Time of Plague*
Alexander Dargomizhsky: *Russalka; The Stone Guest*
Mikhail Glinka: *Russlan and Ludmilla*
Modest Mussorgsky: *Boris Godunov*
Eduard Napravnik: *Dubrovsky*
Sergei Rachmaninov: *Aleko; The Miserly Knight*
Nikolai Rimsky-Korsakov: *The Legend of Tsar Saltan; Le Coq d'Or; Mozart and Salieri*
Igor Stravinsky: *Mavra*
Peter Ilyich Tchaikovsky: *Eugene Onegin; Mazeppa; The Queen of Spades*

NOT-SO-FAMOUS FIRST OPERAS

Some of the most prolific operatic composers got off to a slow start, if their maiden effort is any indication. Here is a list of first operas—virtually all of which have dropped from sight—by famous composers. Excluded are composers who wrote only one opera:

FIRST OPERA	COMPOSER
Adelson e Salvini	Bellini
Le Docteur Miracle	Bizet
Paul Bunyan	Britten
Il Pigmalione	Donizetti
Artaserse	Gluck
Sapho	Gounod
Chatterton	Leoncavallo
La Grand'-Tante	Massenet
La Finta Semplice	Mozart
Pepito	Offenbach
Le Villi	Puccini
Demetrio e Polibio	Rossini
Guntram	R. Strauss
Oberto, Conte di San Bonifacio	Verdi
Die Feen	Wagner

ONE-OPERA COMPOSERS

A substantial number of operatic composers have written only one truly successful work in their lifetime—for example, Gustav Charpentier with *Louise* or even Georges Bizet with *Carmen*. But few qualify as strongly for the One-Opera Club as Ruggiero Leoncavallo (1858–1919) and Pietro Mascagni (1863–1945), both of whom scored a hit with their first effort—and never repeated their success though they spent the rest of their lives trying.

FOURTEEN OPERAS BY LEONCAVALLO BESIDES *PAGLIACCI*

I Medici	*I Zingari*
Chatterton	*La Reginella delle Rose*
La Bohème	*Are You There?*
Zaza	*La Candidata*
Der Roland	*Goffredo Mameli*
Maia	*Prestami tua Moglie*
Malbruk	*Edipo Re*

FOURTEEN OPERAS BY MASCAGNI BESIDES *CAVALLERIA RUSTICANA*

L'amico Fritz	*Amica*
I Ratzau	*Isabeau*
Guglielmo Ratcliff	*Parisina*
Silvano	*Lodoletta*
Zanetto	*Il Piccolo Marat*
Iris	*Si*
Le Maschere	*Nerone*

GILBERT AND/OR SULLIVAN

Few librettist-composer teams were as perfectly matched with each other as William Schwenk Gilbert and Arthur Sullivan, who for nearly a quarter-century produced a series of dazzling operettas that have never gone out of fashion in the English-speaking countries. Despite their artistic affinity, they were never close personal friends, and each tried—generally unsuccessfully—to make a go of it without the other. Here is a listing of their lyric stage works, together and apart:

GILBERT AND SULLIVAN

Thespis; or the Gods Grown Old (1871)
Trial by Jury (1875)
The Sorcerer (1877)
H. M. S. Pinafore (1878)
The Pirates of Penzance (1880)
Patience (1881)
Iolanthe (1882)
Princess Ida (1884)
The Mikado (1885)
Ruddigore (1887)
The Yeomen of the Guard (1888)
The Gondoliers (1889)
Utopia Limited (1893)
The Grand Duke (1896)

GILBERT WITHOUT SULLIVAN

	Music by:
Ages Ago (1869)	Frederic Clay
The Gentleman in Black (1870)	Frederic Clay

Happy Arcadia (1872)	Frederic Clay
Princess Toto (1876)	Frederic Clay
The Mountebanks (1892)	Alfred Cellier
Hark to the Wedding (1893)	George Grossmith
His Excellency (1894)	F. Osmond Carr
Fallen Fairies (1909)	Edward German

SULLIVAN WITHOUT GILBERT

WORDS BY:

Cox and Box (1867)	F. C. Burnand
The Contrabandista (1867)	F. C. Burnand
The Zoo (1875)	B. C. Stephenson (under the pseudonym of Bolton Rowe)
Ivanhoe (grand opera, 1891)	Julian Sturgis
Haddon Hall (1892)	Sydney Grundy
The Chieftain (revision of *The Contrabandista*, 1894)	F. C. Burnand
The Beauty-Stone (1898)	Arthur Pinero
The Rose of Persia (1900)	Basil Hood
The Emerald Isle (completed by Edward German, 1901)	Basil Hood

BIBLICAL OPERAS

Although operatic composers found their earliest sources of inspiration in Greek mythology, it wasn't long before they turned to the Bible for subject matter. Biblical operas have been written in every century since. Here is a sampling, listed chronologically, with titles in the original language:

Johann Thiele: *Adam und Eva* (1678)

Johann Philipp Förtsch: *Kain und Abel; oder der verzweifelnde Brudermörder* (1689)

Antonio Caldara: *Giuseppe* (1722), *La Morte d'Abele* (1732)

Michel Montéclair: *Jepthté* (1732)

Etienne Méhul: *Joseph* (1807)

Giacomo Meyerbeer: *Jephtha's Tochter* (1813)

Gioacchino Rossini: *Mosé in Egitto* (1818), *Moïse* (new version, 1827)

Gaetano Donizetti: *Il Diluvio Universale* (1830)

Giuseppe Verdi: *Nabucco* (or *Nabucodonosor*, 1842)
Charles Gounod: *La Reine de Saba* (1862)
Anton Rubinstein: *Der Thurm zu Babel* (1870), *Die Makkabäer* (1875)
Karl Goldmark: *Die Königen von Saba* (1875)
Camille Saint-Saëns: *Samson et Dalila* (1877)
Jules Massenet: *Hérodiade* (1881)
Jacques Halévy: *Le Déluge* (completed by Bizet, 1885)
Eugène d'Albert: *Kain* (1900)
Richard Strauss: *Salome* (1905)
Felix Weingartner: *Kain und Abel* (1914)
Ildebrando Pizzetti: *Debora e Jaele* (1922)
Arthur Honegger: *Judith* (1926)
Darius Milhaud: *David* (1955)
Arnold Schoenberg: *Moses und Aron* (unfinished, 1957)
Mario Castelnuovo-Tedesco: *Saul* (1960)

HISTORICAL PERSONAGES IN OPERA

Historians might not always recognize them, but famous people from Cleopatra to Einstein have been depicted, more or less melodiously, upon the operatic stage. British royalty, for some reason, is a particular favorite. Here is a sampling of heroes and villains whose careers have inspired operas:

CHARACTER	OPERA (COMPOSER)
John Adams, 2nd President of the United States	*The Mother of Us All* (Thomson)
Alfonso XI, King of Castille	*La Favorita* (Donizetti)
Susan B. Anthony, American suffragist	*The Mother of Us All* (Thomson)
Attila the Hun	*Attila* (Verdi)
Thomas à Becket, Archbishop of Canterbury	*Murder in the Cathedral* (Pizzetti)
Anne Boleyn, Queen of England	*Anna Bolena* (Donizetti)
Simon Bolivar, South American hero	*Bolivar* (Milhaud)
Lizzie Borden, ax-murder suspect	*Lizzie Borden* (Beeson)
Lucrezia Borgia, Duchess of Ferrara	*Lucrezia Borgia* (Donizetti)
William Jennings Bryan, American politician	*The Ballad of Baby Doe* (Moore)
George Gordon, Lord Byron, English poet	*Lord Byron* (Thomson)

CHARACTER	OPERA (COMPOSER)
Benvenuto Cellini, Italian goldsmith	*Benvenuto Cellini* (Berlioz)
Beatrice Cenci, Italian aristocrat	*Beatrix Cenci* (Ginastera)
Thomas Chatterton, English poet	*Tommaso Chatterton* (Leoncavallo)
André Chénier, French poet	*Andrea Chénier* (Giordano)
Cleopatra, Queen of Egypt	*Antony and Cleopatra* (Barber)
Christopher Columbus, Italian explorer	*Cristoforo Colombo* (Franchetti); *Christophe Colomb* (Milhaud)
Hernando Cortez, Spanish explorer	*Fernand Cortez* (Spontini)
Georges Danton, French Revolutionary leader	*Danton's Death* (von Einem)
Jean Jacques Dessalines, Haitian leader	*Troubled Island* (Still)
Robert Devereux, Earl of Essex, English courtier	*Roberto Devereux* (Donizetti)
Elizabeth Doe, miner's wife	*The Ballad of Baby Doe* (Moore)
Albert Einstein, scientist	*Einstein on the Beach* (Glass)
Elizabeth I, Queen of England	*Roberto Devereux* (Donizetti); *Maria Stuarda* (Donizetti); *Gloriana* (Britten)
Francesca da Rimini, Italian noblewoman	*Francesca da Rimini* (Zandonai)
Thomas Gainsborough, English painter	*Gainsborough* (Coates)
Boris Fedorovich Godunov, Czar of Muscovy	*Boris Godunov* (Mussorgsky)
Mathias Grünewald, German painter	*Mathis der Maler* (Hindemith)
Gustavus III, King of Sweden	*A Masked Ball (Verdi)
Henry VIII, King of England	*Henry VIII* (Saint-Saëns)
E. T. A. Hoffmann, German Romantic writer	*The Tales of Hoffmann* (Offenbach)
Ivan IV, "The Terrible," Czar of Russia	*The Maid of Pskov* (Rimsky-Korsakov)
Joan of Arc, French leader	*Giovanna d'Arco* (Verdi); *The Maid of Orleans* (Tchaikovsky)
John of Leyden, Dutch Anabaptist	*Le Prophète* (Meyerbeer)

*Verdi's opera originally was based on the assassination of Gustavus III at a masked ball in Stockholm on March 16, 1872. Its title was to be *Gustavo III*. However, the censor in Rome objected to the depiction on stage of the assassination of a king. The locale accordingly was changed to Boston in Colonial times, with the victim being the English governor Richard (Riccardo), Count of Warwick. It is in this form that the opera is usually given, although the original version is used occasionally.

CHARACTER	OPERA (COMPOSER)
Juana de Castile, Queen of Spain	*Juana la Loca* (Menotti)
Julius Caesar, Roman Emperor	*Giulio Cesare* (Handel)
Johannes Kepler, German astronomer	*Die Harmonie der Welt* (Hindemith)
Mikhail Kutuzov, Russian field marshal	*War and Peace* (Prokofiev)
Adrienne Lecouvreur, French actress	*Adriana Lecouvreur* (Ciléa)
Leonora di Guzman, mistress of Alfonso XI	*La Favorita* (Donizetti)
Marguerite de Valois, French noblewoman	*Les Huguenots* (Meyerbeer)
Mary, Queen of Scots	*Maria Stuarda* (Donizetti); *Mary, Queen of Scots* (Musgrave)
Montezuma, Emperor of Mexico	*Fernando Cortez* (Spontini); *Montezuma* (Sessions)
Wolfgang Amadeus Mozart, composer	*Mozart and Salieri* (Rimsky-Korsakov)
Napoleon Bonaparte, Emperor of France	*Madame Sans-Gêne* (Giordano); *Háry Janos* (Kodály); *War and Peace* (Prokofiev)
Carrie Nation, saloon wrecker	*Carrie Nation* (Moore)
Nero, Roman Emperor	*L'Incoronazione di Poppea* (Monteverdi); *Nerone* (Boito)
Niccolo Paganini, violinist	*Paganini* (Lehár)
Giovanni Pierluigi da Palestrina, composer	*Palestrina* (Pfitzner)
Peter I, "The Great," Czar of Russia	*Zar und Zimmermann* (Lortzing)
Philip II, King of Spain	*Don Carlo* (Verdi)
Pius IV, Pope	*Palestrina* (Pfitzner)
Sir Walter Raleigh, English courtier	*Gloriana* (Britten)
Richard I, King of England	*Richard Coeur de Lion* (Grétry)
Maximilien de Robespierre, French Revolutionary leader	*Robespierre, Overture* (Litolff); *Danton's Death* (von Einem)
Hans Sachs, German poet and Mastersinger	*Die Meistersinger* (Wagner)
Antonio Salieri, composer	*Mozart and Salieri* (Rimsky-Korsakov)
Gianni Schicchi, Florentine rogue	*Gianni Schicchi* (Puccini)
Socrates, Greek philosopher	*Socrate* (Satie)

CHARACTER	OPERA (COMPOSER)
Alessandro Stradella, composer	*Alessandro Stradella* (von Flotow)
Horace Tabor, silver magnate	*The Ballad of Baby Doe* (Moore)
Harriet Tubman, Abolitionist leader	*Harriet: The Woman Called Moses* (Musgrave)
Vasco da Gama, Portuguese explorer	*L'Africaine* (Meyerbeer)
Daniel Webster, American politician	*The Devil and Daniel Webster* (Moore); *The Mother of Us All* (Thomson)
Brigham Young, Mormon leader	*Deseret* (Kastle)

EARNING A LIVING IN OPERA

While operas frequently are about kings, queens, high priestesses, temple virgins, and other exotic creatures, they also deal with persons in ordinary walks of life. Here are some of the more prosaic occupations of operatic characters, with an example of each:

JOB	CHARACTER	OPERA (COMPOSER)
Maid	Adele	*Die Fledermaus* (Johann Strauss)
Pastry cook	Ahmed	*Marouf* (Rabaud)
Greengrocer's assistant	Albert Herring	*Albert Herring* (Britten)
Teamster	Alfio	*Cavalleria Rusticana* (Mascagni)
Photographer	Angèle	*The Czar Has His Photograph Taken* (Weill)
Gardener	Antonio	*The Marriage of Figaro* (Mozart)
Wells-Fargo agent	Ashby	*The Girl of the Golden West* (Puccini)
Dyer	Barak	*Die Frau ohne Schatten* (Richard Strauss)
Spy	Barnaba	*La Gioconda* (Ponchielli)
Landlord	Benôit	*La Bohème* (Puccini)
Housekeeper	Berta	*The Barber of Seville* (Rossini)
Seaman	Billy Budd	*Billy Budd* (Britten)
Cook	Boniface	*Le Jongleur de Notre Dame* (Massenet)
Pullman porter	Brutus Jones	*The Emperor Jones* (Gruenberg)
Goldsmith	Cardillac	*Cardillac* (Hindemith)

JOB	CHARACTER	OPERA (COMPOSER)
Laundress	Catarina	*Madame Sans-Gêne* (Giordano)
Painter	Cavaradossi	*Tosca* (Puccini)
Smuggler	Dancairo	*Carmen* (Bizet)
Rabbi	David	*L'amico Fritz* (Mascagni)
Farmer	Elvino	*La Sonnambula* (Bellini)
School teacher	Ellen	*Peter Grimes* (Britten)
Bullfighter	Escamillo	*Carmen* (Bizet)
Pickpocket	Filch	*The Beggar's Opera* (Gay)
Barber	Figaro	*The Barber of Seville* (Rossini)
Blacksmith	Gennaro	*The Jewels of the Madonna* (Wolf-Ferrari)
Marriage broker	Goro	*Madama Butterfly* (Puccini)
Pimp	Kyoto	*Iris* (Mascagni)
Lighthouse keeper	Lawrence	*The Wreckers* (Smyth)
Innkeeper	Luther	*The Tales of Hoffmann* (Offenbach)
Prostitute	Marie	*Wozzeck* (Berg)
Shoemaker	Marouf	*Marouf* (Rabaud)
Tailor	Matteo del Sarto	*Arlecchino* (Busoni)
Seamstress	Mimi	*La Boheme* (Puccini)
Barmaid	Minnie	*The Girl of the Golden West* (Puccini)
Toy vender	Parpignol	*La Boheme* (Puccini)
Receiver of stolen goods	Mr. Peachum	*The Beggar's Opera* (Gay)
Fisherman	Peter Grimes	*Peter Grimes* (Britten)
U.S. Navy lieutenant	Pinkerton	*Madama Butterfly* (Puccini)
Prison governor	Don Pizarro	*Fidelio* (Beethoven)
Editor	Dr. Schön	*Lulu* (Berg)
U.S. Consul (Nagasaki)	Sharpless	*Madama Butterfly* (Puccini)
Butcher's assistant	Sid	*Albert Herring* (Britten)
Inventor	Spalanzani	*The Tales of Hoffmann* (Offenbach)
Dope dealer	Sportin' Life	*Porgy and Bess* (Gershwin)
Suffragette	Susan B. Anthony	*The Mother of Us All* (Thomson)

JOB	CHARACTER	OPERA (COMPOSER)
Stevedore	Tinca	*Il Tabarro* (Puccini)
Waiter	Tonio	*Conchita* (Zandonai)
Fortune teller	Ulrica	*A Masked Ball* (Verdi)
Chambermaid	Yvonne	*Jonny Spielt Auf* (Krenek)

OPERATIC CHARACTERS NAMED DON

According to the dictionary, a *don* can be a Spanish lord or gentleman; an Italian priest; or a head, fellow, or tutor at a British university. In opera, dons usually fall into the first category, and there are a great many of them. Here is a listing of well-known and not-so-well-known dons, along with the operas they inhabit:

Don Alfonso	Donizetti: *Lucrezia Borgia*
Don Alfonso	Mozart: *Così Fan Tutte*
Don Alhambra del Bolero	Gilbert and Sullivan: *The Gondoliers*
Don Alonzo	Massenet: *Le Cid*
Don Alonzo*	Rossini: *The Barber of Seville*
Don Alvar	Rameau: *Les Indes Galantes*
Don Alvaro	Ghedini: *Re Hassan*
Don Alvaro	Gomes: *Il Guarany*
Don Alvaro	Meyerbeer: *L'Africaine*
Don Alvaro	Verdi: *La Forza del Destino*
Don Andronico	Bizet: *Don Procopio*
Don Annibale Pistacchio	Donizetti: *Il Campanello*
Don Antonio	Gomes: *Il Guarany*
Don Arias	Massenet: *Le Cid*
Don Asdrubale	Ricci: *Crispino e la Comare*
Don Basilio	Mozart: *The Marriage of Figaro*
Don Basilio	Rossini: *The Barber of Seville*
Don Caesar de Bazan	Wallace: *Maritana*
Don Carlo	Verdi: *Ernani*
Don Carlo	Verdi: *La Forza del Destino*
Don Carlo	Verdi: *Don Carlo*
Don Carlos	Cherubini: *L'Hôtellerie Portugaise*
Don Carlos	Dargomizhsky: *The Stone Guest*
Don Carlos	Prokofiev: *The Betrothal in a Monastery*
Don Carlos	Rameau: *Les Indes Galantes*
Don Cassandro	Mozart: *La Finta Semplice*
Don César	Reznicek: *Donna Diana*

*A disguise adopted by the Count Almaviva.

Don César de Bazan	Massenet: *Don César de Bazan*
Don Cesare	Marchetti: *Ruy Blas*
Don Chisciotte	Caldera: *Don Chisciotte e Sancio Panza*
Don Chisciotte	Conti: *Don Chisciotte*
Don Chisciotte	Paisiello: *Don Chisciotte della Mancia*
Don Cléophas	Le Sage: *Le Diable Boiteux*
Don Cristobal de Aranda	Goossens: *Don Juan de Mañara*
Don Curzio	Mozart: *The Marriage of Figaro*
Don Diego	Meyerbeer: *L'Africaine*
Don Diego	Rezniček: *Donna Diana*
Don Diègue	Massenet: *Le Cid*
Don Enriquez	Auber: *Les Diamants de la Couronne*
Don Ettore	Haydn: *La Cantarina*
Don Eugenio	Wolf: *Der Corregidor*
Don Fernando	Beethoven: *Fidelio*
Don Fernando	Granados: *Goyescas*
Don Francisco de la Guerra	Herbert: *Natoma*
Don Gasparo	Donizetti: *La Favorita*
Don Gayferos	de Falla: *El Retablo de Maese Pedro*
Don Giovanni	Alfano: *L'ombra di Don Giovanni*
Don Giovanni	Carnicer: *Don Giovanni Tenorio*
Don Giovanni	Gazzaniga: *Don Giovanni Tenorio*
Don Giovanni	Lattuada: *Don Giovanni*
Don Giovanni	Malipiero: *Don Giovanni*
Don Giovanni	Mozart: *Don Giovanni*
Don Giovanni	Righini: *Il Convitato di Pietra*
Don Giovanni d'Aragona*	Verdi: *Ernani*
Don Gomez	Weber: *Die Drei Pintos*
Don Gomez da Silva	Verdi: *Ernani*
Don Gomez di Feria	Saint-Saëns: *Henry VIII*
Don Gonzales	Gomes: *Il Guarany*
Don Gregorio	Donizetti: *L'ajo nell'imbarazzo*
Don Inigo	Ravel: *L'Heure Espagnole*
Don Jerome	Prokofiev: *The Betrothal in a Monastery*
Don José	Bizet: *Carmen*
Don José de Santarem	Wallace: *Maritana*
Don José Martinez	Delius: *Koanga*
Don Juan	Dargomizhsky: *The Stone Guest*
Don Juan	Goossens: *Don Juan de Mañara*
Don Juan	Graener: *Don Juan's Letzes Abenteur*
Don Juan	Purcell: *The Libertine*
Don Luigi	Rezniček: *Donna Diana*
Don Luis	Goossens: *Don Juan de Mañara*
Don Magnifico	Rossini: *Cenerentola*

*Also known as Ernani.

Don Manolito	Sorozabal: *Don Manolito*
Don Marco	Menotti: *The Saint of Bleecker Street*
Don Marzio	Malipiero: *La Bottega de Caffé*
Don Narciso	Rossini: *The Turk in Italy*
Don Orazio	Galuppi: *L'Amanate di Tutte*
Don Ottavio	Mozart: *Don Giovanni*
Don Pantaleone	Weber: *Die Drei Pintos*
Don Pasquale	Donizetti: *Don Pasquale*
Don Pedre	Rameau: *La Princesse de Navarre*
Don Pedro	Berlioz: *Béatrice et Bénédict*
Don Pedro	Meyerbeer: *L'Africaine*
Don Pelegrio	Haydn: *La Cantarina*
Don Perlimplin	Susa: *The Love of Don Perlimplin*
Don Pietro	Pergolesi: *Lo Frate 'nnamorato*
Don Pimperlin	Rieti: *Don Pimperlin*
Don Pinto	Weber: *Die Drei Pintos*
Don Pippo	Mozart: *L'Oca del Cairo*
Don Pistacchio	Cherubini: *Don Pistacchio*
Don Pizzaro	Beethoven: *Fidelio*
Don Polidoro	Mozart: *La Finta Semplice*
Don Quichotte	Hervé: *Don Quichotte et Sancho Pansa*
Don Quichotte	Ibert: *Le Chevalier Errant*
Don Quichotte	Massenet: *Don Quichotte*
Don Quixote	de Falla: *El Retablo de Maese Pedro*
Don Quixote	Macfarren: *Don Quixote*
Don Quixote	Mendelssohn: *The Wedding of Camacho*
Don Quixote	Purcell: *Don Quixote*
Don Ramiro	Rossini: *Cenerentola*
Don Ranudo	Schoeck: *Don Ranudo de Colibrados*
Don Riccardo	Verdi: *Ernani*
Don Rodrigo	Ginastera: *Don Rodrigo*
Don Rodrigue	Massenet: *Le Cid*
Don Roy Gomez da Silva	Verdi: *Don Carlo*
Don Sallustio	Marchetti: *Ruy Blas*
Don Sanche	Liszt: *Don Sanche*
Don Sebastian	Donizetti: *Don Sebastian, Roi de Portugal*
Don Tammaro	Paisiello: *Il Socrate Imaginario*
Don Tritemio	Galuppi: *Il Filosofo di Campagna*
Don	*Holbrooke: *The Children of Don*

---

*Joseph Holbrooke (1878–1958) was an English composer whose operas, including *The Children of Don* (the first of a trilogy entitled *The Cauldron of Anwyn,* based on Welsh legends) had a brief vogue in the early years of the 20th century. Don is the name of the Earth Goddess and is sung by a soprano. This apparently is the only opera in which Don—all by itself—is a proper name, as well as the first opera in which the Don is a woman.

DON GIOVANNI'S LIST OF CONQUESTS

Of all the operatic Dons, probably the most celebrated is Don Giovanni, or Don Juan, as he is known in the Spanish original. In Act I of Mozart's opera, his sexual successes, totalling 2,065, are recounted by his servant Leporello in the "Catalogue Aria." However, in the opera itself, the Don's atttempts on women bring him only frustration or humiliation, raising the possibility that Leporello's list, delectable as it is to listen to, may be somewhat inflated:

In Italy	640
In Germany	231
In France	100
In Turkey	91
In Spain	1,003
In *Don Giovanni*	0

WAGNERIAN ROSTER

Richard Wagner, who did everything on a big scale, sometimes thought of his protagonists in terms of groups rather than individuals. Here are some of the Wagnerian assemblages:

NINE VALKYRIES

Brünnhilde
Gerhilde
Grimgerde
Helmwige
Ortlinde
Rossweise
Schwertleite
Siegrune
Waltraute

THREE RHINE MAIDENS

Flosshilde
Wellgunde
Woglinde

TWO GIANTS

Fafnir
Fasolt

THIRTEEN MASTERSINGERS AND
THEIR TRADES

Hans Sachs	Cobbler
Veit Pogner	Goldsmith
Kunz Vogelgesang	Furrier
Conrad Nachtigal	Buckle-maker
Sixtus Beckmesser	Town clerk
Fritz Kothner	Baker
Balthasar Zorn	Pewterer
Ulrich Eisslinger	Grocer
Augustin Mosler	Tailor
Hermann Ortel	Soap boiler
Hans Schwarz	Stocking weaver
Hans Foltz	Coppersmith
Walther von Stolzing	Unemployed

The Mastersingers of Wagner's opera *The Mastersingers of Nuremberg* are the working townspeople of the medieval guilds and are so identified in the cast of characters. Walther von Stolzing, who wins their singing contest and thereby obtains both the hand of Pogner's daughter Eva and official designation as a Mastersinger, is listed merely as "a Franconian knight"—apparently his only occupation.

OPERATIC HEROINES

What is the most frequently encountered female name among operatic characters? A quick guess might suggest a toss-up between Leonora and Elvira, but in point of fact, both are outnumbered by Anna, Marguerite, Maria, and Susanna, or their variants. Here are some of the better-known bearers of these names, listed alphabetically with opera (and composer):

NAME	OPERA (COMPOSER)
Anna	*L'Africaine* (Meyerbeer)
Anna	*La Dame Blanche* (Boieldieu)
Anna	*Intermezzo* (Richard Strauss)
Anna	*Nabucco* (Verdi)
Anna	*Les Troyens* (Berlioz)
Anna	*Le Villi* (Puccini)
Donna Anna	*Don Giovanni* (Mozart)
Anna Bolena	*Anna Bolena* (Donizetti)
Anna Gomez	*The Consul* (Menotti)

NAME	OPERA (COMPOSER)
Anna Hope	*The Mother of Us All* (Thomson)
Anna Reich	*The Merry Wives of Windsor* (Nicolai)
Anne	*The Mother of Us All* (Thomson)
Anne (Nanetta) Page	*Falstaff* (Verdi)
Anne Trulove	*The Rake's Progress* (Stravinsky)
Elvira	*Ernani* (Verdi)
Elvira	*L'Italiana in Algeri* (Rossini)
Elvira	*I Puritani* (Bellini)
Elvira	*Masaniello* or *La Muette de Portici* (Auber)
Donna Elvira	*Don Giovanni* (Mozart)
Leonora	*Alessandro Stradella* (Niedemayer)
Leonora	*Fidelio* (Beethoven)
Leonora	*Leonora* (Fry)
Leonora	*Oberto* (Verdi)
Leonora	*Il Trovatore* (Verdi)
Leonora di Gusman	*La Favorita* (Donizetti)
Leonora di Vargas	*La Forza del Destino* (Verdi)
Margared	*Le Roi d'Ys* (Lalo)
Mad Margaret	*Ruddigore* (Gilbert and Sullivan)
Margarethe	*Genoveva* (Schumann)
Margarita	*I Quattro Rusteghi* (Wolf-Ferrari)
Margherita*	*Mefistofele* (Boito)
Margret	*Wozzeck* (Berg)
Marguerite	*La Dame Blanche* (Boieldieu)
Marguerite*	*The Damnation of Faust* (Berlioz)
Marguerite*	*Faust* (Gounod)
Marguerite	*Louise* (Charpentier)
Marguerite de Valois	*Les Huguenots* (Meyerbeer)
Maria	*Friedenstag* (Richard Strauss)
Maria	*Mazeppa* (Tchaikovsky)
Maria	*Porgy and Bess* (Gershwin)
Maria	*West Side Story* (Bernstein)
Maria Golovin	*Maria Golovin* (Menotti)
Marie	*Barbe-Bleu* (Grétry)
Marie	*The Daughter of the Regiment* (Donizetti)
Marie	*Marie* (Herold)

*The heroine of the Faust story appears in many operas, of which only the three most popular are listed here.

NAME	OPERA (COMPOSER)
Marie	*Moïse* (Rossini)
Marie	*Wozzeck* (Berg)
Marie	*Zar und Zimmermann* (Lortzing)
Mariette	*Die Tote Stadt* (Korngold)
Susan	*Hugh the Drover* (Vaughan Williams)
Susan B. Anthony	*The Mother of Us All* (Thomson)
Susanna	*Die Harmonie der Welt* (Hindemith)
Susanna	*Khovantschina* (Mussorgsky)
Susanna	*The Marriage of Figaro* (Mozart)
Susanna	*The Secret of Susanna* (Wolf-Ferrari)
Susannah Polk	*Susanna* (Floyd)
Suzanne	*Louise* (Charpentier)
Suzel	*L'amico Fritz* (Mascagni)
Suzy	*La Rondine* (Puccini)

WOMEN WHO SING MEN'S ROLES

Women singers are frequently called upon to undertake male roles in opera, but the reverse practically never occurs. Some of these so-called "trouser," "pants," or "transvestite" roles are minor, but a good many of them represent important characters who sing notable music. Here are some of the better known:

Cherubino. In Mozart's *The Marriage of Figaro* he (she) embodies the youthful ardor of love. Besides playing an important part in the action, he sings two of the most beautiful arias ever written for mezzo soprano, "Non so più cosa son, cosa faccio" and "Voi che sapete."

Dmitri. This is a minor role for contralto in *Fedora*, a melodramatic opera by Giordano that today seems a bit old-fashioned, not to say old-hat. Dmitri is the groom of Count Vladimir, who is murdered in St. Petersburg on the eve of his marriage to the wealthy Princess Fedora.

Feodor. Feodor, sung by a mezzo-soprano, is the Tsarevitch, the son of Boris Godunov in the opera of that name. He has a pleasant little song to sing in Act II, but his principal function comes at the opera's climax, when he listens to his dying father sing his great farewell aria.

Idamante. Mozart wrote this role in his youthful opera *Idomeneo* for a castrato; nowadays a mezzo-soprano sings it. Idamante is the son of a king of ancient Crete who barely misses being sacrificed by his father in fulfillment of a rash vow. He survives to marry the girl and mount the throne.

Niklausse. Hoffmann's companion and guardian in Offenbach's *The Tales of Hoffmann*, he provides one of the two voices that intertwine in the opera's most famous number, the "Barcarolle."

Octavian. This attractive young hero of Richard Strauss's *Der Rosenkavalier* is regarded by some operagoers as a descendant of Mozart's Cherubino. In fact, the same singers often undertake the two roles, which are quite similar in both their romantic ardor and musical charm.

Orfeo. In Gluck's opera, *Orfeo ed Euridice*, it is Orpheus, lyre in hand and mezzo or alto in voice, who descends into Hades to rescue his beloved Eurydice. In a French version composed by Gluck later for a Paris performance, Orfeo (or Orphée, as he is known) is transformed into a tenor.

Orlofsky. Prince Orlofsky in Johann Strauss's *Die Fledermaus* is most often sung by a mezzo-soprano, though male singers have also been known to undertake the part. Either way, it's a fun role requiring the performer to adopt a heavy Russian accent as he throws a lavish party whose theme is "chacun à son gout."

Oscar. In Verdi's *A Masked Ball* Oscar is a page in the establishment of Riccardo, Count of Warwick, who happens to be the "Governor of Boston" in the Colonial era. Verdi has provided two delightful arias for the role designed for a soprano voice capable of coloratura excursions.

Romeo. In Gounod's *Roméo et Juliette*, the "pants" role is reserved for Stephano, a secondary character (see below), while the hero himself is sung by a tenor. However, in another operatic retelling of Shakespeare's story, Bellini's *I Capuleti e I Montecchi* (The Capulets and the Montagues) the role of Romeo is given to a mezzo-soprano while Giulietta is sung by a soprano.

Sesto. Mozart's *La Clemenza di Tito*, composed in the last year of his life, contains in the part of Sesto, a young Roman patrician, a castrato role nowadays sung by a mezzo-soprano. Another Roman patrician, Annius, is sung by a soprano. The work, long on the operatic shelf, is undergoing a modest modern revival.

Siebel. In Gounod's *Faust*, Siebel is Faust's hopelessly outclassed rival in the quest for Marguerite's affections. In Anglo-Saxon countries, the role is given to a mezzo-soprano, who usually makes the most of her nice little "Flower Song." In France, the part often goes to a regular soprano.

Stephano. *Roméo et Juliette* by Gounod adds to Shakespeare a perky character named Stephano, Romeo's page, who is sung by a soprano. One of Stephano's functions is to hold the ladder upon which Romeo ascends to Juliet's balcony. Musically, Stephano's big moment is a ditty entitled "Que fais-tu, blanche tourterelle" (What are you doing, white dove?) that helps to precipitate the fatal sword fight between Mercutio and Tybalt.

MEN WHO SING WOMEN'S ROLES

A far shorter list, alas, than the above. In fact, it consists of only a single entry. Is this a matter for consideration by the Men's Lib movement?

Cook. The Cook, in Prokofiev's *The Love for Three Oranges*, is a female character designated for a bass voice. Since logic is hardly the keynote of this bizarre, fantastic opera, it seems perfectly reasonable for the huge figure of the Cook (actually a witch named Creonte) to open her mouth and sing in a sonorous basso.*

OPERATIC SPOOKS AND SPECTERS

Supernatural visitors are frequent in opera, often playing pivotal roles (their favorite vocal register is bass). Here is a roster of ghostly characters, listed by opera:

Dalibor (Smetana). Zdenek, a friend of the Bohemian knight Dalibor, has been slain, and in revenge Dalibor kills the murderer. For this he is imprisoned. Zdenek's ghost, playing a violin, appears to Dalibor in his cell. This particular ghost is sung by a soprano.

David (Milhaud). In the course of this opera about the Biblical hero David, King Saul visits the Witch of En-dor who, at his insistence, makes the spirit of the dead prophet Samuel appear.

Der Freischütz (Weber). Max, the forester, is determined to accept diabolical aid to forge magic bullets that can win him the hand of Agathe. In the wild Wolf's Glen scene, the ghost of Max's mother appears to warn him not to do so. Unfortunately, Max doesn't listen.

Don Giovanni (Mozart). Undoubtedly opera's greatest specter is the stone statue of the Commendatore, which accepts Don Giovanni's invitation to supper and stalks in, accompanied by trombones, to

---

*Two operas have male characters who adopt female disguises. In Rossini's *Le Comte Ory*, the Count, a tenor, disguises himself and his followers as nuns to gain access to his lady's castle. In Stravinsky's *Mavra*, Vassily, also a tenor, takes on the guise of a maid named Mavra to enter the household of his beloved, Parasha. However, at the end of both these operas, the tenors regain their original identity—and voices.

convey him to hell. The same episode, of course, also climaxes Don Giovanni or Don Juan operas by other composers.

Hamlet (Thomas). The Ghost of Hamlet's father is a character in Ambroise Thomas's opera, just as it is in most other settings of Shakespeare's play. The operatic version has the Ghost reappear just in time to prevent Hamlet from committing suicide at the bier of Ophelia. Instead, Hamlet stabs Claudius to death.

Macbeth (Verdi). Banquo has been killed by Macbeth's assassins in Act II just after singing a beautiful bass aria. Later in the same act his ghost keeps popping up at a banquet, much to the discomfiture of Macbeth, who is the only one who can see him.

The Medium (Menotti). A dead child's spirit is supposedly raised at a seance staged for her bereaved parents by Madame Flora. Even though the ghost is a fake, impersonated by Flora's daughter Monica, the scene is an eerie one.

Mireille (Gounod). Spirits of dead lovers haunt the wicked Provençal cattle-owner Ourrias as he tries to escape across the Val d'Enfer after stabbing his rival Vincent. Eventually Ourrias is done in by a spectral boatman as he tries to cross a river.

Orfeo ed Euridice (Gluck). Not all ghosts are scary. In Gluck's 1762 opera, Orfeo, after successfully passing Cerberus and the Furies, is greeted by a Happy Shade in the Valley of the Blest in Hades. She and other equally happy shades assure him of their bliss in the Elysian Fields but Orfeo, once he has found Euridice, departs anyway, with deplorable results.

Palestrina (Pfitzner). The composer Palestrina's dead wife Lucretia (a contralto) appears to him as he is writing a mass commissioned by Pope Pius IV. So do the apparitions of Nine Dead Composers (tenor, baritone, bass). These are inspirational ghosts: all do their best to encourage him.

Robert le Diable (Meyerbeer). A chorus of dead nuns rise from their graves in the ruined convent of St. Rosalie to cavort around the churchyard. This spooky scene, performed by ballet dancers, scandalized Paris in the 1830s.

Le Rossignol (Stravinsky). Ghosts representing both good and bad deeds crowd around the bed of a dying Emperor, while Death hovers nearby. The Nightingale arrives, and its beautiful song disperses the ghosts and makes Death itself relent.

Ruddigore (Gilbert and Sullivan). Act II of this operetta presents as splendid an array of ghosts as anyone could wish—an entire picture gallery of the wicked Baronets of Ruddigore that comes to life under the leadership of Sir Roderic Murgatroyd, the wickedest of them all. His suitably scary "The Ghosts' High Noon" could well be adopted as the theme song of operatic spooks everywhere.

Saul and David (Nielsen). This early work by the Swedish composer

Carl Nielsen follows the Old Testament story, with an appearance by the ghost of Samuel as summoned up by the Witch of En-dor.

Semiramide (Rossini). Semiramide, Queen of Babylon, has murdered her husband Nino. His ghost subsequently steps out of his tomb to point the finger of accusation and also to appoint his son as successor.

Les Troyens (Berlioz). A veritable procession of specters appears to order Aeneas to follow his destiny by departing Carthage and heading for Italy to found Rome. Among the ghosts proferring this advice are those of Priam, Chorèbe, Cassandre, and Hector.

The Turn of the Screw (Britten). Two ghosts, both of them malevolent, are the mainspring of this opera. Peter Quint, a butler, and Miss Jessel, a governess, both long since dead, return to an English country house, seeking to dominate two children who knew them in life. The opera, based on a story by Henry James, deals with the new governess' efforts to fight them off.

Le Villi (Puccini). Anna, who has died of a broken heart caused by the faithless Roberto, reappears to him as a spirit amid a crowd of Wilis. She tells him she no longer represents Love but Revenge, and claims his life. Le Villi was Puccini's first opera, and Anna his only ghost.

OPERATIC BREWS AND BEVERAGES

Operatic characters at times display a seemingly unquenchable thirst for drink of all kinds. They consume a variety of potions, poisons, and philtres, and also do a good deal of purely social, not to mention musical, drinking. Here are some instances:

Carmen (Bizet). Carmen is a girl who always knows what she wants. In wine, it's manzanilla, served by her friend Lillas Pastia at his tavern. Manzanilla is a pale, very dry sherry with a particularly bracing and salty character.

Cavalleria Rusticana (Mascagni). "Quel vino è generoso," Turiddu tells Mamma Lucia just before he rushes off for his fatal duel with his love-rival Alfio. The implication is that he's been drinking a *rosso robusto*, and probably too much of it. Undoubtedly, it's a local Sicilian brand, non-vintage.

Così Fan Tutte (Mozart). Chocolate is the ladylike beverage served to the sisters Fiordiligi and Dorabella by their maid Despina, who helps herself to a sip or two en route.

Don Giovanni (Mozart). As might be expected, the Don is a connoisseur in wine no less than in women and song. His exuberant

"Finch' han dal vino" has become known as the Champagne Aria (he invariably tosses off a *coupe* at the end), and in the climactic Supper Scene he praises the "eccellente marsimino" he is drinking. The reference is to an Italian wine, marzemino del Trentino, a fruity red from the north.

L'Elisir d'Amore (Donizetti). "Bordo" (bordeaux) wine is rebottled by Dr. Dulcamara and peddled by him as a universal remedy. Probably not of a very good year, either.

Falstaff (Verdi). Among the Fat Knight's first words in the opera are "Oste! Un'altra bottiglia di Xeres!" (Landlord! Another bottle of sherry!) Later on, after his ducking in the River Thames, he calls for, and receives, a flagon of hot wine—the effects of which ripple through both Sir John and the orchestra.

Faust (Gounod). Only Mephistophélès has the secret of the ingredient that makes Dr. Faust young again when it's popped into his drink.

Die Fledermaus (J. Strauss). At his Act II party, Prince Orlovsky plies his guests with Madeira, jocularly threatening to throw the bottle at anyone failing to keep pace with him. Then he switches to champagne, which he calls "dem König aller Weine" (the king of all wines). His sentiments are echoed by the entire assemblage in the Finale.

Götterdämmerung (Wagner). The spiked drink prepared by Hagen for Siegfried produces such a state of total forgetfulness that it's small wonder no one remembers what went into it.

Hamlet (Thomas). "O vin, dissipe la tristesse," cries Hamlet in one of opera's most rousing drinking songs. The closest translation might be "Oh wine, banish sorrow," especially if one wishes to avoid the double entrendre of "dissipate."

Lucrezia Borgia (Donizetti). Poisoning the wine to get rid of an enemy is an accepted operatic procedure, but Lucrezia wipes out her entire guest list at a banquet. When she discovers that her son Gennaro is among the victims she offers him an antidote, which he selfrighteously refuses—whereupon she drains the poison cup herself.

Madama Butterfly (Puccini). One of the few operas that offer a choice. "Milk punch or whisky?" Lieutenant Pinkerton asks the U.S. Consul who, to his credit, opts for the latter.

Otello (Verdi). As in Shakespeare's play, Iago in Verdi's opera leads the Venetian soldiery on Cyprus in a drinking song, taking particular care to ply Cassio with wine. No particular type is indicated, but a local Cypriote wine would seem the most likely. Curiously, one of today's most popular Cyprus reds is called Othello and bears a picture of the Moor on the label.

The Tales of Hoffmann (Offenbach). Punch—usually pronounced in operatic French as "paunch"—is the favored drink of Hoffmann's student buddies in Luther's tavern. Luther serves it flaming to his customers' cries of "Allumons le punch!"

La Traviata (Verdi). Alfredo's "Libiamo" probably is the most familiar of all operatic *brindisi* (or drinking songs). The place (Paris), circumstances (a fashionable party), and lifestyle of the hostess Violetta Valery ("sempre libera"—always free) all point to one libation—champagne.

Tristan und Isolde (Wagner). Isolde orders up a Death Potion and gets a Love Potion instead. A bartending error or a purposeful switcheroo? Only Brangäne knows.

OPERATIC SUICIDES—A MELANCHOLY LIST

Suicide is second to none as a cause of death in opera. Most of the characters who take their lives do so by such established methods as stabbing or drowning themselves, but some display surprising ingenuity in ending their existences. Here is a survey of some of the better-known instances, listed by the title of the opera in which the suicide takes place:

L'Africaine (Meyerbeer). Selika inhales the perfume of the manchineel tree, deadly to all who breathe it.

Aida (Verdi). Aida conceals herself in the vault in which her lover has been immured so she can share his death by suffocation.

L'Amore dei Tre Re (Montemezzi). Manfredo dies by deliberately kissing the poisoned lips of his murdered wife Fiora in her tomb.

Antony and Cleopatra (Barber). As in Shakespeare, Cleopatra presses an asp to her bosom.

The Consul (Menotti). Magda Sorel seals her kitchen and turns on the gas.

Dido and Aeneas (Purcell). Dido stabs herself and mounts a funeral pyre. (The same ending occurs in Berlioz's *Les Troyens*.)

Ernani (Verdi). Ernani, a nobleman turned bandit, stabs himself in fulfillment of a pledge to die when his enemy Silva sounds his horn.

La Gioconda (Ponchielli). Gioconda the Venetian ballad singer stabs herself to frustrate the lust of the spy Barnaba.

Götterdämmerung (Wagner). Brünnhilde rides her horse Grane onto Siegfried's funeral pyre.

Gwendoline (Chabrier). Gwendoline, an eighth-century Saxon beauty, stabs herself to join her Danish lover, Harald, in death.

Herodiade (Massenet). Salome stabs herself upon learning that John the Baptist has been executed.

L'incoronazione di Poppea (Monteverdi). Seneca the philosopher opens his veins in the bath at the command of the Emperor Nero.

Iris (Mascagni). Iris, a poor but beautiful Japanese girl, unjustly accused of becoming a geisha, throws herself into a sewer.

Khovantschina (Mussorgsky). Marfa and Andrea and other members of the Old Believers climb a funeral pyre and perish in the flames.

Lady Macbeth of Mzensk (Shostakovich). Katerina Ismailova drowns herself in a river enroute to a prison camp in Siberia.

Lakmé (Délibes). Lakmé, daughter of a Brahmin, poisons herself with the juice of an exotic flower when she loses her lover, the English officer Gerald.

Lucia di Lammermoor (Donizetti). Edgardo kills himself with a dagger at Lucia's tomb.

Madama Butterfly (Puccini). Harakiri is the method selected by Cio-Cio-San.

Masaniello (Auber). Fenella, the mute girl of Portici, throws herself into the sea when she learns that her heroic brother Masaniello has been killed.

Norma (Bellini). Another funeral-pyre case. This time the Roman officer Pollione voluntarily joins the Druid priestess in death.

Otello (Verdi). Otello stabs himself with a dagger he has been carrying in reserve after his sword has been taken from him following his murder of Desdemona.

Pique Dame (*The Queen of Spades,* Tchaikovsky). Herman, an officer given to gambling, stabs himself when he sees the ghost of an old countess whose death he has caused. The old woman's daughter Lisa has previously drowned herself.

Le Roi d'Ys (Lalo). Margared, daughter of the King of Ys, leaps from a precipice in attempted expiation for the crime of helping an enemy open the dikes that protect her city from the sea.

Romeo and Juliet (Gounod). Both lovers die in the traditional fashion.

Samson and Delila (Saint-Saëns). Samson brings down the Temple of Dagon upon all its occupants, including himself. In some productions there is one survivor—the little child who has guided Samson to the central pillars and who is warned by the blinded hero to escape.

Snegurochka (*The Snow Maiden,* Rimsky-Korsakov). Mizguir, a young Tartar merchant, flings himself into a lake when his beloved Snow Maiden is melted by an inopportune ray of sunlight.

Suor Angelica (Puccini). Sister Angelica swallows a poisonous potion she has concocted from the herbs in her convent's garden.

Tosca (Puccini). Tosca leaps to her death from the parapet of the Castle of Sant' Angelo in Rome after her lover has been shot by a firing squad.

Il Trovatore (Verdi). Leonora takes poison from a ring and swallows it rather than submit to the Count di Luna.

Turandot (Puccini). The slave-girl Liu stabs herself rather than reveal under torture the name of the Unknown Prince, Calaf.

La Wally (Catalani). The heroine throws herself from a precipice during an avalanche in the Alps.

Werther (Massenet). The lovelorn Werther shoots himself with a pistol.

Wozzeck (Berg). Wozzeck stabs his wife with a knife, then, after visiting a tavern, walks into a pond and drowns himself.

OPERATIC DOCTORS AT WORK

Although physicians abound in opera, few are shown actually practicing their profession. Of those who actually treat patients—one way or another—the following may be noted:

Dr. Dulcamara (L'Elisir d'Amore). A quack, though a most endearing one. His cure-all is "bordo," or Bordeaux wine, effective against everything from aches to lovesickness.

Dr. Grenvil (La Traviata). A fashionable Paris practitioner. He tries to cheer up the dying Violetta Valery, then quietly tells her maid the patient has only a few hours to live.

Dr. Miracle (The Tales of Hoffmann). Accurately described as "a gravedigger, an assassin" by Crespel, the father of his patient, Antonia. His "remedy" for her illness consists of certain mysterious flagons that should be drunk every morning.

Dr. Spinellocchio (Gianni Schicchi). A doddering old Florentine physician called in to "treat" a corpse. Deceived when a live body replaces the dead one, he departs rejoicing in the virtues of the Bolognese School of Medicine.

Doctor, unnamed (Così Fan Tutte). Another quack, actually the maid Despina in disguise. She professes to be a disciple of Dr. Franz Anton Mesmer, the discoverer of mesmerism, and "cures" two supposed victims of poison by waving a magnet over them.

Doctor, unnamed (La Forza del Destino). A Spanish military surgeon at the Battle of Velletri, August 11, 1744 who successfully extracts a bullet from the breast of the wounded Don Alvaro, thereby saving his life, in one of opera's most notable medical triumphs.

Doctor, unnamed (Macbeth). Observes Lady Macbeth while she is sleepwalking, but offers no remedies.

Doctor, unnamed (*Pelléas and Mélisande*). Sympathetic but helpless, he attends Melisande on her deathbed. He has no advice to offer other than to open the window to let in some fresh air.

Doctor, unnamed (*Wozzeck*). A military physician, obsessed with new theories and spouting medical terminology, but without the least idea of how to treat his patient. An obvious candidate for a malpractice suit.

VOCAL TYPES

The four basic categories of the singing voice are soprano, alto, tenor, and bass. However, this is only the beginning of an intricate series of classifications; some "sopranos," for instance, are mezzo-sopranos, and some "basses" are bass-baritones. In addition, there are many subdivisions and specialties. Following are some of the more commonly—as well as less commonly—encountered vocal types:

SOPRANO

The word derives from the Italian "sovrano," meaning highest, chief, or head—a designation that would be challenged by few sopranos in any era. This is the highest natural adult female voice, although boy sopranos may emulate it before puberty. Normal range: approximately two octaves upward from the B-flat below middle C. Three basic types of soprano exist:

Coloratura. The highest range of all, requiring an ability to sing with agility and even acrobatically.
Lyric. Light, pleasant and flexible, usually with a bright quality.
Dramatic. Marked by power and declamatory ability.

In addition, the following soprano designations are encountered, though less frequently:

Dugazon. A singer who specializes in soubrette roles, usually involving intelligent acting. The name comes from a French exponent of the type, Louise Rosalie Dugazon (1735–1821), who created 60 roles at the Opera-Comique. Depending upon the age of the character portrayed, a dugazon part may be either a "jeune dugazon" or a "mère dugazon." The role of Ellen in Délibes' opera *Lakmé* is listed in the cast of characters not as a soprano but as a dugazon.

Falcon. A type of dramatic soprano named after Marie-Cornélie Falcon (1812–1897), another Parisian favorite. Roles to which the designation is applied include Rachel in Halévy's *La Juive*, Alice in Meyerbeer's *Robert le Diable* and Valentin in Meyerbeer's *Les Huguenots*.

Leggiero. Light; the Italian term for a lyric soprano.

Sfogato. A very high, light, thin (vocally, at least) soprano. Comes from the Italian word for "unburdened."

Spinto. A lyric voice capable of being made to sound powerful or dramatic at climactic moments. Derived from the Italian for "pushed." For sopranos, the full term is lirico spinto, with Mimi in Puccini's *La Bohème* a favorite spinto role. For tenors, see below.

MEZZO-SOPRANO

A female voice between the soprano and the alto (see below), sharing some of the range of both. Although some mezzos move up permanently to the soprano classification, this type of in-between voice is usually considered a shade closer to the alto. The supreme mezzo-soprano role is Bizet's *Carmen.*

ALTO OR CONTRALTO

The terms are interchangeable. This is the lowest normal female voice. The derivation is from "high" (the Latin word is *altus*) but this refers to the high male voice, nowadays called counter-tenor (see below), employed in early church music. The female alto voice has an essential role in choral music and also is important in opera. Normal range: approximately two octaves upward from the E or F below middle C.

TENOR

The highest natural adult male voice. The word comes from the Italian *teneo*—(I hold)—indicating that the tenor kept the tune in ancient music, no less than in the recent kind. Normal range: approximately two octaves upward from the C an octave below middle C. The following types may be noted:

Counter-tenor. A very high, often a falsetto, voice; sometimes cultivated rather than natural. Originally, a male alto.

Heldentenor. German for a voice of heroic quality and quantity; the typical Wagnerian protagonist.

Spinto. The tenor equivalent of the soprano lirico spinto above. Alfredo in Verdi's La Traviata may be cited as a tenor spinto role.

Tenore buffo. The second tenor of a company; one who specializes in comic roles.

Tenor di forza. A heroic, powerful voice; equivalent to the German Heldentenor. In English, a dramatic tenor. Verdi's *Otello* is a typical role.

Tenore di grazia. Light and graceful; a lyric tenor. Verdi's Duke of Mantua in *Rigoletto* is an example.

Tenore robusto. Slightly less powerful than the tenore di forza; the terms are almost interchangeable.

Trial. A high, thin, nasal tenor. The term does not reflect the difficulty of listening to this voice; it derives from Antoine Trial, a popular operatic tenor in Paris in the 18th century. In Ravel's opera *L'Heure Espagnole* the dramatis personae calls for a trial to sing the role of Torquemada, the clockmaker.

BARITONE

The male voice lower than a tenor and higher than a bass. This intermediate status has not prevented it from assuming major status among the vocal types, with its power and ringing brilliance endearing it especially to operatic composers. Normal range: approximately two octaves upward from the A a tenth below middle C. The word derives from the Greek for "of heavy tone" and was formerly spelled barytone.

Baritone-Martin. A high baritone, bordering on the tenor range. It is a type of voice particularly valued in France, and is named for Jean Blaise Martin (1769–1837), who allegedly could reach high C with ease. The role of Ramiro in Ravel's *L'heure Espagnole* is specified for a baritone-martin.

Bass-baritone. Between the baritone and bass registers and sharing some of the characteristics of each. Useful in opera; Mozart's Don Giovanni is frequently sung by a bass-baritone.

BASS

The lowest male voice, often encountered under the Italian designation of *basso.* Normal range: approximately two octaves upward from the E an octave and a sixth below middle C. Several varieties exist:

Basso buffo. An agile, flexible bass, adaptable to comic roles in opera.

Basso cantante. Literally, singing bass; a voice suited to lyric roles.

Basso profondo. The lowest of the low. At home alike in Sarastro's arias in Mozart's *The Magic Flute* and Henry W. Petrie's "Asleep in the Deep."

Contra-basso. Another term for basso profondo; often used for Russian singers with especially strong low notes.

THE CASTRATI

The castrati, now vanished from the musical scene, were one of the most remarkable group of singers that ever existed. They were male sopranos (occasionally contraltos) whose testicles had been surgically removed in boyhood, leaving them with the high voices of their childhood projected by adult lung-power. Enormously popular in the 18th century, they often attained stardom and riches, with adulatory audiences reportedly crying out "Evviva il coltello!" (Long live the little knife) when they executed a particularly florid or brilliant passage. Here, in chronological order, are eight castrati whose names have survived:

Senesino (c.1680–c.1750). Real name, Francesco Bernardi; "Senesino" was a name he took from his birthplace, Siena. A contralto by some accounts and mezzo-soprano by others, he was a particular favorite of George Frideric Handel and sang in his operas in London for 15 years.

Farinelli (1705–1782). Real name, Carlo Broschi. This soprano was the most famous of the castrati, with the artist William Hogarth depicting in his *The Rake's Progress* a lady at the opera crying out: "One God and one Farinelli!" According to one story, his teacher Niccolò Porpora kept him singing the same sheet of vocal exercises for six years, then told him: "Go, my son, you are now the first singer in Italy." His brother wrote an aria for him so difficult it became known as the *Concerto for Larynx.* For his unusual services to a King of Spain, see listing under MUSIC AND SLEEP.

Caffarelli (1710–1783). Real name, Gaetano Majorano. Also a pupil of Porpora, he enjoyed a brilliantly successful career despite being criticized several times for offensive behavior, including what one manager called "lasciviousness with one of the female singers." When he built himself a palace in southern Italy he inscribed in Latin over the portal: "Amphion built Thebes, I this house," to which a ribald neighbor added the words: "He with, you without."

Gaetano Guadagni (1725–1792). A contralto who also sang for Handel in London. Perhaps his greatest distinction is that he created the part of Orfeo in Gluck's opera *Orfeo ed Euridice,* thereby becoming the first singer ever to sing the celebrated aria "Che faro senza Euridice."

Gasparo Pacchiarotti (1740–1821). A singer with an enormous range (some contemporaries call him a soprano, others a contralto), he also had an acting ability that could move an audience to tears.

He sang at the opening of two of Italy's most famous opera houses, La Scala in Milan, in 1778, and La Fenice, Venice, in 1792.

Luigi Marchesi (1754–1829). One of the most handsome of the castrati, he also was one of the most vain and demanding. He insisted on wearing lavish costumes, including helmets with plumes a yard high. His career took him as far as St. Petersburg, Russia, where he sang at the court of Catherine the Great.

Vincenzo dal Prato (1756–1828). Not one of the great castrati, his claim to fame is that, at the age of 24, he sang the role of Idamante in Mozart's opera *Idomeneo*. Mozart, who had great trouble working with the rather awkward and inept singer, ironically called him "mio molto amato castrato dal Prato" (my much beloved castrato dal Prato).

Alessandro Moreschi (1858–1922). The last of the castrati, he sang at the Sistine Chapel in the Vatican until his retirement in 1913. His voice, which brought him the nickname of "l'angelo di Roma" (the angel of Rome) may still be heard on records.

CARUSO AT THE MET

Enrico Caruso, generally regarded as the greatest of 20th-century tenors, sang 18 seasons at the Metropolitan Opera House, from 1903 to 1920. He died August 2, 1921, at the age of 48. In his years at the Met, Caruso appeared in the leading tenor roles of 37 operas. Here they are, with dates, in the order of his first appearance in each:

> *Rigoletto* (Verdi) November 23, 1903
> *Aida* (Verdi) November 30, 1903
> *Tosca* (Puccini) December 2, 1903
> *La Bohème* (Puccini) December 5, 1903
> *Pagliacci* (Leoncavallo) December 9, 1903
> *La Traviata* (Verdi) December 23, 1903
> *Lucia di Lammermoor* (Donizetti) January 8, 1904
> *L'Elisir d'Amore* (Donizetti) January 23, 1904
> *La Gioconda* (Ponchielli) November 28, 1904
> *Lucrezia Borgia* (Donizetti) December 5, 1904
> *A Masked Ball* (Verdi) January 27, 1905
> *Les Huguenots* (Meyerbeer) February 3, 1905
> *La Favorita* (Donizetti) November 29, 1905
> *La Sonnambula* (Bellini) December 15, 1905
> *Faust* (Gounod) January 3, 1906
> *Martha* (Flotow) February 9, 1906

Carmen (Bizet) February 20, 1906
Fedora (Giordano) December 25, 1906
L'Africaine (Meyerbeer) January 11, 1907
Manon Lescaut (Puccini) January 18, 1907
Madama Butterfly (Puccini) February 11, 1907
Adriana Lecouvreur (Ciléa) November 28, 1907
Iris (Mascagni) December 6, 1907
Il Trovatore (Verdi) February 16, 1908
Cavalleria Rusticana (Mascagni) December 17, 1908
Germania (Franchetti) January 22, 1910
Armide (Gluck) November 19, 1910
La Fanciulla del West (Puccini) December 10, 1910
Manon (Massenet) January 22, 1913
Julien (Charpentier) February 26, 1914
Samson et Dalila (Saint-Saëns) November 15, 1915
Les Pêcheurs des Perles (Bizet) November 3, 1916
Lodoletta (Mascagni) January 12, 1918
Le Prophète (Meyerbeer) February 7, 1918
L'amore dei Tre Re (Montemezzi) March 19, 1918
La Forza del Destino (Verdi) March 25, 1919
La Juive (Halévy) November 22, 1920

UNLIKELY OPERATIC DEBUT ROLES

Many opera stars begin their careers with minor companies, but most of them make their debuts in roles—or at least in repertory—that will later be associated with them. Thus, Beverly Sills launched her career by singing Micaela in Carmen with the Philadelphia Opera; Luciano Pavarotti with Rodolfo in La Bohème at the Municipal Theater of Reggia Emilia in Italy; and Placido Domingo with Alfredo in La Traviata at the Monterrey Opera of Mexico. Some singers, however, made their debuts in works that gave very little indication of the kind of roles that would eventually make them famous. Here are some instances:

SINGER	ROLE AND OPERA	PLACE AND YEAR
Enrico Caruso	Francesco in L'Amico Francesco*	Naples, 1894
Kirsten Flagstad	Nuri in Tiefland	Oslo, 1913**
Marilyn Horne	Hata in The Bartered Bride	Los Angeles, 1954

*L'Amico Francesco was an opera by one Mario Morelli, which was performed twice and disappeared forever.
**Flagstad didn't get to the Metropolitan Opera for another 22 years.

SINGER	ROLE AND OPERA	PLACE AND YEAR
Lauritz Melchior	Canio in *Pagliacci*	Copenhagen, 1913
Ezio Pinza	King Marke in *Tristan und Isolde*	Rome, 1920***
Leontyne Price	Mme. Lidoine in *Dialogues des Carmelites*	San Francisco, 1957
Titta Ruffo	The Herald in *Lohengrin*	Rome, 1898
Leonie Rysanek	Manon in *Manon*	Klagenfurt, Austria, 1950
Joan Sutherland	The First Lady in *The Magic Flute*	London, 1952
Shirley Verrett	Zigeunerin in *Rasputins Tod*	Cologne, 1960

*** Pinza's Metropolitan Opera debut in 1926 was as Pontifex Maximus in Spontini's *La Vestale*.

TWENTY TOP BROADWAY MUSICALS

The Broadway—and Off-Broadway—musical show is regarded by many as America's homegrown opera, or at least operetta. This list of 20 singles out shows that have had broad influence, artistic impact, or spectacular success—sometimes all three—and whose qualities have, in many cases, led to continuing revivals, some on the operatic stage. They are in chronological order:

Jerome Kern: *Show Boat* (1927)
George and Ira Gershwin: *Of Thee I Sing* (1931)
Harold Rome: *Pins and Needles* (1937)
Marc Blitzstein: *The Cradle Will Rock* (1937)
Richard Rodgers and Lorenz Hart: *Pal Joey* (1940)
Kurt Weill and Moss Hart: *Lady in the Dark* (1941)
Richard Rodgers and Oscar Hammerstein II: *Oklahoma!* (1943)
Richard Rodgers and Oscar Hammerstein II: *Carousel* (1945)
Cole Porter: *Kiss Me, Kate* (1948)
Richard Rodgers and Oscar Hammerstein II: *South Pacific* (1949)
Frank Loesser: *Guys and Dolls* (1950)
Richard Rodgers and Oscar Hammerstein II: *The King and I* (1951)
Kurt Weill and Marc Bitzstein: *The Threepenny Opera* (American version, 1951)
Frank Loesser: *The Most Happy Fella* (1956)
Alan Jay Lerner and Frederick Loewe: *My Fair Lady* (1956)
Leonard Bernstein and Stephen Sondheim: *West Side Story* (1957)

Sheldon Harnick and Jerry Bock: *Fiddler on the Roof* (1964)
Galt McDermott: *Hair* (1967)
Michael Bennett and Marvin Hamlish: *A Chorus Line* (1975)
Stephen Sondheim: *Sweeney Todd, the Demon Barber of Fleet Street* (1979)

PART V
MEDLEY

SHAKESPEARE'S PLAYS IN MUSIC

William Shakespeare's plays have been an inexhaustible source and inspiration to musicians. In fact, no other literary source has provided the impetus for as many operas, songs, overtures, fantasias, and popular shows. The plays most frequently set to music are *Romeo and Juliet*, *Hamlet*, and—perhaps most surprising—*The Tempest*.

The German composer Manfred Gurlitt (1890–1973) even wrote a "Shakespeare Symphony" for five solo voices and orchestra, with each of its five movements based upon a play—*Antony and Cleopatra*, *Henry IV*, *Julius Caesar*, *Richard II*, and *Richard III*. Composed in 1954, it is rarely heard today.

This list, extensive as it is, does not pretend to be complete. None could, for musical adaptations or approximations of Shakespeare seem countless. But here are some you may have encountered—and some you probably never will:

All's Well That Ends Well.
Edmond Audran: *Gillotte de Narbonne* (opera, 1882)
Mario Castelnuovo-Tedesco: *Tutto è Bene Quello Finisce Bene* (opera, 1958)
SONGS: William Linley, Virgil Thomson
Antony and Cleopatra.
Vincent d'Indy: *Antoine et Cléopâtre* (overture, 1877)
Gian Francesco Malipiero: *Antonio e Cleopatre* (opera, 1938)
Anton Rubinstein: Overture (1890)
Franz Schubert: "Come thou, monarch of the vine" (song, 1826)
Ethel Smyth: Overture (1890)
INCIDENTAL MUSIC: Henry Bishop, Jacques Ibert, Quincy Porter, Florent Schmitt, Virgil Thomson
As You Like It.
John Alden Carpenter: *The Seven Ages* (symphonic suite, 1945)
John Knowles Paine: Overture (1876)
Francesco Veracini: *Rosalinda* (opera, 1744)
William Walton: Film score (1936)
INCIDENTAL MUSIC: Henry Bishop, Arthur Bliss, Roger Quilter, Julius Rietz, Ernest Toch, Hermann Zilcher
SONGS: Thomas Arne, Frederick Delius, John Hilton, Thomas Morley, Horatio Parker, Hubert Parry, Roger Quilter, Edmund Rubbra, Franz Schubert, Arthur Sullivan, Ralph Vaughan Williams, Peter Warlock

The Comedy Of Errors.
Isa Krejčí: *The Revolt at Ephesus* (opera, 1946)
Richard Mohaupt: *Zwillingskomodie* (opera, English title *Double Trouble*, 1954)
Richard Rodgers and Lorenz Hart: *The Boys from Syracuse* (show, 1938)
Stephen Storace: *Gli Equivoci* (opera, 1786)
INCIDENTAL MUSIC: Henry Bishop, Yuri Shaporin, Hermann Zilcher
Coriolanus.
August Baeyens: *Coriolanus* (opera, 1940)
Ludwig van Beethoven: *Coriolan Overture* (1810)*
Mario Castelnuovo-Tedesco: Overture (1947)
INCIDENTAL MUSIC: Alexander Mackenzie, August Söderman
Cymbeline.
William Boyce: Dirge (1746)
Arne Eggen: *Cymbelin* (opera, 1951)
Rudolphe Kreutzer: *Imogene ou la Gageuse Indiscrète* (opera, 1796)
SONGS: William Boyce, Mario Castelnuovo-Tedesco, Constant Lambert, Hubert Parry, Roger Quilter, Franz Schubert, Ralph Vaughan Williams
Hamlet.
Hector Berlioz: *Mort d'Ophélie* (funeral march 1850)
Boris Blacher: Ballet and symphonic poem (1950)
Johannes Brahms: *Five Ophelia Songs* (1873)
Luigi Caruso: *Amleto* (opera, 1789)
Franco Faccio: *Amleto* (opera, 1865)
Niels Gade: Overture (1861)
Wenzel Robert von Gallenberg: *Amleto* (ballet score, 1815)
Edward German: Symphonic poem (1897)
Joseph Joachim: Overture (1855)
Constant Lambert: Ballet music (1940)
Guillaume Lekeu: Symphonic study for orchestra (1890)
Franz Liszt: Symphonic poem (1858)
Edward MacDowell: *Hamlet and Ophelia* (symphonic poem, 1885)
George Macfarren: Overture (1856)
Saverio Mercadante: *Amleto* (opera, 1860)
Bernard Rogers: Prelude for orchestra (1928)
Domenico Scarlatti: *Amleto* (1715)
Humphrey Searle: *Hamlet* (opera, 1968)

---

*Beethoven's overture actually was written not for Shakespeare's play, but for a drama on the same story by Heinrich Joseph von Collin, a contemporary of the composer. Nevertheless, the Overture remains the most familiar score associated with the name of this Shakespearean hero.

William Shakespeare: Dramatic overture*
Richard Strauss: *Three Ophelia Songs* (1918)
Peter Ilyich Tchaikovsky: *Hamlet* (fantasy-overture, 1888)
Ambroise Thomas: *Hamlet* (opera, 1869)
William Walton: Film score (1947)
INCIDENTAL MUSIC: Arthur Honegger, Darius Milhaud, Gabriel Pierné, Dmitri Shostakovich, Virgil Thomson
SONGS: Mario Castelnuovo-Tedesco, Karl Loewe

Henry IV, Parts I and II.
Edward Elgar: *Falstaff* (symphonic study 1913)
Gustav Holst: *At the Boar's Head* (opera, 1925)
Joseph Joachim: Overture (1855)
Saverio Mercadante: *La Gioventù di Enrico V* (opera, 1834)
(See also *The Merry Wives of Windsor*)

Henry V.
Rutland Boughton: *Agincourt* (dramatic scene, 1918)
Walter Macfarren: Overture (1881)
William Walton: Film score (1944)

Henry VI, Parts I, II and III.
Frank Bridge: "God's goodness hath been great to thee" (song, 1916)
Aaron Copland: Incidental music for Orson Welles's *Five Kings* (1939)**

Henry VIII.
INCIDENTAL MUSIC: Edward German, Arthur Sullivan
SONGS: Mario Castelnuovo-Tedesco, Roger Quilter, William Schuman, Ralph Vaughan Williams

Julius Caesar.
Mario Castelnuovo-Tedesco: Overture (1934)
Georg Frideric Handel: *Guilio Cesare* (opera, 1724)
Gian-Francesco Malipiero: *Guilio Cesare* (opera, 1936)
Robert Schumann: Overture (1852)
INCIDENTAL MUSIC: Marc Blitzstein, Hans von Bülow, John Ireland, Darius Milhaud

King John.
Mario Castelnuovo-Tedesco: Overture (1942)

King Lear.
Granville Bantock: Overture for Brass Band (1936)
Hector Berlioz: Overture (1831)
Paul Dukas: Overture (1883)
Alberto Ghislanzoni: *Re Lear* (opera, 1937)
Henry Litolff: *König Lear* (opera, 1890)

---

*This William Shakespeare (1849–1931) was an English tenor, singing teacher, and composer. His Dramatic Overture to Hamlet is listed as his Opus 15.
**The other monarchs in Welles's stage piece *Five Kings* are Henry IV and V and Richard II and III.

Aribert Reimann: *Lear* (opera, 1978)

Felix Weingartner: Symphonic poem

INCIDENTAL MUSIC: Mily Balakirev, Claude Debussy, Felipe Pedrell, Yuri Shaporin

SONGS: Mario Castelnuovo-Tedesco

Love's Labours Lost.

Adrian Welles Beecham: *Love's Labours Lost* (opera, 1936)

INCIDENTAL MUSIC: Henry Bishop, Herbert Menges

SONGS: Thomas Arne, Mario Castelnuovo-Tedesco, Hubert Parry, Roger Quilter, Igor Stravinsky, Ralph Vaughan Williams

Macbeth.

Ernest Bloch: *Macbeth* (opera, 1909)

Lawrance Collingwood: *Macbeth* (opera, 1934)

William Henry Fry: *Overture and Witches' Incantation* (1862)

Edvard Grieg: "Watchman's Song" (lyric piece for piano, 1867)

Henry Hugh Pearson: *Macbeth* (symphony, 1874)

Dmitri Shostakovich: *Lady Macbeth of Mzensk**

Bedřich Smetana: *Macbeth and the Witches* (for piano, 1859)

Richard Strauss: Symphonic poem (1890)

Nicolas Tcherepnin: *Witches' Scene* (for orchestra)

Guiseppe Verdi: *Macbeth* (opera, 1847)

INCIDENTAL MUSIC: Granville Bantock, Norman Demuth, Aram Khachaturian, Darius Milhaud, Johann Friedrich Reichardt, Arthur Sullivan

Measure for Measure.

Richard Wagner: *Das Liebsverbot* (opera, 1836)

INCIDENTAL MUSIC: Dimitry Kabalevsky

SONGS: Mario Castelnuovo-Tedesco, Hubert Parry, Roger Quilter, Edmund Rubbra, Ralph Vaughan Williams, Peter Warlock

The Merchant of Venice.

Mario Castelnuovo-Tedesco: *Il Mercante di Venezia* (opera, 1961)

Gabriel Fauré: *Shylock* (incidental music, 1889)

Josef Bohuslav Foerster: *Jessika* (opera, 1905)

Reynaldo Hahn: *Le Marchand de Venise* (opera, 1935)

George Macfarren: Overture (1834)

Ralph Vaughan Williams: *Serenade to Music* (1938)

INCIDENTAL MUSIC: Elliott Carter, Engelbert Humperdinck, Henri Rabaud, Karol Rathaus, Arthur Sullivan

SONGS: Thomas Arne, Mario Castelnuovo-Tedesco, Carl Maria von Weber

The Merry Wives of Windsor.

Adolphe Adam: *Falstaff* (opera, 1856)

---

*Shostakovich's opera has nothing to do with Shakespeare's play, aside from the allusion in the title.

Michael Balfe: *Falstaff* (opera, 1838)
Karl Ditters von Dittersdorf: *Die Lustigen Weiber von Windsor* (opera, 1796)
Otto Nicolai: *Die Lustigen Weiber von Windsor* (opera, 1849)
François André Philidor: *Herne le Chasseur* (opera, 1773)
Antonio Salieri: *Falstaff* (opera, 1799)
Ralph Vaughan Williams: *Sir John in Love* (opera, 1929)
Giuseppe Verdi: *Falstaff* (opera, 1893)
INCIDENTAL MUSIC: Henry Bishop, Arthur Sullivan
SONGS: Mario Castelnuovo-Tedesco
A Midsummer Night's Dream.
Dennis Arundell: *A Midsummer Night's Dream* (opera)
Benjamin Britten: *A Midsummer Night's Dream* (opera, 1960)
Claude Debussy: *La Danse de Puck* (Preludes, Book I, No. 11)
Marcel Delannoy: *Puck* (opera, 1949)
Ruggero Leoncavallo: *Songe d'une Nuit d'Été* (unproduced opera, *c.1880*)
Luigi Mancinelli: *Songo di una Notte d'Estate* (opera, 1917)
Henry Purcell: *The Fairy Queen* (stage music, 1692)
Erik Satie: *Cinq Grimaces pour le Songe d'une Nuit d'Été* (orchestrated by Darius Milhaud, 1914)
John Christopher Smith: *The Fairies* (opera, 1754)
Franz von Suppé: *Sommernachtsstraum* (operetta, 1844)
Carl Maria von Weber: *Oberon* (opera, 1826)
Hugo Wolf: *Elfenlied* (choral work, 1891)
INCIDENTAL MUSIC: Henry Bishop, Ernst Krenek, Felix Mendelssohn, Carl Orff,* Bernhard Paumgartner.
SONGS: Mario Castelnuovo-Tedesco, Ralph Vaughan Williams
Much Ado About Nothing.
Hector Berlioz: *Béatrice et Bénédict* (opera, 1862)
Reynaldo Hahn: *Beaucoup de Bruit pour Rien* (opera, 1936)
Charles Villiers Stanford: *Much Ado About Nothing* (opera, 1901)
INCIDENTAL MUSIC: Edward German, Tikhon Khrennikov, Erich Korngold
SONGS: Mario Castelnuovo-Tedesco, Peter Warlock
Othello.
Antonin Dvořák: Overture (1892)
Zdenko Fibich: *Othello* (symphonic poem, 1873)
Henry Hadley: Overture (1919)
Walter Macfarren: Overture (1896)
Gioacchino Rossini: *Otello* (opera, 1816)
Giuseppe Verdi: *Otello* (opera, 1887)

---

*Carl Orff's Incidental Music for *A Midsummer Night's Dream* was written for a competition sponsored by the Nazis, who had banned Felix Mendelssohn's famous score, and were seeking a replacement. Orff later wrote an operatic version (1952).

INCIDENTAL MUSIC: Samuel Coleridge-Taylor
SONGS: Mario Castelnuovo-Tedesco, Carl Loewe, Hubert Parry,
Ralph Vaughan Williams
Pericles.
    Alan Hovhannes: Overture (1973)
Richard II.
    INCIDENTAL MUSIC: Henry Purcell
Richard III.
    Gaston Salvayre: *Riccardo III* (opera, 1883)
    Bedřich Smetana: *Richard III* (symphonic poem 1862)
    William Walton: Film score (1954)
    INCIDENTAL MUSIC: Edward German, Robert Volkmann
Romeo and Juliet.
    Herbert Bedford: *Queen Mab* (suite, 1900)
    Vincenzo Bellini: *I Capuletti ed I Montecchi* (opera, 1830)
    Georg Benda: *Romeo und Julie* (singspiel, 1776)
    Hector Berlioz: *Roméo et Juliette* (choral symphony, 1839)
    Leonard Bernstein: *West Side Story* (show, 1957)
    Boris Blacher: *Romeo und Julia* (chamber opera, 1943)
    William Boyce: *Dirge* (1750)
    Nicolas Dalayrac: *Tout pour l'amour* (opera, 1792)
    Frederick Delius: *A Village Romeo and Juliet* (opera, 1907)*
    Charles Gounod: *Roméo et Juliette* (opera, 1867)
    Constant Lambert: Ballet score (1926)
    George Macfarren: Overture (1840)
    Gian Francesco Malipiero: *Romeo e Giulietta* (section of radio drama,
1950)
    Melesio Morales: *Romeo y Julieta* (opera, 1863)
    Serge Prokofiev: Ballet score (1940)
    Heinrich Sutermeister: *Romeo und Julia* (opera, 1940)
    Johan Svendsen: Fantasy-overture (1876)
    Peter Ilyich Tchaikovsky: Fantasy-overture (1869, revised 1880)
    Nicola Vaccai: *Giulietta e Romeo* (opera, 1825)
    Riccardo Zandonai: *Giulietta e Romeo* (opera, 1922)
    Nicola Antonio Zingarelli: *Giulietta e Romeo* (opera, 1796)
    INCIDENTAL MUSIC: Henry Bishop, David Diamond, Edward
German, Engelbert Humperdinck, Dmitri Kabalevsky, Frank Martin,
Darius Milhaud
    SONGS: Thomas Arne, Matthew King
The Taming of the Shrew.
    Mario Castelnuovo-Tedesco: Overture (1930)
    Vittorio Giannini: *The Taming of the Shrew* (opera, 1953)
    Cole Porter: *Kiss Me Kate* (show, 1948)

---

*The subject is a tragic love affair, but the resemblance to Shakespeare is purely
titular.

Hermann Goetz: *Der Widerspaenstigen Zaehmung* (opera, 1874)
Walter Macfarren: Overture (1845)
Alick Maclean: *Petruccio* (opera, 1895)
Spiro Samara: *La Furia Domata* (opera, 1895)
Vissarion Shebalin: *Ukroshchenie Stroptivoi* (opera, 1957)
Ermanno Wolf-Ferrari: *Sly* (opera, 1927)
INCIDENTAL MUSIC: Richard Addinsell, Hermann Zilcher

The Tempest.
Kurt Atterberg: *Stormen* (opera, 1949)
Ludwig van Beethoven: Piano Sonata No. 17 in D Minor, "Tempest" (1802)*
Hector Berlioz: Fantasy in *Lélio* (1832)
William Boyce: Masque (1757)
John Eaton: *The Tempest* (opera, 1985)
Arthur Farwell: Caliban (masque, 1915)
Zdeněk Fibich: Bouře (*The Tempest*, opera, 1895)
Fromental Halévy: *La Tempesta* (opera, 1850)
Arthur Honegger: Orchestral prelude and two songs (1923)
Lars-Erik Larsson: Four vignettes for orchestra (1923)
Felice Lattuada: *La Tempestà* (opera, 1922)
Matthew Locke: *The Tempest* (1673)
Frank Martin: *Der Sturm* (opera, 1956)
John Knowles Paine: Symphonic poem (1876)
Henry Purcell: *The Tempest, or the Enchanted Isle* (opera, 1695)
Johann Friedrich Reichardt: *Die Geisterinsel* (Singspiel, 1798)
John Christopher Smith: *The Tempest* (opera, 1756)
Heinrich Sutermeister: *Die Zauberinsel* (opera, 1942)
Peter Ilyich Tchaikovsky: Orchestral fantasy (1873)
Johann Rudolf Zumsteeg: *Die Geisterinsel* (opera, 1798)
INCIDENTAL MUSIC: Malcolm Arnold, Arthur Bliss, Ernest Chausson, David Diamond, Engelbert Humperdinck, Jan Sibelius
SONGS: Thomas Arne, John Bannister, Mario Castelnuovo-Tedesco, John Ireland, Henry Purcell, Ralph Vaughan Williams

Timon of Athens.
David Diamond: Portrait (1950)
Leopold I, Holy Roman Emperor: *Timone Misantropo* (opera, 1696)
Martin Lunssens: *Timon d'Athènes* (symphonic poem)
Henry Purcell: Incidental music and songs (1694)
Arthur Sullivan: Overture (1857)

Titus Andronicus.
Jeremiah Clarke: Overture and act-tune (c.1700)
Norman Demuth: Incidental music (radio presentation)

---

*When his friend Anton Schindler asked Beethoven what the first movement of this sonata meant, the composer replied: "Read Shakespeare's *The Tempest*."

Troilus and Cressida.
  William Walton: *Troilus and Cressida* (opera, 1954)*
  Winfred Zillig: *Troilus und Cressida* (opera, 1951)
Twelfth Night.
  David Amram: *Twelfth Night* (opera, 1968)
  Mario Castelnuovo-Tedesco: Overture and three songs (1933)
  Amedeo de Filippi: *Malvolio* (opera, 1937)
  Fritz Hart: *Malvolio* (opera, 1913)
  Hal Hester and Danny Apolinar: *Your Own Thing* (show, 1968)
  Bedřich Smetana: *Viola* (unfinished opera, performed 1954)
  Wilhelm Taubert: *Cesario* (opera, 1874)
  Karel Weis: *Viola* (opera, 1892)
  INCIDENTAL MUSIC: Henry Bishop, Paul Bowles, J. B. Foerster, Engelbert Humperdinck, Bernhardt Paumgartner
  SONGS: Thomas Arne, Johannes Brahms, Peter Cornelius, Joseph Haydn, Gustav Holst, Hubert Parry, Roger Quilter, Jan Sibelius, Ralph Vaughan Williams, Peter Warlock
The Winter's Tale.
  William Boyce: Music for Florizel and Perdita (Garrick's adaptation, 1756)
  Max Bruch: *Hermione* (opera, 1872)
  Mario Castelnuovo-Tedesco: Overture (1938)
  Karl Goldmark: *Ein Wintermaerchen* (opera, 1908)
  John Harbison: *The Winter's Tale* (opera, 1979)
  Josef Nesvera: *Perditta* (opera, 1897)
  Josef Suk: Overture (1894)
  INCIDENTAL MUSIC: Frederick von Flotow, Engelbert Humperdinck, Darius Milhaud, Hermann Zilcher
  SONGS: Thomas Arne, John Ireland
Two Gentlemen of Verona.
  Galt MacDermott: *Two Gentlemen of Verona* (show, 1971)
  SONGS: Henry Bishop, Mario Castelnuovo-Tedesco, Richard Leveridge, Edmund Rubbra, Franz Schubert

FAUST IN MUSIC

Few subjects have appealed as strongly to composers as the legend of Dr. Faust, who sold his soul to the Devil. The tale first appeared in print in Germany around 1587, then made its way to England, where Christopher Marlowe published his *Tragical History of the Life and Death of Doctor Faust* in 1593. Musicians took to the story

---

*Walton's opera actually is based on Chaucer's version, not Shakespeare's.

quickly—a musical pantomime, "Harlequin Faustus," was staged in London in 1715—and operatic settings soon followed. Goethe's famous philosophical drama, published in 1808, inspired many subsequent compositions in many lands. These Fausts are listed in chronological order. All are operas unless otherwise specified:

Karl Hanke. *Doktor Faust's Zaubergürtel* (*Dr. Faust's Magic Belt*, Vlissingen, 1794).

Ignaz Walter. *Faust* (Hanover, 1797).

Antoni Henryk, Prince Radziwill. *Compositions for Goethe's Dramatic Poem of Faust* (Berlin, 1810). Radziwill was a Polish aristocrat, politician, and cellist. His music for Faust consisted of 25 separate pieces.

Ludwig Spohr. *Faust* (Prague, 1818). This opera was based on the old legend rather than Goethe's play. Its first conductor was Carl Maria von Weber.

Henry Rowley Bishop. *Faustus* (London, 1827). An English version.

Alexei Verstovsky. *Pan Tvardovsky* (Moscow, 1828). Tvardovsky is the Polish Faust figure.

Louise-Angélique Bertin. *Faust* (Paris, 1831). The first Faust opera by a woman. The supernatural must have had a strong appeal to Bertin, a contralto and a pianist as well as a composer, for she also wrote an opera entitled *Le Loup-garou*.

Gaetano Donizetti. *Fausta* (Naples, 1832). For Donizetti, who wrote 70 operas, the subject was too good to miss. However, his *L'elisir d'Amore*, performed only four months later, was far more successful.

Augustin de Pellaert. *Faust* (Brussels, 1834).

Julius Rietz. Incidental music to Goethe's play (Düsseldorf, 1836).

Luigi Gordigiani. *Fausto* (Florence, 1837).

Pietro Raimondi. *Il Fausto Arrivo* (Naples, 1837).

Richard Wagner. *A Faust Overture* (Dresden, 1844; rev. 1855).

Hector Berlioz. *La Damnation de Faust* (Paris, 1846). Called an "opéra de concert" by its composer, it was successfully adapted to the operatic stage by Raoul Gunsbourg in 1893.

Robert Schumann. *Scenes from Goethe's Faust* (Dresden, 1849). These instrumental and vocal pieces were written over a nine-year period starting in 1843. A portion were performed in Dresden during the centenary of Goethe's birth.

Peter Joseph von Lindpaintner. Overture to Faust (Stuttgart, 1854). Another composer attracted to the supernatural—Lindpaintner also composed an opera called *Der Vampyr*.

Henry Hugh Pierson. Incidental music to the second part of Goethe's Faust (Hamburg, 1854).

Franz Liszt. *Faust Symphony* (Weimar, 1857). A three-movement tone poem, with sections devoted to Faust, Gretchen, and Mephistopheles, inspired by the Goethe drama. Liszt also composed two orchestral works based on another Faust by the Austro-Hungarian poet Nikolaus Lenau. The second of these is the *Mephisto Waltz*, which he wrote in both orchestral and piano versions. It is best known in the latter form as a piece of devilish difficulty. Liszt also composed three other *Mephisto Waltzes* and a *Mephisto Polka*, and transcribed for piano the waltzes from Gounod's *Faust* (see below).

Charles Gounod. *Faust* (Paris, 1859). For generations of opera fans, this was *the* Faust opera. In Germany, it's sometimes called *Margarete* in an effort to disassociate it from the Goethe drama.

Arrigo Boito. *Mefistofele* (Milan, 1868). The librettist of Verdi's *Otello* and *Falstaff*, Boito was a composer skilled enough to produce a Faust opera that survives to the present.

Hervé (real name Florimond Ronger). *Le Petit Faust* (Paris, 1869). A frothy version by the composer of the operetta *Mam'zelle Nitouche*.

Eduard Lassen. Incidental music to Goethe's Faust, Parts I and II (Weimar, 1876). A Danish composer who settled in Germany. His Faust score retained its popularity there for many years.

Giovanni von Zaytz (original name Iva Zajc). *Pan Tvardovsky* (Zagreb, 1880). Like the Russian composer Verstovsky (see above) this Croatian composer, who took a half-Italian, half-German name, used Tvardovsky, the Polish Faust, for his operatic protagonist.

Heinrich Zollner. *Faust* (Munich, 1887).

Lili Boulanger. *Faust et Hélène* (Paris, 1913). This cantata won the Prix de Rome for Lili, sister of Nadia Boulanger.

Ferruccio Busoni. *Doktor Faust* (unfinished; posthumous performance Dresden, 1925). Although it is rarely performed, Busoni's *Faust*, completed by his pupil Philipp Jarnach, is regarded by some authorities as a masterful work.

Gertrude Stein. *Doctor Faustus Lights the Lights* (Paris, 1938). This is a libretto for an opera commissioned from Gertrude Stein by Lord Berners (Gerald Tyrwhitt), English composer and litterateur (1883–1950). He never wrote the music for it, and it was published in Stein's *Last Operas and Plays*.

Hanns Eisler. *Johannes Faustus* (East Berlin, 1953). Communist critics in the German Democratic Republic criticized this opera for the complexity of its score and the mysticism of its libretto, with the result that it has not been performed since its premiere.

Sergei Prokofiev. *The Fiery Angel* (Paris, 1954). Faust and Mephistopheles are only secondary characters, appearing as guests at an inn. Their vocal ranges are reversed from the Gounod opera, Faust being a bass and Mephisto a tenor.

Havergal Brian. *Doktor Faust* (1956). Brian was an eccentric English composer who lived nearly a century, from 1876 to 1972, and wrote an enormous amount of music, most of it unperformed. His Faust opera is based on Goethe.

Henri Pousseur. *Vôtre Faust* (Milan, 1969). Pousseur, a Belgian modernist, composed an aleatory (improvisational) "fantasy in the style of an opera" in which Faust is a young composer and Méphisto a director who commissions an opera from him. The audience is invited to decide the ending.

H. Wesley Balk. *Faust Counter Faust* (Minneapolis, 1971). A musical collage that pits the story of a modern-day Faust against the images created by Berlioz and Gounod.

[Note: A great many other works, such as Douglas Moore's *The Devil and Daniel Webster* (1938) and Igor Stravinsky's *L'histoire du Soldat* (1918) and *The Rake's Progress* (1951) are based on the intervention of the Devil in human affairs, but the foregoing list is limited to cases involving his dealings with a Faustian figure.]

MUSIC AND ART

Music has sometimes been described as painting in sound, just as architecture has been defined as frozen music. Whatever the accuracy of such statements, there have been instances where composers have found inspiration in the visual arts. Here are some examples:

Antheil: Symphony No. 6. George Antheil's Symphony No. 6, given its world premiere in San Francisco under Pierre Monteux in 1949, was inspired by Eugene Delacroix's painting *Liberty Leading the People.* The composer said the first movement depicted "the smoke of battle, courage, despair, and hope, all marching into the future."

Badings: The Night Watch. Dutch composer Henk Badings's 1942 opera bears the title of one of Rembrandt's most celebrated paintings, but the hero is the artist himself. Another opera about Rembrandt is Paul von Klenau's *Rembrandt van Rijn* (1937).

Carpenter: Krazy Kat. One of the few symphonic scores inspired by a comic strip. Chicago composer John Alden Carpenter wrote a jazzy ballet piece based on George Herriman's "Krazy Kat" strip in 1921. It was so successful that Serge Diaghilev commissioned him to write another "American" ballet, which turned out to be his *Skyscrapers.*

Granados: Goyescas. Granados's admiration for the paintings of his countryman, Francisco Goya, led him to compose a sequence of piano pieces entitled *Goyescas* (in the manner of Goya). "I am enamored with the psychology of Goya," Granados wrote, "with his palette, with him, with his muse the Duchess of Alba, with his quarrels with his models, his loves and flatteries." The composer later adapted his piano pieces into an opera of jealousy involving two pairs of lovers and ending in a fatal duel.

Henze: *Das Floss der Medusa.* Theodore Gericault's 1819 painting, *The Raft of the Medusa,* a grim portrayal of a group of people struggling for survival after a shipwreck, impelled Hans Werner Henze to compose an oratorio of the same title dedicated to the memory of Che Guevara. At its premiere in Hamburg in 1968 the composer's insistence on placing red flags on the stage provoked a demonstration that led to the performance's cancellation.

Hindemith: *Mathis der Maler.* Two works by Paul Hindemith bear the title *Matthias the Painter,* an opera and a symphony, both dating from 1934. They deal with Matthias Grünewald, the early 16th-century German painter. The symphonic score in particular attempts to recreate in the listener the emotions produced by a viewing of Grünewald's most famous work, the 11-panel altar of the church of St. Anthony in Isenheim, Germany. The three movements are "Angelic Concert" (also the Overture to the opera), "The Entombment of Christ" and "The Temptation of St. Anthony."

Liszt: *Totentanz.* On a visit to Italy in the late 1830s, Franz Liszt saw at the Campo Santo in Pisa Andrea Orcagna's fresco *The Triumph of Death,* a grotesque, grisly fantasy of Death as the wrecker of human joys—with the figure of Death itself a bat-winged woman. He began working at once on his Totentanz, or "Dance of Death," a set of variations for piano and orchestra based on the ancient plainsong Dies Irae theme. He kept revising the score, and only in 1859 did he produce the version that has remained in the repertory ever since.

Mahler: *Symphony No. 1 in D.* In a synopsis that Mahler provided for early performances of his First Symphony—but which he later withdrew—he said the grotesque third movement was "a funeral march in the manner of Callot." The reference was to Jacques Callot (1592–1635), a French etcher and engraver who specialized in grotesque figures. Mahler had seen one of Callot's drawings, the funeral procession of a hunter with the corpse surrounded by gaily dancing animals, in an old German fairy-tale book.

Menotti: *Amahl and the Night Visitors.* This was the first opera composed specifically for television (1951), and thanks to its many broadcast repetitions, it may be the opera viewed by more people than any other ever written. Menotti's inspiration was Hieronymus Bosch's *The Adoration of the Magi,* with the opera's costumes and sets influenced by that painting.

Mussorgsky: *Pictures at an Exhibition.* After the eminent Russian painter Victor Hartmann died in 1873, his close friend Modest Mussorgsky decided to pay tribute to him. He did so by composing a set of 10 piano pieces, each depicting in music a picture shown at a memorial exhibition of Hartmann's watercolors and drawings at the Academy of Arts in St. Petersburg. Maurice Ravel later made an orchestral transcription, as have several other composers. The work is introduced by a Promenade theme, followed by depictions of 10 pictures:

Gnomus. A clumsy dwarf.
The Old Castle. A medieval castle before which a troubador sings.
Tuileries. Children and nurses in the Paris gardens.
Bydlo. An ox-drawn Polish wagon.
Ballet of Chicken in Their Shells. A drawing for the ballet *Trilby.*
Samuel Goldenberg and Schmulye. Two Polish Jews, one wealthy, one poor.
Limoges: The Market-Place. Women arguing.
Catacombs. Those in Paris are depicted.
The Hut on Fowl's Legs. A witch's dwelling.
The Great Gate at Kiev. Hartmann's design for a massive gate to the city.

Rachmaninov: *The Isle of the Dead.* The subtitle of this symphonic poem, Sergei Rachmaninov's Opus 29, reads: "To the Picture by A. Böcklin." Arnold Böcklin (1827–1901) was a Swiss Romantic painter whose *Isle of the Dead* depicts a small boat bearing a coffin, with a white-shrouded figure standing in the prow, as it glides toward a mysterious island of rocks and cypress trees. Rachmaninov creates a similarly desolate and foreboding mood in his score. Böcklin's oil painting is in the Metropolitan Museum of Art in New York City.

Reger: *Four Tone-Poems after Böcklin.* German composer Max Reger (1873–1916) also found inspiration in the paintings of Arnold Böcklin. Of these four tone-poems for orchestra, one, like Rachmaninov's, is based on *The Isle of the Dead.* The others are *The Hermit With a Violin, Sport Among the Waves,* and *The Bacchanal.* Composed in 1913, the work is rarely heard today.

Schumann: *Symphony No. 3 in E-flat, Op. 97.* Robert Schumann said that his "Rhenish" Symphony was first conceived when he saw Cologne Cathedral. However, he broadened its scope to depict various aspects of life along the Rhine, and remarked that in music "a general impression of a work of art is better" than an attempt to reproduce it in exact detail.

Sondheim: *Sunday in the Park With George.* Stephen Sondheim's 1984 Broadway show is an attempt to bring to life the French neo-

135

impressionist Georges Seurat, notably his *Un Dimanche d'Été à l'Isle de la Grande Jatte.*

R. Strauss: *Friedenstag.* The inspiration for Strauss's opera *Friedenstag* (The Day of Peace), about the siege of Breda during the Thirty Years' War, is ascribed to a viewing of Velazquez's painting, *The Surrender at Breda.*

Stravinsky: *The Rake's Progress.* The impulse for Igor Stravinsky's 1951 opera came from William Hogarth's 18th-century engravings depicting the moral descent of the libertine Tom Rakewell. The libretto is by W. H. Auden and Chester Kallman.

Thompson: *The Peaceable Kingdom.* Randall Thompson's *The Peaceable Kingdom,* a choral work, was inspired by a painting of the early American folk artist Edward Hicks (1780–1849) showing the lion and the calf together, as in Isaiah 11, with William Penn signing a treaty with the Indians in the background. Thompson's score is a setting of seven verses from the Book of Isaiah.

WORLD WAR II IN MUSIC

Wars invariably give rise to musical works, and World War II was no exception. More than most other wars, however, it was marked by a large proportion of elegaic or commemorative pieces, as distinguished from the customary martial variety. This list includes examples of both types:

Walter Damrosch: *Dunkirk* (1943). A setting of Robert Nathan's poem, for baritone, chorus, and small orchestra.

Dmitri Kabalevsky: *At Moscow* (1943). Kabalevsky's opera celebrates the defeat of the Germans before the Soviet capital. In 1947 it underwent revision and received a new title, *In the Fire.*

Bohuslav Martinu: *Memorial to Lidice* (1943). A Czech composer's tribute to the village and people destroyed by the Nazis in retaliation for the assassination of Reinhard Heydrich. At its climax this orchestral piece uses the Beethoven's Fifth motif that symbolized European resistance to the Germans.

Vano Muradeli: *Symphony No. 2* (1946). Subtitled "The War of Liberation," this symphony won its Soviet composer a Stalin Prize. However, his opera *The Great Friendship* in 1947 led to an official condemnation of modernistic trends in Soviet music. Subsequent works by Muradeli regained party approval.

Ian Parrott: *El Alamein* (1944). This symphonic prelude was written by a British composer who actually served in the Royal Signal Corps in North Africa during the war.

Krzysztof Penderecki: Threnody for the Victims of Hiroshima (1960). This composition for 52 string instruments with its unconventional techniques has proved to be one of the most frequently performed pieces stemming from World War II.

Walter Piston: Fanfare for the Fighting French (1942). A short piece in honor of the troops led by General Charles de Gaulle.

Francis Poulenc: C (1940). This powerful song, composed by Poulenc after the French collapse in 1940, is about the four "Caesar bridges" at the town of Angers, where the Gauls were defeated by the Romans in 51 B.C. and the French by the Germans nearly 2,000 years later.

Richard Rodgers: South Pacific (1949). A Broadway show, with lyrics by Oscar Hammerstein II, that captured the mood and achievements of U.S. forces in the Pacific, and has undergone innumerable revivals over the years.

Richard Rodgers: Victory at Sea (1952). A television score that has attained concert performances and recording.

Arnold Schoenberg: A Survivor from Warsaw (1947). Schoenberg was impelled to write this graphic cantata for narrator, men's chorus, and orchestra, his Opus 46, by revelations of Nazi concentration camp atrocities.

William Schuman: Symphony No. 9, 'Le Fosse Ardeatine" (1969). A symphonic commemoration of another Nazi atrocity, the slaying of Italian civilian hostages in the Ardeatine Caves near Rome.

Dmitri Shostakovich: Symphony No. 7, "Leningrad" (1942). Extravagantly praised, this musical tribute to the defenders of Leningrad during its siege by the Germans was first conducted in the United States by Arturo Toscanini, who beat out Leopold Stokowski for the honor. Later it was championed by Serge Koussevitzky in Boston, but it has virtually dropped out of the repertory.

Dmitri Shostakovich: Symphony No. 13, "Babi Yar" (1962). The finale of this symphony, a setting of Yevgeny Yevtushenko's poem about the massacre by the Nazis of 200,000 Jews at a ravine near Kiev in 1943, produced a powerful effect upon audiences that heard it at its first performances both in Russia and the United States. Later, the Soviet authorities demanded changes in the text to indicate that others besides Jews had also been murdered.

SPORTS IN MUSIC

Sports may not be among the prime interests of composers, yet various games and pastimes have managed to make an appearance in musical works. Here are some instances:

SPORT	COMPOSITION	COMPOSER
Archery	*William Tell* (opera)	Rossini
Baseball	*Casey at the Bat* (opera)	Schuman
Boxing	*Partita a Pugni* (Boxing Match, opera)	Tosatti
Bullfighting	*Carmen* (opera)	Bizet
Chess	*Checkmate* (ballet)	Bliss
Crap-shooting	*Porgy and Bess* (opera)	Gershwin
Fishing	*Die Forellen* (song)	Schubert
Hunting	*Quartet No. 17 in B-flat*	Mozart
Ice-skating	*The Skaters Waltz*	Waldteufel
Poker	*Jeu de Cartes* (ballet)	Stravinsky
Rugby	*Rugby* (symphonic movement)	Honegger
Soccer	*Half-Time* (orchestral work)	Martinu
Tennis	*Jeux* (ballet)	Debussy
Yachting	*La Regata Veneziana* (songs)	Rossini

DISHES NAMED AFTER MUSICIANS

While the starving musician is a figure well-known in folklore, in actual life many musicians have managed to eat so well that they've either created new dishes themselves or had gustatory delights named after them. Here are a dozen of the best-known:

Chicken Tetrazzini. Cubed chicken cooked with mushrooms in broth, cream, and sherry, then sprinkled with cheese, baked in a casserole, and served with spaghetti. It was named for soprano Luisa Tetrazzini, whose ample figure attested to her taste for it.

Consommé Bizet. Chicken consommé thickened with tapioca and garnished with tiny chicken dumplings.

Melba toast. Auguste Escoffier, the master chef, toasted thin bread in an oven and named the resultant wafers for Dame Nellie Melba, the Australian soprano, when she expressed her liking for this form of light nourishment.

Mozart Kugeln. A confection of chocolate and marzipan made by Reber of Bad Reichenhall, Germany.

Oeufs Auber. Halved tomatoes stuffed with chopped chicken and truffles, topped with a soft-boiled or poached egg, garnished with white sauce.

Oeufs Berlioz. Croustades (hollowed-out potato puffs) with a filling of truffles and mushrooms in madeira sauce, topped with soft-boiled or poached eggs.

Oeufs Massenet. Croustades prepared as above, but with a filling of chopped-up string beans, topped with soft-boiled or poached eggs in a white wine sauce.

Oeufs Meyerbeer. Cooked eggs garnished with a grilled lamb kidney.

Pêches Melba. Peaches served on ice cream and topped with a raspberry sauce, properly served in a silver dish. Invented by Escoffier in honor of Dame Nellie, who thus holds the rare distinction of having both slenderizing and calorific delicacies named for her. For *poires Melba,* substitute pears for peaches.

Spaghetti Caruso. Spaghetti prepared with chicken livers. The great tenor's association with the dish is a matter of controversy. Some say he loved it, others that it basically was a specialty of the Caruso restaurant chain of New York.

Suprêmes de volaille Verdi. Sauteed chicken served in a pastry shell filled with diced macaroni in purée de foie gras, topped with sliced truffles, and lightly coated in marsala sauce.

Tournedos Rossini. Sliced beefsteak sautéed in butter, arranged on croutons, and topped with a slice of foie gras and truffles. Rossini's love for foie gras was notorious, and a vast variety of dishes garnished with goose liver, or approximations thereof, bear his name—poularde à la Rossini, escalope de ris de veau Rossini, cotelettes d'agneau Rossini, timbales à la Rossini, omelette Rossini, oeufs brouillés Rossini, salade Rossini, and others.

NON-MUSICAL WORKS WITH MUSICAL TITLES

Musical allusions abound in literature, and often make their way into titles of works that have nothing, or little, to do with music. Here is a sampling of musical titles from fiction, poetry, drama and films.

Aimez-vous Brahms? by Françoise Sagan (novel)
Alexandria Quartet by Lawrence Durrell (novels)
L'Allegro by John Milton (poem)
Autumn Sonata by Barbara Pym (novel)
The Bald Soprano by Eugene Ionescu (play)
The Blue Harpsichord by Francis Steegmuller (mystery)
The Bushwhacked Piano by Thomas McGuane (novel)
Chamber Music by James Joyce (poems)
Fanfare for Two Pigeons by H. W. Heinsheimer (memoirs)
Four Quartets by T. S. Eliot (poems)
The G-String Murders by Gypsy Rose Lee (mystery)
Hebrew Melodies by George Gordon, Lord Byron (poems)
Intermezzo (film, Ingrid Bergman)
Irish Melodies by Thomas Moore (poems)
The Kreutzer Sonata by Leo Tolstoy (short story)
The Lobster Quadrille by Lewis Carroll (poem)

The Man With the Blue Guitar by Wallace Stevens (poem)
A Night at the Opera (film, The Marx Brothers)
The Parsifal Mosaic by Robert Ludlum (novel)
Pavannes and Divigations by Ezra Pound (poems and essays)
Peter Quince at the Clavier by Wallace Stevens (poem)
The Phantom of the Opera by Eugene Sus (novel)
Point Counter Point by Aldous Huxley (novel)
The Radetzky March by Joseph Roth (novel)
Ragtime by E. L. Doctorow (novel)
Rameau's Nephew by Denis Diderot (satire)
Requiem for a Nun by William Faulkner (novel)
Rothschild's Fiddle by Anton Chekhov (short story)
Serenade by James M. Cain (novel)
Symphonie Pastorale by André Gide (novel)
A Toccata of Galuppi's by Robert Browning (poem)
The Waltz of the Toreadors by Jean Anouilh (play)

MUSICAL TASTES OF FICTIONAL CHARACTERS

In some cases fictional personages have strong musical tastes that provide a key to their characters. Following are some well-known figures from novels and short stories whose musical inclinations are worthy of note. They are listed by author and title:

Max Beerbohm: Zuleika Dobson. **Zuleika Dobson,** the beautiful charmer for whom every Oxford undergraduate is ready to drown himself, apparently is the first to utter one of the most famous—and fatuous—of musical sayings. "I don't know anything about music, really," she says. "But I know what I like."

Samuel Butler: The Way of All Flesh. **Ernest Pontifex,** who has been given a rigorous upbringing by his pompous, pious clergyman father, cherishes above all the music of George Frideric Handel. In the last chapter he confesses, "I would like modern music, if I could; I have been trying all my life to like it." When he is asked, "And pray, where do you consider modern music to begin?" he replies, "With Sebastian Bach."

James M. Cain: Serenade. **Captain Conners,** the sea-captain who tries to help a broken-down opera star in this 1937 novel, loves Beethoven but detests Rossini and all other Italian opera composers. He gets into an argument with the singer, who wins with this tirade: "Listen, symphonies are not all of music. When you get to the overtures, Beethoven's name is not at the top and Rossini's is

. . . . Rossini loved the theater, and that's why he could write an overture."

Arthur Conan Doyle: *The Adventures of Sherlock Holmes.* **Sherlock Holmes,** the great detective, was surely one of the most remarkable musicians who never lived. He could play and improvise fantastically on the violin, he was a regular concert- and opera-goer, and he authored a monograph on "The Polyphonic Motets of Lassus," which according to his faithful amanuensis, Dr. Watson, was "the last word upon the subject"—and maybe also the first.

Gustave Flaubert: *Madame Bovary.* **Emma Bovary** displays her romantic sentimentality, among other places, at the opera in Rouen, where she goes to hear *Lucia di Lammermoor.* Although her bourgeois husband is bored and wants to leave, she is carried away by the romance on the stage before her. But when her former lover, Léon, unexpectedly appears during an intermission, she abruptly goes off with him for some of the real article.

E. M. Forster: *Howards End.* The entire **Schlegel family,** the central figures in this 1910 novel about class relationships in England, is deeply sensitive to music. They display the range of their feelings at a performance of Beethoven's Fifth Symphony, Margaret being fascinated by its intellectual side, her sister Helen by its romantic, and their brother Tibby by its technical. The result is an unusually vivid musical analysis within a work of fiction.

James Joyce: *Ulysses.* **Leopold Bloom** has a nice taste in music, being especially partial to Mozart's opera *Don Giovanni.* On several occasions he sings to himself such snatches as the Statue's reply to the Don's invitation to dinner. But his favorite quotation seems to be the peasant girl Zerlina's answer when the Don attempts to break down her resistance: "I would and yet I would not." It is a phrase that characterizes Mr. Bloom himself all too well.

Thomas Mann: *Dr. Faustus.* **Adrian Leverkühn,** the composer-hero of Thomas Mann's next-to-last novel *Doctor Faustus,* and one of the most detailed and convincing of fictional musicians, is fascinated from his boyhood by the ambiguous relationships among chords and keys—but also by a desire for lost, uncivilized naiveté. His last work, a cantata entitled *The Lamentation of Doctor Faustus,* is described as based upon a 12-tone row.

Marcel Proust: *Remembrance of Things Past.* **Charles Swann,** a fashionable young man, finds his life intertwined with a theme by the composer Vinteuil that he has heard at a soirée. The little phrase of seven notes becomes almost the theme song of his passionate love affair with the rather dubious Odette de Crécy. Vinteuil is supposedly modeled by Proust upon the composer César Franck.

Romain Rolland: *Jean Christophe.* Rolland's 10-volume series is about a German-born musician, **Jean Christophe Kraft,** who settles in Paris. The novel, as one might imagine, is filled with allusions to music. Among other observations, Jean Christophe is distressed at the Parisian public's indifference to new or adventurous music: "At every concert he found the same names and the same pieces . . . . virtually nothing before Beethoven, almost nothing after Wagner. And in between, what gaps! . . . His inquiring mind was bold and unprejudiced; he was consumed with a desire to hear something new and to admire the works of genius."

William Shakespeare: *A Midsummer Night's Dream.* Shakespeare, who wrote so sensitively and beautifully about music, also produced at least one character who didn't know much about it, but knew what he liked. This is **Nick Bottom,** the weaver, who tells the assembled company in Act IV: "I have a reasonable good ear in music. Let's have the tongs and the bones."

Leo Tolstoy: War and Peace. Among her other attributes, **Natasha Rostova** embodies the amateur singer at her best. After a winter of vocal studies "she no longer sang like a child and one no longer heard the clumsy efforts of a pupil." But her voice still lacks technique. All the same, connoisseurs "involuntarily yielded to the pleasure that this same voice afforded . . . . One could sense in it a sweet, virginal purity, and unconsciousness of its power."

MUSICIANS WITH NAMES OF THREE LETTERS OR LESS

The composer with the longest name probably is Mario Castelnuovo-Tedesco (1895–1968), though Mikhail Ippolitov-Ivanov gives him a good run. However, musicians in general seem to flourish best with short names rather than long, to which the following list attests:

Evald Aav (1900–1939) Estonian composer
Franz Abt (1819–1885) German composer
Emanuel Ax (1949–   ) American pianist
Jesus Bal y Gay (1905–   ) Spanish composer
Arnold Bax (1883–1953) British composer
Coenraad Bos (1875–1955) Dutch pianist and accompanist
César Cui (1835–1918) Russian composer
Ikuma Dan (1924–   ) Japanese composer
Claire Dux (1885–1967) Polish-born soprano
Werner Egk (1901–   ) German composer
Gunnar Ek (1900–   ) Swedish composer

Donald Erb (1927–   ) American composer
William Henry Fry (1813–1864) American composer
Johann Joseph Fux (1660–1741) German composer
Hans Gal (1890–   ) Austrian composer and scholar
Maria Gay (1879–1943) Spanish-born contralto
Hershy Kay (1919–   ) American composer and arranger
Ulysses Simpson Kay (1917–   ) American composer
Francis Scott Key (1779–1843) American lawyer and song-writer (one song)
Young-Uck Kim (1948–   ) Korean violinist
Andrew Law (1749–1821) American singing teacher and composer
Leonardo Leo (1694–1744) Italian composer and teacher
Yo-Yo Ma (1955–   ) American cellist
Yves Nat (1890–1956) French pianist
Elly Ney (1882–1968) German pianist
Joaquin Nin (1879–1949) Spanish composer
Odo de Clugny, Saint (? –942) musical theorist and writer
Adele Aus der Ohe (1864–1937) German pianist
Shulamit Ran (1948–   ) Israeli composer
Klaus George Roy (1924–   ) American composer and musicologist
Adolphe Sax (1814–1894) Inventor of the saxophone
Ferdinand Sor (1778–1839) Spanish composer
Joseph Tal (1910–   ) Israeli composer
Christopher Tye (1500–1572) British composer
Bela Ujj (1873–1942) Hungarian composer
Paul de Wit (1852–1925) Dutch cellist
Pietro Yon (1886–1943) American organist
Yakov Zak (1913–1976) Soviet pianist

MUSICIANS' REAL NAMES

Name changes for artistic (or other) reasons are by no means unique to musicians. If you don't immediately recognize the ladies and gentlemen in the first column, try the second:

Isidore Balin	Irving Berlin
Borge Rosenbaum	Victor Borge
Maria Calogeropoulos	Maria Callas
Joseph Guttoveggio	Paul Creston
Robert Zimmerman	Bob Dylan
Reba Fiersohn	Alma Gluck
Byron Yanks	Byron Janis
Reg Dwight	Elton John

Helen Porter Armstrong	Nellie Melba
Peter Mennini	Peter Mennin
Jeno Blau	Eugene Ormandy
Jacob Pincus Perelmuth	Jan Peerce
Elisabeth Sättler	Elisabeth Rethberg
Ruffo Titta	Titta Ruffo
Lucie Hickenlooper	Olga Samaroff
Belle Silverman	Beverly Sills
Richard Starkey	Ringo Starr
Anastasia Strataki	Teresa Stratas
Emperatriz Chavarri	Yma Sumac
Ernst Sieffert	Richard Tauber
Reuben Ticker	Richard Tucker

MUSICAL ASTROLOGY

Few composers appear to have paid much attention to astrology, or to have consulted their horoscopes before launching on a new project. Nevertheless, here are the zodiacal signs—along with the commonly accepted characteristics of each—under which various composers of the past and present were born, together with their birth dates:

ARIES
(MARCH 20–APRIL 19)

Adventurous, decisive, fearless, confident, leadership capabilities.

Johann Sebastian Bach (March 21, 1685)
Béla Bartók (March 25, 1881)
Richard Rodney Bennett (March 29, 1936)
William Bergsma (April 1, 1921)
Pierre Boulez (March 26, 1925)
Ferruccio Busoni (April 1, 1866)
Mario Castelnuovo-Tedesco (April 3, 1895)
Dennis Russell Davies (April 16, 1944)
Ferde Grofé (March 27, 1892)
Franz Joseph Haydn (March 31, 1732)
Andrew Imbrie (April 6, 1921)
Vincent d'Indy (March 27, 1851)
Johann Kuhnau (April 6, 1660)
Marin Marais (March 31, 1656)
Modest Mussorgsky (March 21, 1839)
Sergei Rachmaninoff (April 1, 1873)

Albert Roussel (April 5, 1869)
Miklós Rózsa (April 18, 1907)
Ludwig Spohr (April 5, 1784)
Morton Subotnick (April 14, 1933)
Franz von Suppé (April 18, 1819)
Germaine Tailleferre (April 19, 1892)
William Walton (March 29, 1902)
Richard Yardumian (April 5, 1917)

TAURUS
(APRIL 20–MAY 20)

Loyal, tenacious, earthy, fertile, practical.

Milton Babbitt (May 10, 1916)
Arthur Berger (May 15, 1912)
Irving Berlin (May 11, 1888)
Johannes Brahms (May 7, 1833)
Albert Coates (April 23, 1882)
Duke (Edward Kennedy) Ellington (April 29, 1899)
Gabriel Fauré (May 12, 1845)
Jerzy Fitelberg (May 20, 1903)
Friedrich von Flotow (April 26, 1812)
Johann Jakob Frohberger (May 18, 1616)
Karl Goldmark (May 18, 1830)
Louis Moreau Gottschalk (May 8, 1829)
Franz Lehár (April 30, 1870)
Ruggero Leoncavallo (March 18, 1858)
Anatol Liadov (May 10, 1855)
Padre Giambattista Martini (April 24, 1706)
Jules Massenet (May 12, 1842)
Peter Mennin (May 17, 1923)
Nikolai Miaskovsky (April 20, 1881)
Giovanni Paisiello (May 9, 1740)
Hans Pfitzner (May 5, 1869)
Sergei Prokofiev (April 23, 1891)
Emil Rezniček (May 4, 1860)
Wallingford Riegger (April 29, 1885)
Erik Satie (May 17, 1866)
Alessandro Scarlatti (May 2, 1660)
Harold Shapero (April 29, 1920)
Ethel Smyth (April 23, 1858)
Harvey Sollberger (May 11, 1938)
Leo Sowerby (May 1, 1895)
Karl Stamitz (May 7, 1745)

William Grant Still (May 11, 1895)
Arthur Sullivan (May 13, 1842)
Peter Ilyich Tchaikovsky (May 7, 1840)

GEMINI
(MAY 21–JUNE 20)

Tending toward dual personality, brilliant, restless, versatile, quick-witted, open-minded, articulate.

Tomaso Albinoni (June 8, 1671)
Carlos Chávez (June 13, 1899)
Edward Elgar (June 2, 1857)
Jean Françaix (May 23, 1912)
Mikhail Glinka (June 1, 1804)
Charles Gounod (June 17, 1818)
Edvard Grieg (June 15, 1843)
Fromental Halévy (May 27, 1799)
Werner Josten (June 12, 1885)
Aram Khatchaturian (June 6, 1903)
Erich Korngold (May 29, 1897)
Otto Luening (June 15, 1900)
Carl Nielsen (June 9, 1865)
Jacques Offenbach (June 20, 1819)
Vincent Persichetti (June 6, 1915)
Edmund Rubbra (May 23, 1901)
Robert Schumann (June 8, 1810)
Johann Stamitz (June 19, 1717)
Igor Stravinsky (June 17, 1882)
Antonio Vivaldi (June 11, 1669)
Richard Wagner (May 22, 1813)
Charles Wuorinen (June 9, 1935)
Yannis Xenakis (May 29, 1922)

CANCER
(JUNE 21–JULY 22)

Sentimental, sincere, sensitive, patient, shrewd.

George Antheil (July 8, 1900)
Jack Beeson (July 15, 1921)
Georg Anton Benda (June 30, 1772)
Paul Ben-Haim (July 5, 1897)
Gustave Charpentier (June 25, 1860)
Avery Claflin (June 21, 1898)
David Diamond (July 9, 1915)

Jacob Druckman (June 26, 1928)
Stephen Foster (July 4, 1826)
Christoph Willibald von Gluck (July 2, 1714)
Percy Grainger (July 8, 1882)
Hans Werner Henze (July 1, 1926)
Josef Holbrooke (July 5, 1878)
Leoš Janáček (July 3, 1854)
Meyer Kupferman (July 3, 1926)
Gustav Mahler (July 7, 1860)
Étienne Méhul (June 22, 1763)
Gian Carlo Menotti (July 7, 1911)
Carl Orff (July 10, 1895)
Harry Partch (June 24, 1901)
Ottorino Respighi (July 9, 1879)
Richard Rodgers (June 28, 1902)
Jean-Jacques Rousseau (June 28, 1712)
Ruth Crawford Seeger (July 3, 1901)
Bernard Wagenaar (July 18, 1894)

LEO
(JULY 23–AUGUST 22)

Dignified, brave, warm-hearted, inspired, noble, generous.

Anton Arensky (August 11, 1861)
Granville Bantok (August 7, 1868)
Arthur Bliss (August 2, 1891)
Ernest Bloch (July 24, 1880)
Carrie Jacobs Bond (August 11, 1862)
Lili Boulanger (August 21, 1893)
Alfredo Casella (July 25, 1883)
Cécile Chaminade (August 8, 1857)
Samuel Coleridge-Taylor (August 15, 1875)
Claude Debussy (August 22, 1862)
Ernst von Dohnányi (July 27, 1877)
Georges Enesco (August 19, 1881)
John Field (July 26, 1782)
Lukas Foss (August 15, 1922)
Alexander Glazunov (August 10, 1865)
Enrique Granados (July 27, 1867)
Louis Gruenberg (August 3, 1884)
Karel Husa (August 7, 1921)
Jacques Ibert (August 15, 1890)
John Ireland (August 13, 1879)
André Jolivet (August 8, 1905)

*Leonardo Leo (August 5, 1694)
Benedetto Marcello (July 24, 1686)
Douglas Moore (August 10, 1893)
Alexander Mossolov (August 10, 1900)
Jacopo Peri (August 20, 1561)
Gabriel Pierné (August 16, 1863)
Antonio Salieri (August 15, 1750)
William Schuman (August 4, 1910)
Karlheinz Stockhausen (August 22, 1928)
Ambroise Thomas (August 5, 1811)
Ben Weber (July 23, 1916)

VIRGO
AUGUST 23–SEPTEMBER 22

Practical, systematic, conscientious, helpful, tending toward perfectionism.

Johann Christian Bach (September 5, 1735)
Leonard Bernstein (August 25, 1918)
Henry Brant (September 15, 1913)
Anton Bruckner (September 4, 1824)
Luigi Cherubini (September 14, 1760)
Peter Maxwell Davies (September 8, 1934)
Antonin Dvořák (September 8, 1841)
Charles Tomlinson Griffes (September 17, 1884)
Gustav Holst (September 21, 1874)
Francis Hopkinson (September 21, 1737)
Engelbert Humperdinck (September 1, 1854)
Niccolò Jommelli (September 10, 1714)
Ernst Krenek (August 23, 1900)
Constant Lambert (August 23, 1905)
Pietro Locatelli (September 3, 1695)
Frank Martin (September 15, 1890)
Giacomo Meyerbeer (September 5, 1791)
Darius Milhaud (September 4, 1892)
Moritz Moszkowski (August 23, 1854)
Horatio Parker (September 15, 1863)
Ildebrando Pizzetti (September 20, 1880)
Amilcare Ponchielli (August 31, 1834)
Eric Salzman (September 8, 1933)
Arnold Schoenberg (September 13, 1874)
Clara Schumann (September 13, 1819)
Robert Ward (September 13, 1917)

---

*For this composer to have been born under any other sign would be unthinkable.

LIBRA
(SEPTEMBER 23–OCTOBER 22)

Diplomatic, sensitive, peaceful, tactful, in love with beauty.

William Billings (October 7, 1746)
Paul Creston (October 10, 1906)
Paul Dukas (October 1, 1865)
Baldassare Galuppi (October 18, 1706)
George Gershwin (September 28, 1898)
Charles Ives (October 20, 1874)
Franz Liszt (October 22, 1811)
Jean-Philippe Rameau (September 25, 1683)
Steve Reich (October 3, 1936)
Camille Saint-Saëns (October 9, 1835)
Heinrich Schütz (October 8, 1585)
Dmitri Shostakovich (September 25, 1906)
Charles Villiers Stanford (September 30, 1852)
Karol Szymanowski (October 6, 1882)
Ralph Vaughan Williams (October 12, 1872)
Giuseppe Verdi (October 10, 1813)
Hugo Weisgall (October 13, 1912)

SCORPIO
(OCTOBER 23–NOVEMBER 21)

Self-controlled, intense, magnetic, passionate, a survivor.

David Amram (November 17, 1930)
Arnold Bax (November 8, 1883)
Vincenzo Bellini (November 3, 1801)
Luciano Berio (October 24, 1925)
Alexander Borodin (November 11, 1833)
Aaron Copland (November 14, 1900)
François Couperin (November 10, 1668)
George Crumb (October 24, 1929)
Karl Ditters von Dittersdorf (November 2, 1739)
Alexander Gretchaninov (October 25, 1864)
W. C. Handy (November 16, 1873)
Howard Hanson (October 28, 1896)
Paul Hindemith (November 16, 1895)
Johann Nepomuk Hummel (November 14, 1778)
Mikhail Ippolitov-Ivanov (November 19, 1859)
Emmerich Kálmán (October 24, 1882)
Hershy Kay (November 17, 1919)

Albert Lortzing (October 23, 1801)
Daniel Gregory Mason (November 20, 1873)
Ignace Jan Paderewski (November 18, 1860)
Henri Rabaud (November 10, 1873)
Ned Rorem (October 23, 1923)
Hans Sachs (November 5, 1494)
Domenico Scarlatti (October 26, 1685)
John Philip Sousa (November 6, 1854)
Gasparo Spontini (November 14, 1774)
Johann Strauss, Jr. (October 25, 1825)
Louise Talma (October 31, 1906)
Vladimir Ussachevsky (November 3, 1911)
Philippe de Vitry (October 31, 1291)
Carl Maria von Weber (November 18, 1786)
Eugen Zador (November 5, 1894)

SAGITTARIUS
(NOVEMBER 22–DECEMBER 20)

Optimistic, wise, straight-talking, vibrant, an explorer.

Wilhelm Friedemann Bach (November 22, 1710)
Ludwig van Beethoven (December 16, 1770)
Hector Berlioz (December 11, 1803)
Benjamin Britten (November 22, 1913)
Elliott Carter (December 11, 1908)
Domenico Cimarosa (December 17, 1949)
Gaetano Donizetti (November 29, 1797)
Manuel de Falla (November 23, 1876)
Irving Fine (December 3, 1914)
César Franck (December 10, 1822)
Morton Gould (December 10, 1913)
Henry Hadley (December 20, 1871)
Scott Joplin (November 24, 1868)
Zoltán Kodály (December 16, 1882)
Charles Koechlin (November 27, 1867)
Jean-Baptiste Lully (November 28, 1632)
Edward MacDowell (December 18, 1861)
Bohuslav Martinu (December 8, 1890)
Pietro Mascagni (December 7, 1863)
Olivier Messiaen (December 10, 1908)
Krzysztof Pendercki (November 23, 1933)
Gaetano Pugnani (November 27, 1731)
Gunther Schuller (November 22, 1925)
Rodion Shchedrin (December 16, 1932)

Jean Sibelius (December 8, 1865)
Antonio Soler (December 3, 1729)
Virgil Thomson (November 25, 1896)
Joaquin Turina (December 9, 1882)
Anton von Webern (December 3, 1883)

CAPRICORN
(DECEMBER 21–JANUARY 19)

Economical, slow, careful, patient, secretive, ambitious, diplomatic, practical, hard-working.

Henk Badings (January 17, 1907)
Mily Balakirev (January 2, 1837)
Boris Blacher (January 3, 1903)
Paul Bowles (December 30, 1910)
Max Bruch (January 6, 1838)
Charles Wakefield Cadman (December 24, 1881)
Emmanuel Chabrier (January 18, 1841)
Frederick S. Converse (January 5, 1871)
Donald Erb (January 17, 1927)
Peggy Glanville-Hicks (December 29, 1912)
Reinhold Glière (January 11, 1875)
Ulysses Simpson Kay (January 7, 1917)
Lowell Mason (January 8, 1792)
Nikolai Medtner (January 5, 1880)
John Knowles Paine (January 9, 1839)
Giovanni Battista Pergolesi (January 7, 1710)
Niccoló Piccinni (January 16, 1728)
Francis Poulenc (January 7, 1899)
Giacomo Puccini (December 22, 1858)
Xaver Scharwenka (January 6, 1850)
Roger Sessions (December 28, 1896)
Elie Siegmeister (January 15, 1909)
Christian Sinding (January 11, 1856)
Robert Starer (January 8, 1924)
Alexander Tanayev (January 17, 1850)
Deems Taylor (December 22, 1885)
Michael Tippett (January 2, 1905)
Edgar Varèse (December 22, 1885)
Jaromir Weinberger (January 8, 1896)
Ermanno Wolf-Ferrari (January 12, 1876)
Johann Rudolf Zumsteeg (January 10, 1760)

AQUARIUS
(JANUARY 20–FEBRUARY 18)

Progressive, independent, inventive, utopian goals, spontaneous.

Daniel-Francois-Esprit Auber (January 29, 1782)
Georges Auric (February 15, 1899)
Alban Berg (February 9, 1885)
Thomas Campion (February 12, 1567)
Pier Francesco Cavalli (February 14, 1602)
Ernest Chausson (January 20, 1855)
Muzio Clementi (January 23, 1752)
Luigi Dallapiccola (February 3, 1904)
Walter Damrosch (January 30, 1862)
Frederick Delius (January 29, 1862)
Norman Dello Joio (January 24, 1913)
Henri Duparc (January 21, 1848)
Gottfried von Einem (January 24, 1918)
Edward German (February 17, 1862)
Philip Glass (January 31, 1937)
André Grétry (February 8, 1741)
Roy Harris (February 12, 1898)
Victor Herbert (February 1, 1859)
Lee Hoiby (February 17, 1926)
Jerome Kern (January 27, 1885)
Leon Kirchner (January 24, 1919)
Édouard Lalo (January 27, 1823)
Witold Lutaslowski (January 25, 1913)
Felix Mendelssohn (February 3, 1809)
Wolfgang Amadeus Mozart (January 27, 1756)
Luigi Nono (January 29, 1924)
Walter Piston (January 20, 1894)
Mel Powell (February 12, 1923)
Michael Praetorius (February 15, 1571)
Vittorio Rieti (January 28, 1898)
Bernard Rogers (February 4, 1893)
Franz Schubert (January 31, 1793)
Alexander Tcherepnin (January 20, 1899)
Henri Vieuxtemps (February 17, 1820)

PISCES
(FEBRUARY 19–MARCH 19)

Creative, idealistic, imaginative, generous, pure of mind, compassionate.

Thomas Arne (March 12, 1710)
Carl Philipp Emanuel Bach (March 8, 1714)
Samuel Barber (March 9, 1910)
Marc Bitzstein (March 2, 1905)
Luigi Boccherini (February 19, 1743)
Arrigo Boito (February 24, 1842)
Frank Bridge (February 26, 1879)
Frédéric Chopin (February 22, 1810)
Henry Cowell (March 11, 1897)
Carl Czerny (February 20, 1791)
Mario Davidovsky (March 4, 1934)
Léo Delibes (February 21, 1836)
David del Tredici (March 16, 1937)
Arthur Foote (March 5, 1853)
Niels Gade (February 22, 1817)
George Frideric Handel (February 23, 1685)
Arthur Honegger (March 10, 1892)
Alan Hovhaness (March 8, 1911)
Hubert Parry (February 27, 1848)
Maurice Ravel (March 7, 1875)
Max Reger (March 19, 1873)
Anton Reicha (February 26, 1770)
Nikolai Rimsky-Korsakov (March 18, 1844)
Gioacchino Rossini (February 29, 1792)
Carl Ruggles (March 11, 1876)
Bedřich Smetana (March 2, 1824)
Oscar Straus (March 6, 1870)
Johann Strauss, Sr. (March 14, 1804)
Carlos Surinach (March 4, 1915)
Georg Philipp Telemann (March 14, 1681)
Heitor Villa-Lobos (March 5, 1887)

MUSICAL MARRIAGES

Musicians marry musicians—or at least members of other musical families—with considerable frequency. Here is a list of some of the

better-known musical marriages, many (though not all) of which
proved to be permanent:

Husband	Wife
Wolfgang Amadeus Mozart, composer	Constanze Weber, a cousin of Carl Maria von Weber
Georges Bizet, composer	Genevieve Halévy, daughter of Fromental Halévy
Robert Schumann, composer	Clara Wieck, pianist
Charles de Beriot, violinist	Maria Malibran, contralto
Richard Wagner, composer	Cosima von Bülow, daughter of Franz Liszt, wife of Hans von Bülow
Richard Strauss, composer	Pauline de Ahna, soprano
Arnold Rosé, violinist	Justine Mahler, sister of Gustav Mahler
Eugène d'Albert, composer and pianist	Theresa Carreño, pianist, was his first wife; 5 others followed
Arnold Schoenberg, composer	Mathilde von Zemlinsky, sister of Alexander von Zemlinsky; following her death, married Gertrud Kolisch, sister of Rudolf Kolisch
Josef Suk, violinist	Otilie Dvořák, daughter of Antonin Dvořák
Leopold Stokowski, conductor	Olga Samaroff, pianist—first of his 3 wives
Pierre Luboshutz, duo-pianist	Genia Nemenoff, duo-pianist
Efrem Zimbalist, violinist	Alma Gluck, soprano
Eugene Ormandy, conductor	Stephanie Goldner, harpist
Wilfred Pelletier, conductor	Rose Bampton, soprano
Robert Casadesus, pianist	Gaby Casadesus, pianist
Kurt Weill, composer	Lotte Lenya, singer
Xavier Cugat, band leader	Carmen Castillo, Lorraine Allen, and Abbe Lane, all singers
Andre Kostelanetz, conductor	Lilly Pons, soprano
Jan Kiepura, tenor	Martha Eggerth, soprano
Rudolf Serkin, pianist	Irene Busch, daughter of Adolf Busch
Vladimir Horowitz, pianist	Wanda Toscanini, daughter of Arturo Toscanini
Eugene Istomin, pianist	Martita Casals, widow of Pablo Casals
James McCracken, tenor	Sandra Warfield, soprano

Mstislav Rostropovich, cellist and conductor

Thomas Stewart, baritone

Richard Bonynge, conductor

Henry Lewis, conductor

Daniel Barenboim, pianist and conductor

Pinchas Zukerman, violinist and conductor

Galina Vishnevskaya, soprano

Evelyn Lear, soprano

Joan Sutherland, soprano

Marilyn Horne, mezzo-soprano

Jacqueline du Pré, cellist

Eugenia Zukerman, flutist

MUSICIANS WHO ESCAPED THE NAZIS

The advent of the Hitler regime in Germany in 1932 led to an emigration of musicians and musical personalities that continued into World War II. Many left Germany or Austria because they were Jewish, but there also were non-Jews who found themselves unable to conform to the Nazis's artistic tenets. Some refugees settled in Britain or other countries, and a number returned to Germany after the war. But most came to the United States and remained there permanently, strengthening and enriching American musical life. Among the refugees were:

Maurice Abravanel, conductor
Kurt Adler, conductor, pianist
Kurt Herbert Adler, San Francisco Opera director
Peter Hermann Adler, NBC Opera director
Carl Bamberger, conductor
Béla Bartók, composer
Rudolf Bing, Metropolitan Opera director
Victor Borge, pianist, comedian
Robert Breuer, critic
Adolf Busch, violinist
Fritz Busch, conductor
Paul Dessau, composer
Alfred Einstein, musicologist
Hanns Eisler, composer
Bruno Eisner, pianist
Emanuel Feuermann, cellist
Lukas Foss, conductor, composer, pianist
Paul Fromm, Fromm Music Foundation
Karl Geiringer, musicologist, biographer
Szymon Goldberg, violinist
Manfred Gurlitt, conductor, composer
John Gutman, opera executive

Hans W. Heinsheimer, editor, writer
Paul Hindemith, composer
Bronislaw Huberman, violinist
Erich Kleiber, conductor
Rudolph Kolisch, violinist
Otto Klemperer, conductor
Erich Wolfgang Korngold, composer
Ernst Krenek, composer
Efrem Kurtz, conductor
Hugo Leichtentritt, musicologist, composer
Erich Leinsdorf, conductor
Kurt List, composer, critic
Nikolai Lopatnikov, composer
Edward Lowinsky, musicologist
Thomas P. Martin, conductor, translator
Darius Milhaud, composer
Richard Mohaupt, composer
Hans Moldenhauer, musicologist
Paul Nettl, musicologist, writer
Paul Amadeus Pisk, composer, teacher
André Previn, conductor
Karol Rathaus, composer
Arnold Rosé, violinist
Joseph Rosenstock, conductor
Julius Rudel, conductor, New York City Opera director
Max Rudolf, conductor
Curt Sachs, musicologist
Felix Salzer, musicologist
George Schick, conductor
Artur Schnabel, pianist
Alexander Schneider, violinist, conductor
Arnold Schoenberg, composer
Boris Schwarz, violinist
Erna Schwerin, president, Friends of Mozart (New York)
Rudolf Serkin, pianist
Tossy Spivakovsky, violinist
Eduard Steuermann, pianist
William Steinberg, conductor
Fritz Stiedry, conductor
Ignace Strasfogel, conductor
George Szell, conductor
Henryk Szeryng, violinist
Walter Taussig, conductor
Ernst Toch, composer
Frederick Waldmann, conductor

Bruno Walter, conductor
Kurt Weill, composer
Jaromir Weinberger, composer
Eric Werner, musicologist
Stefan Wolpe, composer
Alexander von Zemlinsky, composer

MUSICIANS WHO DID NOT ESCAPE THE NAZIS

Karel Ancerl (1908–1973). A Czech conductor who was music director of the Prague Radio when Czechoslovakia was occupied by the Nazis in 1939. As a Jew he was removed from his post and sent first to the Theresienstadt (Terezin) and then to the Auschwitz concentration camps. At Auschwitz his entire family was put to death, but Ancerl survived, and in 1950 was appointed conductor of the Czech Philharmonic. In 1970 he became conductor of the Toronto Symphony.

Henryk Gadomski (1907–1941). Polish composer born in St. Petersburg, Russia, and trained at the Warsaw Conservatory. He was seized by the Gestapo and sent to Auschwitz, where he died. He wrote for films, radio, and theater; he also wrote chamber and piano music.

Pavel Haas (1899–1944). Czech composer, born in Brno and a soldier in the Austrian Army in World War I. In 1941 he was sent to Terezin and then to Auschwitz, where he was put to death. He continued composing to the end. Among his works are an opera, *The Charlatan*, and chamber and incidental music.

Kurt Huber (1893–1943). Swiss musicologist who taught at Munich University. He was executed by the Gestapo in Munich on July 13, 1943, for participating in student protests against the Nazi government. He published several volumes, including a collection of Bavarian folksongs.

Rudolf Karel (1880–1945). Czech composer and the last student of Antonin Dvořák. Active in the Czech Resistance, he was caught and sent to Terezin, where he died. His output included 4 symphonies, chamber music, opera, oratorio, and songs. His last work, *Three Hairs of the Wise Old Man*, a "musical fairy tale," sketched out in the concentration camp, was arranged and performed in Prague posthumously in 1948.

Joseph Koffler (1896–1943). Polish composer killed with his wife and child during a street roundup of Jews near Cracow. A pupil of Arnold Schoenberg and a graduate of the University of Vienna, he was the first Polish 12-tone composer. His music includes three symphonies and many songs.

Hans Krása (1899–1944). Czech composer who spent many years in Germany, conducting at the Kroll Opera in Berlin. In 1942 he was sent to Terezin, where he continued to compose and led performances by Jewish inmates. In 1944 he was transferred to Auschwitz and killed. His opera *Betrothal in a Dream* received a Czech State Prize in 1933. Some of his orchestral music was played by the Boston Symphony in 1926, and his string trio was performed posthumously at Aspen, Colorado, in 1951. His children's opera *Brundibar*, given in Terezin in 1943, was presented at the Hartford Atheneum in Connecticut in June, 1985.

Simon Laks (1901–   ). Polish composer who studied at the Warsaw and Paris Conservatories. In 1941 he was sent to Auschwitz, but survived and settled in Paris in 1945. Many of his works are on Polish or Jewish themes.

Zygmunt Moczynski (1871–1941). Polish organist and composer who died in a German concentration camp. He wrote church music and songs, and was the recipient of a Polish Gold Medal of Merit.

Arno Nadel (1878–1943). Lithuanian-born German composer and critic. Born in Vilna, he settled in Berlin, where he became choral conductor for the Jewish community and wrote for several newspapers. In 1943 he was transported to Auschwitz and died the same year. He compiled anthologies of Jewish songs.

Roman Padlewski (1915–1944). Polish composer who joined the Underground and was killed by the Germans during the Warsaw uprising of 1944. His works included three string quartets.

Albert van Raalte (1890–1952). Dutch conductor, who studied in Germany with Arthur Nikisch and Max Reger. He conducted opera in Leipzig and the Hague, and also the Hilversum Radio Orchestra. Under the German occupation of Holland he was sent to a concentration camp for his "Jewish associations"; after the Liberation he resumed conducting at Hilversum.

Karel Reiner (1910–   ). Czech composer and pianist. A leader in Prague musical circles, he was sent by the Nazis successively to Terezin, Dachau, and Auschwitz, but managed to survive them all. After the war he resumed his activities as a composer and pianist in Prague.

Nico Max Richter (1915–1945). Dutch composer who studied with Hermann Scherchen and conducted student orchestras. A member of the Dutch Resistance, he was seized by the Germans and sent to Dachau for three years. He survived the war but died a few months afterwards from the effects of his ill-treatment.

Willi Schmid (died July 1934). Dr. Willi Schmid was the music critic of the *Neueste Nachrichten*, a Munich daily. He was taken from his home one evening and murdered by members of the S.S. elite corps who had mistaken him for another man with a similar name. William L. Shirer recounts the incident in his *The Rise and Fall of the Third Reich.*

Erwin Schulhoff (1894–1942). A Czech composer and pianist who studied with Max Reger in Germany and became active in modern music circles. He traveled as a pianist through France, England, and Russia, and several of his works were played at contemporary music festivals. His compositions included an opera and a ballet. He settled in Prague and was sent by the Nazis to a concentration camp at Wülzburg, Germany, where he died.

James Simon (1880–1944). German composer and musicologist. He moved to Zurich when the Nazis came to power in Germany, but later moved again to Amsterdam. The Nazis seized him there after their conquest of Holland, and sent him to Terezin and then to Auschwitz, where he was put to death on arrival. His compositions include opera, symphony, chamber music, and songs.

Kurt Singer (1885–1944). A doctor of medicine as well as a musician, his books included one entitled *Diseases of the Musical Profession.* When the Nazis deprived him of his musical posts he became music director of Jewish cultural groups. In 1939 he left Germany for Holland, but was arrested there by the Nazi invaders, and died at the Terezin concentration camp.

Leo Smit (1900–1944). Dutch composer seized by the Nazis and interned in the Westerbork concentration camp in Holland. Later he was sent to Poland, where he perished, but the exact date and place are unknown. He had lived in Paris for some years and his music showed a strong French influence. He should not be confused with the American pianist and composer of the same name.

Alfred Stadler (1889–1943). Polish composer and conductor, arrested as a hostage in Lwow and shot by the Germans in 1943. His works included the opera *Varsovienne* and many choral compositions.

Eric Steinhard (1886–1942). Czech musicologist. A native of Prague, he studied in Germany as well as in his own country. He was an editor, a critic, and librarian of the University of Prague. In 1941 he was transported to a concentration camp at Lodz, Poland, where he died.

MUSICIANS WHO LEFT THE SOVIET UNION

Soviet emigré musicians have been playing an increasing role in the musical life of the West. Some have defected while traveling abroad; some have simply never returned while holding Soviet passports; others have received exit permits and emigrated by legal means. All three types are represented in the following list. Most of those named have settled in the United States:

Yuri Ahronovitch, conductor
Vladimir Ashkenazy, pianist
Renata Babak, soprano
Rudolph Barshai, conductor
Nina Beilina, violinist
Boris Belkin, violinist
Emanuel Borok, violinist
Yefim Bronfman, pianist
Semyon Bychkov, conductor
Bella Davidovich, pianist
Youri Egorov, pianist
Boris Goldstein, violinist
Lazar Gosman, conductor, Soviet Emigré Orchestra
Marina Gusak, pianist
Vakhtang Jordania, conductor
Felix Krugilov, conductor
Albert Markov, violinist
Alexander Markov, violinist
Viktoria Mullova, violinist
Mstislav Rostropovich, cellist, conductor
Maxim Shostakovich, conductor
Dimitry Sitkovetsky, violinist
Alexander Toradze, pianist
Galina Vishnevskaya, soprano
Oxana Yablonskaya, pianist

BLACK MUSICIANS

Although it is only in recent years that blacks have begun to get their due as serious musicians, they are the heirs of an ancient and distinguished tradition. Here are 10 black musicians, most of them forgotten today, who were active prior to the 20th century, followed by a listing of some of the outstanding figures of the modern era:

PRE-20TH CENTURY

Thomas Green Bethune, American pianist and composer (1849–1908). The original "Blind Tom," he was born sightless and a slave in Columbus, Georgia. Self-taught, he wrote piano and vocal pieces and became a masterful pianist and improviser. He toured Europe and the United States, making a fortune for his master (later his guardian), James Bethune.

James Bland, American songwriter (1854–1911). Born in Flushing, New York, he entered Howard University but left to perform and compose. Among his 600 songs were "Carry Me Back to Old Virginny," "In the Evening by the Moonlight," "Dem Golden Slippers" and "Hand me Down my Walking Cane."

Thomas Bowers, American tenor (1836–1885). His voice had qualities that won him the sobriquet of "the Black Mario," the comparison being to the great Giovanni Mario. Bowers, a Philadelphian, said he deliberately set out to prove that "colored men and women could sing classical music as well as the members of that other race that has so villified us."

George Bridgetower, British violinist (1780–1860). Bridgetower's chief claim to fame is that he and Beethoven together gave the first performance of the "Kreutzer" Sonata in Vienna on May 17, 1803. For a time, apparently, Beethoven considered dedicating the sonata to Bridgetower, who was the son of a black self-styled "African prince" and a Polish woman.

Samuel Coleridge-Taylor, British composer (1875–1912). A prolific composer, he is best remembered for his "Hiawatha's Wedding Feast," part of a trilogy "The Song of Hiawatha." Coleridge-Taylor made three visits to the United States in the early 1900s. His father was a native of Sierra Leone, his mother English.

Sissieretta Jones, American soprano (1868–1933). Called "the Black Patti" in a comparison with the great Adelina, Madam Jones made a triumphal tour of Europe in the 1890s. Later she established her own company, the Black Patti Troubadors, and remained its head for 19 years. Her real name was Matilda Joyner.

Ignacio Parreiras Neves, Brazilian composer (c.1730–c.1793). Born in Vila Rica, Brazil, he was a member of that city's Brotherhood of St. Joseph of Colored Men. A Credo and a Christmas Oratorio by him are still extant. He also was a singer and a conductor.

Joseph Boulogne Chevalier de Saint-Georges, French violinist (1745–1799). Son of an African mother and a French father, St. Georges was born on the Caribbean island of Guadeloupe and was sent to Paris to study. He became a matinée idol as a violinist and also composed extensively for his instrument. In 1792, during the French Revolution he was appointed colonel of an all-black regiment called Les Hussards Américains et du Midi.

Marie Selika, American soprano. Her name was Mrs. Sampson Williams, but she borrowed her stage name from Selika, the heroine of Meyerbeer's *L'Africaine*, an opera in which she scored a European success. Of her singing the Paris newspaper *Le Figaro* said:

"She has a very strong voice, of depth and compass, rising with perfect ease from C to C . . . . Her range is marvelous and her execution and style show perfect cultivation."

Elizabeth Taylor-Greenfield, American soprano (1809–1876). Born a slave in Natchez, Mississippi, this singer became known as "the Black Swan" and was likened by some to Jenny Lind. She toured in the United States but, like most of her race at that time, won much of her success in Europe, particularly in Britain, where she gave a command performance for Queen Victoria. Eventually she moved to Philadelphia, where she opened a vocal studio.

MODERN ERA

Black musicians today make vital contributions to virtually every phase of musical life. The following is only a partial listing of those who achieved recognition in the recent past or are continuing to do so today:

COMPOSERS

Gilbert Allen	Ulysses Simpson Kay
Henry T. Burleigh	Hale Smith
Roque Cordero	William Grant Still
Duke (Edward Kennedy) Ellington	Howard Swanson
Scott Joplin	George Walker

CONDUCTORS

Dean Dixon	Henry Lewis
Isaiah Jackson	Leonard de Paur
Hall Johnson	James de Preist
Everett Lee	Calvin Simmons

PIANISTS

Leon Bates	Philippa Schuyler
Natalie Hinderas	André Watts

SOPRANOS AND MEZZO-SOPRANOS

Adele Addison	Carol Brice
Roberta Alexander	Grace Bumbry
Betty Allen	Clamma Dale
*Marian Anderson	Ellabella Davis
Martina Arroyo	Gloria Davy
Kathleen Battle	Alteouise DeVaughn

*The first black singer ever to appear at the Metropolitan Opera, in the role of Ulrica in Verdi's *The Masked Ball,* January 7, 1955.

Mattiwilda Dobbs	Leona Mitchell
Reri Grist	Jessye Norman
Cynthia Haymon	Leontyne Price
Barbara Hendricks	Florence Quivar
Esther Hinds	Faye Robinson
*Caterina Jarboro	Joy Simpson
Isola Jones	Shirley Verrett
Marvis Martin	Felicia Weathers
Inez Matthews	Camilla Williams
Dorothy Maynor	

TENORS

Vinson Cole	Charles Holland
Roland Hayes	Seth McCoy
Kenn Hicks	George Shirley

BARITONES AND BASSES

Jules Bledsoe	Ben Holt
McHenry Boatwright	Robert McFerrin
Todd Duncan	Paul Robeson
Simon Estes	William Warfield
	Lawrence Winters

OTHER PERFORMERS

Elayne Jones, timpanist   Wynton Marsalis, trumpeter

*The first black singer ever to appear with an American opera company, in the title role of Verdi's *Aida* with Alfredo Salmaggi's Chicago Opera Company in April 1933.

HOW CONDUCTORS GET STARTED

Although today's conservatories and music schools teach conducting as a regular course, many leading conductors have begun their careers as instrumentalists and then graduated to the podium. Some traditionalists still doubt that the art of directing an orchestra can really be taught. Eugene Ormandy, for nearly 50 years the music director of the Philadelphia Orchestra, used to tell the story of the novice who approached the great Arthur Nikisch and pleaded with him for conducting lessons. "Of course," replied Nikisch, "I'd be very glad to teach you. It's really very simple. 1–2–3–4, 1–2–3, 1–2. The rest you have to do yourself."

Nikisch himself began life as a violinist. Here's how some others got started:

Daniel Barenboim	piano
Pablo Casals	cello

Saul Caston	trumpet
Charles Dutoit	violin, viola
Harold Farberman	percussion
Lukas Foss	piano
Serge Koussevitzky	double-bass
Neville Marriner	violin
André Previn	jazz piano
Eugene Ormandy	violin
Mstislav Rostropovich	cello
Hermann Scherchen	viola
Gerard Schwarz	trumpet
Leopold Stokowski	organ
George Szell	piano
Arturo Toscanini	cello
Alfred Wallenstein	cello

MUSICAL RIOTS AND REVOLUTIONS

Music can arouse not only emotions but passions—some of them quite extraneous to the work in question or to the composer's intentions in writing it. Following, in chronological order, are some examples of musical performances of works that led to unexpectedly violent results:

Grétry: *"O Richard! O mon roi!"* from *Richard, Coeur de Lion*. This aria from André Grétry's opera *Richard the Lion-Hearted* played a part in precipitating the French Revolution. The song is sung by Blondel, the minstrel of the imprisoned king, lamenting his captivity and expressing a resolve to free him. The opera achieved great popularity after its premiere in Paris in 1784. Four years later, on October 1, 1788, Marie Antoinette, the Queen of France, attended a banquet of the officers of the Versailles garrison and, glass in hand, walked among them singing Grétry's famous aria—which had become a kind of Royalist anthem for those who favored the regime of Louis XVI. When news of her action reached Paris, indignant mobs marched to Versailles to demand that the royal family return to Paris. They did so—bringing them one step closer to the scaffold.

Rossini: *The Barber of Seville*. Rossini's famous *Barber* had one of the most riotous receptions in operatic history when it was unveiled at the Teatro Argentina in Rome on February 20, 1816. The cause of the disturbance is uncertain, and those present disagreed afterward as to details. But apparently there were some who resented the attempt by the young (age 23) composer to set a subject already treated by the venerable and highly respected Giovanni Paisiello—even though Rossini had been careful to pay his respects to his predecessor, and even tried to give his opera a different title, *Almaviva*, or *The Vain Precaution*. In addition, all sorts of things went wrong on opening night. One of the strings on Almaviva's guitar snapped during an aria; the Basilio tripped over a trapdoor and had to sing his "Calumny" aria with a bloody nose; during the finale a cat wandered onto the stage and evaded the effort of the singers to catch it. At each contretemps the audience hooted and hissed; Rossini said he left the theater fearing he might be assassinated. On the second night he remained home pretending to be ill, and when he heard a hubbub in the street he thought a mob was coming after him. However, it turned out to be a crowd of Romans rushing to congratulate him—the second night had been a howling success, which the *Barber* has remained ever since.

Auber: *Masaniello or La Muette de Portici*. This work by Daniel Auber, first given in Paris in 1828, is one of the few operas that has gone down in history with two titles that serve it equally well. It also bears the distinction of having helped to bring a nation into being. Its subject was a revolt in Naples against Spanish occupying forces in 1647, with the climax occurring during the eruption of Mount Vesuvius (an event that actually occurred in 1631.) When *La Muette de Portici* was given for the first time in Brussels, then occupied by the Dutch, its scenes of patriotic fervor ignited a popular uprising against the foreign soldiers, starting a chain of events that led to the establishment of Belgium as an independent state.

Verdi: *A Masked Ball*. This 1859 opera by Verdi about the assassination of a ruler ran into trouble with the official censors, who objected to the depiction on stage of a royal personage being killed. Consequently Verdi changed the identity of the victim from King Gustavus III of Sweden to a mythical "Governor of Boston" named Riccardo of Warwick. However, the controversy helped stir up patriotic feelings among Italians, who regarded their own rulers as antidemocratic. Many of them began shouting Verdi's name in the streets and scrawling it on walls—not only because they loved the composer but because the letters V-E-R-D-I formed an acronym for Vittorio Emmanuele Re d'Italia—Victor Emanuel, King of Italy—the symbol of Italian liberation and unification. Verdi willingly lent his support to this struggle and eventually became an Italian senator.

Stravinsky: *The Rite of Spring*. Possibly the most celebrated riot on purely musical grounds took place at the Théâtre des Champs-Elysées in Paris the night of May 29, 1913, when Igor Stravinsky's *Le Sacre du Printemps* received its premiere. The score was in-

165

stantly recognized as revolutionary, and there were plenty of counter-revolutionists in the audience. Catcalls and stamping of feet greeted the early measures, while supporters rose to defend the music with shouts of their own. Fistfights and shoving matches broke out, and conductor Pierre Monteux had all he could do to keep the piece going. Controversy over *Le Sacre* persisted for years, but this seems to have been the only performance that produced actual violence.

Fritz Kreisler's Cornell Concert. In December of 1919, Fritz Kreisler, the great violinist, had a concert scheduled at Cornell University in Ithaca, New York, as part of his first U.S. concert tour after World War I. During the war he had served briefly in the Austrian Army, being invalided out. His arrival in Ithaca was greeted with denunciations by a fanatically patriotic segment of the populace, led by the city's mayor. When the actual concert was underway, some one cut the electrical wires, plunging the hall into darkness. Kreisler continued to play in the blackout, and despite fisticuffs in the audience, which led to the police being called, he managed to complete the concert. Twenty years later he returned to Bailey Hall at Cornell for a recital, and was greeted with a warm welcome.

NATIONAL ANTHEMS

National anthems are a comparatively new phenomenon, with most receiving their formal designations only in the 19th or 20th centuries. Some have never been given official status, but have become adopted through usage. This list gives either the title or the opening words of each country's anthem, together with the year of official designation, if any:

Afghanistan. "As long as the earth and heavens exist" (1974).
Albania. "The flag that in battle unites us" (1912).
Algeria. "We swear by the lightning" (1963).
Andorra. "The great Charlemagne, my father, liberated me from the Saracen" (1914).
Argentina. "Hear, O mortals, the sacred cry" (1813).
Australia. "Advance, Australia Fair" (1974).
Austria. "Land of mountains, land of streams" (1947). The music is from Mozart's *Little Masonic Cantata* (K. 623).
Bahama. "March on, Bahamaland" (1973).
Bangladesh. "My Bengal of gold, I love you" (1972).
Barbados. "In plenty and in time of need" (1966).
Belgium. "La Brabançonne" (1938). The name derives from the province of Brabant, in which Brussels is located.

Benin. "L'Aube Nouvelle" (The New Dawn).

Bolivia. "Bolivians, propitious fate has crowned our hopes" (1842).

Botswana. "Blessed be this noble land" (1966).

Boukina Fasso. "Against the humiliating bars, a thousand years ago." This African country, formerly known as Upper Volta, changed its name and its national anthem in 1984. The old one started out "Proud Volta of our forefathers."

Brazil. "A cry rang out from peaceful Ipiranga's banks" (1922).

Brunei. "O God, long live His Majesty the Sultan" (1951).

Bulgaria. "Stara Planina's peaks proudly rise" (1964).

Burma. "We shall love evermore Burma, land of our fathers" (1948).

Burundi. "Dear Burundi, O pleasant land" (1962).

Cambodia. See Kampuchea.

Cameroon. "Chant de Ralliement" (Rallying Song, 1957).

Canada. "O Canada" (1967).

Central African Republic. "O Central Africa, cradle of the Bantus" (1960).

Chad. "La Tchadienne" (The Song of Chad, 1960).

Chile. "Chile, your blue skies are pure" (1941).

China. "March on, brave people of our nation" (music 1949, words 1978).

Colombia. "O unfading glory, O immortal joy" (1920).

Congo. "La Congolaise" (The Song of the Congo, 1960).

Costa Rica. "Noble country, your beautiful flag" (1853).

Cuba. "Rush to the fray, men of Bayamo" (1902). Written and sung during the Battle of Bayamo against the Spanish in 1868.

Czechoslovakia. "Where Is My Home?" and "On Tatra Mountains Lightning Strikes"—two songs combined into the state anthem (1919).

Denmark. "King Christian stood by the lofty mast."

Dominican Republic. "Brave men of Quisqueya, let us raise our song" (1883).

Ecuador. "Hail to thee a thousand times, Oh fatherland!" (1948).

Egypt. "O my weapon, how I long to clutch thee!" (1860).

El Salvador. "Let us proudly salute our country" (1953).

Ethiopia. March Forward, Dear Mother Ethiopia" (1975).

Finland. "Maamme" (Our Land, 1848).

France. "La Marseillaise" (1795). Words and music by Claude-Joseph Rouget de Lisle; sung by a battalion of volunteers from Marseilles during the French Revolution.

Gabon. "United in concord and fraternity" (1960).

Gambia. "For Gambia our homeland we strive and work and play" (1965).

German Democratic Republic (East Germany). "Arisen from the ruins and looking to the future" (1949). Music by Hanns Eisler.

German Federal Republic (West Germany). "Unity, right and freedom for the German Fatherland" (1950). The music is by Joseph Haydn, written in 1797 as the national anthem of Austria and incorporated into his String Quartet in C, Op. 76, No. 3, the "Emperor." From 1922 to 1950 it was used with a text beginning "Deutschland, Deutschland über alles."

Ghana. "God bless our homeland Ghana" (1966).

Great Britain. "God Save the King/Queen." The author of neither words nor music is known, nor has it ever been officially adopted. The first known public performance was in 1745.

Greece. "Hymn to Liberty" (1863). The words are from a poem by Dionysius Solomos, with 158 stanzas, of which only 2 are sung in the anthem.

Grenada. "Hail Grenada, land of ours" (1974).

Guatemala. "Happy Guatemala, may your altars never be profaned" (1896).

Guinea. "Glory to our ancestors' and our elders' struggle for Africa's independence" (1958).

Guinea-Bissau. "Sun, sweat, verdure and sea" (1974).

Guyana. "Dear land of Guyana, of rivers and plains" (1966).

Haiti. "La Dessalinienne" (The Song of Dessalines, 1903). Jean-Jacques Dessalines was the island's liberator and first emperor.

Honduras. "Your flag, your flag is a strip of sky" (1915).

Hungary. "God bless the Hungarians" (1845). The music by Ferenc Erkel was chosen in a public competition.

Iceland. "O God of our land" (1874).

India. "Thou rulest the minds of all people" (1950). Words and music are by Rabindranath Tagore.

Indonesia. "Indonesia, our native land" (1945).

Iran. The Islamic Republic of Iran has no national anthem. Prior to the advent of the Ayatollah Khomeini it was "Long live the Shah."

Iraq. "Salute of the Republic" (1959).

Ireland. "Soldiers are we whose lives are pledged to Ireland" (1926).

Israel. "Hatikvah" (The Hope, 1948). The melody was adapted from a folksong; the words are by Naftali Herz Imber. Before being adopted by the Jewish State upon its formation, the song was the anthem of the Zionist movement.

Italy. "Italian brothers, Italy has arisen" (1946). Written by Goffredo Mameli (words) and Michele Novaro in 1847, this is Italy's first authentic national anthem. Such previous numbers as the "Garibaldi Hymn" and the Fascist party song "La Giovinezza" (Youth) never had official status. The "Mameli Hymn" was adopted with the establishment of the post-World War II Italian Republic.

Ivory Coast. "We salute you, land of hope" (1960).

Jamaica. "Eternal Father, bless our land" (1962).

Japan. "The Reign of Our Emperor" (1888).

Jordan. "Long live the King, his position is sublime" (1946).

Kampuchea. "Khmers are known throughout the world as descendants of a nation of glorious warriors" (1977). Replaces "Heaven protects our King," the anthem adopted in 1941 when the country was called Cambodia.

Kenya. "O God of all creation" (1963).

Korean Democratic People's Republic (North Korea). "Let morning shine on the silver and gold of this land" (1947).

Korean Republic (South Korea). "Until Pakdro Mountain wears away" (1948).

Laos. "Our Laotian race once knew great renown in Asia" (1947).

Lebanon. "All of us are for the country" (1927).

Lesotho. "Lesotho, land of our fathers" (1967).

Liberia. "All hail Liberia, hail."

Liechtenstein. "High above the German Rhine" (1951). The music is that of "God Save the King."

Luxembourg. "Where slow you see the Alzette flow, the Sura play wild pranks" (1895).

Malagasy Republic. "O, beloved land of our fathers" (1958).

Malawi. "O God bless the land of Malawi" (1964).

Malaysia. "My country, my native land" (1957). Each of the 13 princely states of Malaysia also has its own anthem.

Maldive Republic. "We salute you in this national unity" (1972).

Mali. "At your call, Mali, for your prosperity, faithful to your destiny, we all will be united."

Malta. "Guard her, O Lord, as ever thou hast guarded" (1941).

Mauritius. "Glory to thee, Motherland" (1968).

Mexico. "Mexicans, at the call of war take up your swords and bridles" (1943). The anthem was first sung in 1854. An official decree forbids any alteration in words or music.

Monaco. "Principality of Monaco, my country."

Mongolia. "The beautiful and magnificent land of Mongolia."

Morocco. "Hymn of the Sharif."

Mozambique. "Long live Frelimo, guide of the Mozambican people" (1975).

Nepal. "May glory crown you, courageous sovereign, you the gallant Nepalese" (1952).

Netherlands. "I am William of Nassau, of Dutch descent" (1932). Mozart's 7 Variations on "Wilhelmus van Nassouwe" (K. 25), composed at the age of 10, also use the melody, which is of great antiquity.

New Zealand. "God Save the Queen." The country also has a widely sung "National Song" entitled "God Defend New Zealand," but it has never been accorded the status of an official anthem.

Nicaragua. "Hail to thee, Nicaragua, on thy native soil" (1939).

Niger. "Beside the mighty Niger which beautifies Nature" (1961).

Nigeria. "Arise, O compatriots, Nigeria's call obey" (1978).

Norway. "Yes, we love this land" (1864).

Oman. "God save our Sultan Said."

Pakistan. "Blessed be the sacred land, the bounteous realm" (1954).

Panama. "We have at last achieved victory" (1925).

Papua New Guinea. "O arise all you sons of this land" (1975).

Paraguay. "To the peoples of unhappy America" (1934).

Peru. "We are free, let us be so forever" (1821). Chosen in a public competition, with the text declared unalterable.

Philippines. "Beloved land, pearl of the Orient."

Poland. "Poland still is ours forever, as long as Poles remain" (1927). The music is from a Polish folk song.

Portugal. "Heroes of the sea" (1910).

Romania. "We praise thee, Fatherland Romania" (1953).

Rwanda. "My Rwanda, land that gave me birth" (1962).

San Marino. "Honor to thee, honor, O ancient republic" (1894).

Saudi Arabia. "Long live our glorious King" (1950).

Senegal. "Everyone pluck the koras and strike the balafos, the red lion has roared" (1960). The kora and the balafo are Senegalese musical instruments. The words are by Leopold Sédar Senghor.

Seychelles. "Seychellois both staunch and true, the nation now has need of you" (1976).

Sierra Leone. "High we exalt thee, land of the free" (1961).

Singapore. "Let us, the people of Singapore, march forward" (1959).

Solomon Islands. "God save our Solomon Islands" (1978).

Somalia. "Long Live Somalia" (1960).

South Africa. "The Call of South Africa" (1938).

Spain. "Marcha Real" (Royal March, 1942). This march is known to have been in use as far back as 1770.

Sri Lanka. "Sri Lanka, we worship thee" (1952).

Sudan. "We are soldiers of God, we are soldiers of the country" (1955).

Swaziland. "O God, who bestows blessings on the Swazi" (1968).

Sweden. "Thou ancient, unconquered, rock-towered north" (1961).

Switzerland. "On the mountains, when the sun proclaims a radiant morn" (1961). The "Swiss Hymn" is known as the "Schweitzer Psalm" in German, "Cantique Suisse" in French, "Salmo Svizzero" in Italian, and "Psalm Svizzer" in Romansch.

Syria. "Defenders of the homeland, greetings" (1939).

Taiwan. "The three principles of democracy our party does revere." The words are from a speech by Sun Yat Sen and were carried over from the mainland of China.

Tanzania. "God bless Africa, bless its leaders" (1964).

Thailand. "Hail to our king, blessings on our king" (1934).

Togo. "We salute you, land of our fathers" (1960).

Tonga. "O Almighty God above, Thou art our Lord and sure defense."

Trinidad and Tobago. "Forged from the love of liberty" (1962).

Tunisia. "Immortal and precious the blood we have shed" (1958).

Turkey. "Fear not and be not dismayed, the crimson flag will never fade" (1921).

Uganda. "Pearl of Africa" (1962).

Union of Soviet Socialist Republics. "Unbreakable union of freeborn republics" (1944). This "Hymn of the Soviet Union" replaced the "Internationale," in use since the Bolshevik Revolution in 1917.

United States of America. "The Star-Spangled Banner" (1931). Francis Scott Key wrote the words on September 14, 1814, after watching the unsuccessful British bombardment of Fort McHenry in Baltimore Harbor. The music he used was "To Anacreon in Heaven," a song by the British composer John Stafford Smith. Puccini quotes a snatch of "The Star-Spangled Banner" in his opera *Madama Butterfly.*

Uruguay. "Uruguayans, the country or the tomb!" (1845).

Vatican City. "Immortal Rome, of martyrs and saints" (1950). Charles Gounod wrote this "Pontifical Hymn" (originally "Pontifical March") in 1869.

Venezuela. "Glory to the nation that shook off the yoke" (1881).

Vietnam. "Forward, soldiers!"

Yemen Arab Republic. "Peace to the land."

Yugoslavia. "Fellow Slavs, the spirit of your ancient breed still triumphs" (1945).

Zaire. "We are from Zaire, a people united in our new-found peace" (1971).

Zambia. "Stand and sing of Zambia" (1964). The music is that of a Bantu song, also used for the national anthem of Tanzania.

MUSIC AND SLEEP

Music has long been known as a useful tool for inducing sleep—deliberately or otherwise. It also can produce a generally soothing effect, helpful in assuaging mental or physical upsets, as reflected in William Congreve's remark "Music has charms to soothe a savage breast"—often misquoted as "savage beast." Many composers have written music aimed at putting children to sleep, employing the titles (depending on their language) berceuse, Wiegenlied, cradle-song, or lullaby. That the same technique can be used on an adult level is demonstrated by three notable cases involving noble patrons suffering from insomnia and allied afflictions:

King Saul of Israel. The Old Testament records (I Samuel 16) how this tormented monarch employed David son of Jesse, "a cunning player on a harp . . . . a man that can play well" to perform music to quiet his troubled spirit. "So Saul was refreshed, and was well." However, the cure was only temporary, for during a subsequent performance, Saul threw a javelin at David, causing him to flee and eventually to replace him on the throne.

King Philip V of Spain. Withdrawn, melancholy, and restless, this unbalanced monarch could achieve a modicum of normality only when sung to by the great male soprano Farinelli (see listing of CASTRATI). His Queen, Elizabeth Farnese, accordingly engaged Farinelli to take up residence at the Spanish court in 1737. Farinelli said that he sang the same four songs to the king every night for the next 10 years—two arias from Johann Hasse's opera *Artaserse*, a minuet by Attilio Aristi, and a song imitating a nightingale by Geminiano Giacomelli. In 1746 Philip died and Farinelli was able to retire to Italy with a fortune.

Count Hermann Carl von Kaiserling. This former Russian Ambassador to the Court of the Elector of Saxony frequently lived in Leipzig, where a member of his household was an organist and harpsichordist named Johann Gottlieb Goldberg. Kaiserling was sickly and suffered from sleepless nights. On such occasions he asked Goldberg to play the harpsichord in an adjoining room. In 1742 Kaiserling commissioned Johann Sebastian Bach to compose some clavier pieces for Goldberg "which should be of such a soft and somewhat lively character that he might be a little cheered up with them in his sleepless nights." Bach responded with the monumental work known ever since as the *Goldberg Variations*. The music must indeed have put the Count to sleep, for he responded by giving Bach one of the richest presents he ever received, "a golden goblet, filled with 100 Louis d'ors."

MUSIC FOR CHILDREN

Not all of these works were composed specifically for children, yet all have achieved a wide audience among youngsters, either because of the nature of their subject matter or the piquancy of their music:

Berezowsky: *Babar the Elephant*
Britten: *Noye's Fludde* (one-act opera)
Britten: *The Young Person's Guide to the Orchestra*
Copland: *The Second Hurricane* (opera)
Debussy: *Children's Corner Suite* (piano)

Haydn: *Toy Symphony**
Humperdinck: *Hansel and Gretel* (opera)
Kleinsinger: *Tubby the Tuba*
Knussen: *Where the Wild Things Are* (opera)
Poulenc: *The Story of Babar the Little Elephant*
Prokofiev: *Peter and the Wolf*
Saint-Saëns: *Carnival of the Animals*
Tchaikovsky: *The Nutcracker* (ballet)
Weill: *Der Jasager* (opera)
Wilder: *Miss Chicken Little* (opera)

TWELVE OFFBEAT MUSICAL ORGANIZATIONS

A great many organizations are dedicated to the furthering of music, and some of them, like the American Symphony Orchestra League (ASOL) and the Metropolitan Opera Guild, are nationally known. However, there are some that operate in narrower spheres and have more intriguing names. A complete list with addresses may be found in the *Encyclopedia of Associations,* published by Gale Research Company of Detroit, Michigan. Here is a sampling of a dozen, with their home bases:

American Accordion Musicological Society	Pitman, New Jersey
American Friends of Scottish Opera	New York, New York
American Guild of English Handbell Ringers	Dayton, Ohio
Catgut Acoustical Society	Montclair, New Jersey
Detroit Waldhorn Society	Ferndale, Michigan
Fretted Instrument Guild of America	Chicago, Illinois
Musica Nostra et Vostra	New York, New York
North American Guild of Change Ringers	Bradford, Massachusetts
Sweet Adelines	Tulsa, Oklahoma
Tamburitza Association of America	St. Louis, Missouri
Tubists Universal Brotherhood Association	Lexington, Kentucky
United In Group Harmony Association	Clifton, New Jersey

*Sometimes ascribed to Leopold Mozart, the father of Wolfgang.

MAKERS OF MUSICAL LISTS

Dr. Samuel Johnson, who published the first great *Dictionary of the English Language* in 1755, cheerfully defined a lexicographer as "a harmless drudge." Much the same description might be applied to compilers of musical lists. However, recognition is due to those musicologists who have catalogued the works of great composers, making it easier to identify and classify individual pieces. They do so by assigning a number to each work, usually preceded with their own initial. Thus, Mozart's works are invariably identified by their "K" (for Köchel) number. These are some of the better-known cataloguers, together with their composers:

Deutsch (Schubert). Otto Erich Deutsch (1883–1967) catalogued in chronological order the works of Franz Schubert, with a total of 998 "D" numbers. Of these the "Unfinished" Symphony is D. 759 and the "Great" C Major is D. 944.

Hoboken (Haydn). Anthony van Hoboken (1887–   ), a Dutch musical bibliographer, published his thematic catalogue of the works of Joseph Haydn in two volumes in 1957 and 1971. The usual designation is "Hob."

Kirkpatrick (Scarlatti). American harpsichordist Ralph Kirkpatrick published a catalogue of Domenico Scarlatti's more than 600 keyboard sonatas in 1953, giving each a "K" number, not to be confused with Köchel's for Mozart. For another Scarlatti cataloguer, see Longo below.

Köchel (Mozart). The most famous and frequently used of all musical lists is that compiled by Ludwig von Köchel (1800–1877) of the works of Wolfgang Amadeus Mozart—626 in all. Köchel's list has been revised and supplemented, notably by musicologist Alfred Einstein (1880–1952), but his "K" numbers remain the basic Mozart identity tag. (Sometimes the designation is "KV," standing for Köchel-Verzeichnis (Köchel listing).

Longo (Scarlatti). Alessandro Longo (1864–1945) was an Italian editor and pianist whose Domenico Scarlatti catalogue has been largely superseded by Ralph Kirkpatrick's. Nevertheless, "Longo" or "L" numbers are still encountered.

Ryom (Vivaldi). Of the several efforts that have been made to catalogue the prodigious output of Antonio Vivaldi, that by Peter Ryom, published in Paris in 1977, is the most comprehensive. Consequently, identification is made by "R" numbers. However "P" numbers and "F" numbers may also be found, referring to previous lists by Marc Pincherle and Antonio Fanna.

Schmieder (Bach). Wolfgang Schmieder (1901–   ) is one of the rare cataloguers whose own initial is not usually applied to the works he numbered. Instead, his catalogue of the compositions of Johann Sebastian Bach employs the symbol "BWV" for Bach-Werke-Verzeichnis (list of Bach's Works). It was published in 1950, the 200th anniversary of Bach's death. Altogether it enumerates 1,080 authenticated works.

A LIST OF MUSICAL LISTS

Emanuel List (1891–1967)	Austrian basso
Eugene List (1918–1985)	American pianist
Garrett List (1943–)	American composer
Kurt List (1913–1970)	Austrian critic and composer
Magister Nikolaus Listenius (c.1500– ?)	German theoretician
Bernhard Listemann (1841–1917)	German violinist and conductor
Franz Listemann (1873–1930)	American cellist
Konstantin Listov (1900–)	Soviet composer
Franz Liszt (1811–1886)	Hungarian pianist and composer

PART VI
STATISTICS AND REFERENCE

UNITED STATES AND CANADIAN SYMPHONY ORCHESTRAS

Well over 1,500 symphony orchestras are currently active in the United States and Canada, performing in cities, towns, and on college campuses. The American Symphony Orchestra League has grouped them in classifications of which the top two are Major and Regional. (Others include Urban, Community, College, etc.) Ratings are determined by the size of annual budgets. Following are the orchestras in the top two categories:

MAJOR ORCHESTRAS (ANNUAL INCOME OVER $3,250,000)

ORCHESTRA	MUSIC DIRECTOR*	YEAR OF FOUNDING
Atlanta Symphony	Robert Shaw	1933
Baltimore Symphony	David Zinman	1916
Boston Symphony	Seiji Ozawa	1881
Buffalo Philharmonic	Semyon Bychkor	1891
Chicago Symphony	Georg Solti	1891
Cincinnati Symphony	Michael Gielen	1895
Cleveland Orchestra	Christoph von Dohnanyi	1918
Dallas Symphony	Eduardo Mata	1914
Denver Symphony	Philippe Entremont	1933
Detroit Symphony	Gunther Herbig	1914
Houston Symphony	Sergiu Comissiona	1930
Indianapolis Symphony	John Nelson	1930
Los Angeles Philharmonic	André Previn	1919
Milwaukee Symphony	Lukas Foss	1959
Minnesota Orchestra	Neville Marriner	1903

*Music Director is a comparatively recent title. In this and succeeding lists the designation indicates the musical head or chief conductor of the orchestra.

MAJOR ORCHESTRAS (ANNUAL INCOME OVER $3,250,000)

ORCHESTRA	MUSIC DIRECTOR*	YEAR OF FOUNDING
Montreal Symphony (official name: Orchestre Symphonique de Montréal)	Charles Dutoit	1934
National Arts Centre Orchestra (Ottawa)	Franco Mannino	1969
National Symphony (Washington, D.C.)	Mstislav Rostropovich	1931
New Orleans Philharmonic-Symphony	Philippe Entremont	1935
New York Philharmonic	Zubin Mehta	1842
Oregon Symphony	James DePreist	1896
Philadelphia Orchestra	Riccardo Muti	1900
Pittsburgh Symphony	Lorin Maazel (consultant)	1895
Rochester Philharmonic	Jerzy Semkow	1923
St. Louis Symphony	Leonard Slatkin	1880
St. Paul Chamber Orchestra	Pinchas Zukerman	1968
San Antonio Symphony	Sixten Ehrling	1939
San Diego Symphony	David Atherton	1927
San Francisco Symphony	Herbert Blomstedt	1909
Seattle Symphony	Gerard Schwarz	1903
Syracuse Symphony	Christopher Keene	1961
Toronto Symphony	Andrew Davis	1918
Utah Symphony	Joseph Silverstein	1926
Vancouver Symphony	Rudolf Barshai	1919

REGIONAL ORCHESTRAS (ANNUAL INCOME OVER $900,000)

Alabama Symphony	Amerigo Marino
American Symphony Orchestra	John Mauceri
Austin Symphony	Sung Kwak
Charlotte Symphony	Leo Driehuys
Colorado Springs Symphony	Charles Ansbacher
Columbus Symphony	Christian Badea
Edmonton Symphony	Uri Mayer
Flint Symphony	Isaiah Jackson
Florida Gulf Coast Symphony	Irwin Hoffman

Florida Symphony	Sidney Rothstein
Fort Worth Symphony	John Giordano
Grand Rapids Symphony	Semyon Bychkov
Hamilton Philharmonic	Boris Brott
Hartford Symphony	Arthur Winograd
Honolulu Symphony	Donald Johanos
Jacksonville Symphony	William McNeiland
Long Beach Symphony	Murry Sidlin
Los Angeles Chamber Orchestra	Gerard Schwarz
Louisville Orchestra	Lawrence Leighton Smith
Memphis Symphony	Vincent de Frank
Nashville Symphony	Kenneth Schermerhorn
New Jersey Symphony	George Manahan
New Mexico Symphony	Yoshimi Takeda
North Carolina Symphony	Gerhardt Zimmerman
Oakland Symphony	Richard Buckley
Oklahoma Symphony	Luis Herrera de la Fuente
Omaha Symphony	Bruce Hangen
Phoenix Symphony	Theo Alcantara
Puerto Rico Symphony	John Barnett
Richmond Symphony	Jacques Houtmann
Sacramento Symphony	Carter Nice
San Jose Symphony	George Cleve
Spokane Symphony	Gunther Schuller
Springfield Symphony	Robert Gutter
Toledo Symphony	Yuval Zuliak
Tulsa Philharmonic	Bernard Rubenstein
Virginia Orchestra Group	Richard Williams
Wichita Symphony	Michael Palmer
Winnipeg Symphony	Kazuhiro Koizumi

SYMPHONIC REPERTORY

Which music is played most often by symphony orchestras in the United States? Since orchestras—unlike opera companies—have no uniform system of keeping records of performances, comparative figures are hard to come by. Nevertheless, the lists that follow give a picture of symphonic performances as represented by the "Big Five" American orchestras—Boston, Chicago, Cleveland, New York, and Philadelphia. In a way, the very diversity of reporting methods serves to add to the comprehensiveness of the overall survey.

CLEVELAND ORCHESTRA

Founded: 1918
Home: Severance Hall
(capacity 2,000)

MUSIC DIRECTORS:

Nikolai Sokoloff 1918–1933
Arthur Rodzinski 1933–1943
Erich Leinsdorf 1943–1946
George Szell 1946–1970
Pierre Boulez (musical advisor) 1970–1972
Louis Lane (resident conductor) 1970–1972
Lorin Maazel 1972–1982
Yoel Levi (resident conductor) 1983
Christoph von Dohnanyi 1984–

Following are the compositions performed most frequently by the Cleveland Orchestra from its inception through May 1984. Included are only regular season performances at Severance Hall:

COMPOSER AND WORK	TOTAL PERFORMANCES
1. Brahms: *Symphony No. 1*	83
2. Beethoven: *Symphony No. 5*	75
3. Beethoven: *Symphony No. 7*	72
4. Brahms: *Symphony No. 2*	71
5. Beethoven: *Symphony No. 3*	70
Wagner: *Tannhäuser Overture*	70
6. Brahms: *Symphony No. 4*	66
7. Beethoven: *Violin Concerto*	64
Tchaikovsky: *Symphony No. 6, "Pathetique"*	64
8. Smetana: *Bartered Bride,* excerpts	62
Wagner: *Die Meistersinger Prelude*	62
9. Mendelssohn: *Violin Concerto*	60
Schubert: *Symphony No. 8, "Unfinished"*	60
Stravinsky: *Firebird Suite*	60
10. Brahms: *Violin Concerto*	58
11. Mendelssohn: *Midsummer Night's Dream* music	57
12. R. Strauss: *Till Eulenspiegel*	56
Tchaikovsky: *Violin Concerto*	56
Weber: *Oberon Overture*	56
13. Debussy: *La Mer*	55
Tchaikovsky: *Symphony No. 4*	55
14. Ravel: *Daphnis and Chloe, Suite No. 2*	53
R. Strauss: *Don Juan*	53

COMPOSER AND WORK	TOTAL PERFORMANCES
15. Brahms: *Piano Concerto No. 2*	52
Dvořák: *Symphony No. 9, "New World"*	52
R. Strauss: *Death and Transfiguration*	52

NEW YORK PHILHARMONIC

Founded: 1842
Home: Avery Fisher Hall, Lincoln Center
(capacity 2,739)

MUSIC DIRECTORS:

Ureli Corelli Hill 1842–1848
(From 1842 to 1852 the Philharmonic was led by a variety of conductors, many of them members of the orchestra.)

Theodore Eisfeld 1852–1856
Carl Bergmann 1856–1876
Leopold Damrosch 1876–1877
Theodore Thomas 1877–1891
Adolph Neuendorff 1878–1879
Anton Seidl 1891–1898
Emil Paur 1898–1902
Walter Damrosch 1902–1903
Wassily Safanoff 1906–1909
Gustav Mahler 1909–1911
Josef Stransky 1911–1923
Willem Mengelberg 1923–1929
Arturo Toscanini 1929–1936
John Barbirolli 1937–1941
Arthur Rodzinski 1943–1947
Bruno Walter 1947–1949
Leopold Stokowski 1949–1950
Dimitri Mitropoulos 1949–1958
Leonard Bernstein 1958–1969
George Szell 1969–1970
Pierre Boulez 1971–1977
Zubin Mehta 1978–

The following lists show total performances since 1842 by the New York Philharmonic of some of the most popular symphonic works. The totals include performances by the New York Symphony prior to its merger in 1928 with the Philharmonic. The figures are for regular season concerts through June 1984:

NINE BEETHOVEN SYMPHONIES

No. 5	360
No. 7	324
No. 3	308
No. 8	205
No. 6	167
No. 2	159
No. 4	134
No. 9	132
No. 1	114

FOUR BRAHMS SYMPHONIES

No. 1	326
No. 2	289
No. 4	249
No. 3	165

POPULAR SYMPHONIES BY OTHER COMPOSERS (SELECTED)

Dvořák: *Symphony No. 9, "New World"*	216
Tchaikovsky: *Symphony No. 6, "Pathetique"*	216
Franck: *Symphony in D Minor*	184
Schubert: *Symphony No. 8, "Unfinished"*	174
Mozart: *Symphony No. 41, "Jupiter"*	121
Mozart: *Symphony No. 40*	115
Mahler: *Symphony No. 1*	80

FIVE BEETHOVEN PIANO CONCERTOS

No. 5, "Emperor"	159
No. 4	151
No. 3	114
No. 1	66
No. 2	29

TWO BRAHMS PIANO CONCERTOS

No. 2	129
No. 1	109

FOUR MOZART PIANO CONCERTOS

No. 20 in D Minor, K. 466	65
No. 23 in A, K. 488	54
No. 24 in C Minor, K. 491	45
No. 21 in C, K. 467	44

PIANO CONCERTOS BY OTHER COMPOSERS (SELECTED)

Schumann: in A Minor, op. 54	155
Tchaikovsky: No. 1 in B-flat minor	122
Grieg: Piano Concerto in A Minor	75
Rachmaninov: No. 2 in C Minor	54

VIOLIN CONCERTOS (SELECTED)

Brahms: in D, op. 77	214
Beethoven: in D, op. 61	210
Mendelssohn: in E Minor	173
Tchaikovsky: in D, op. 35	132

PHILADELPHIA ORCHESTRA

Founded: 1900
Home: Academy of Music
(capacity 3,000)

MUSIC DIRECTORS:

Fritz Scheel 1900–1907
Karl Pohlig 1907–1912
Leopold Stokowski 1912–1938
Eugene Ormandy 1938–1982
Riccardo Muti 1982–

Totals for Philadelphia Orchestra listings are for all performances of each work, including tours and festivals, through June 1984:

NINE BEETHOVEN SYMPHONIES

No. 5	418
No. 7	370
No. 3	207
No. 8	143
No. 1	119
No. 6	117
No. 4	110
No. 2	101
No. 9	81

FOUR BRAHMS SYMPHONIES

No. 1	405
No. 2	403
No. 4	333
No. 3	207

No. 6	304
No. 4	297
No. 5	277

THE PHILADELPHIA ORCHESTRA'S "TOP 20"

These are the 20 compositions most frequently played by the Philadelphia Orchestra since its inception. No individual totals are available, so the pieces are listed by composer in alphabetical order:

Bach: *Toccata and Fugue in D Minor*
Beethoven: *Leonora Overture No. 3*
Beethoven: *Symphony No. 5*
Beethoven: *Symphony No. 7*
Brahms: *Symphony No. 1*
Brahms: *Symphony No. 2*
Brahms: *Symphony No. 4*
Debussy: *L'après-midi d'un Faun*
Franck: *Symphony in D Minor*
Mussorgsky: *Pictures at an Exhibition*
Prokofiev: *Classical Symphony*
Ravel: *Daphnis et Chloe, Suite No. 2*
R. Strauss: *Don Juan*
R. Strauss: *Rosenkavalier Suite*
Stravinsky: *Firebird Suite*
Tchaikovsky: *Symphony No. 4*
Tchaikovsky: *Symphony No. 5*
Tchaikovsky: *Symphony No. 6*
Wagner: *Die Meistersinger Prelude*
Wagner: *Tristan und Isolde, Prelude and Liebestod*

CHICAGO SYMPHONY ORCHESTRA

Founded: 1891*
Home: Orchestra Hall
(capacity 2,574)

MUSIC DIRECTORS:

Theodore Thomas 1891–1905
Frederick Stock 1905–1942
Désire Defauw 1943–1947

---

*The name Chicago Symphony Orchestra was adopted in 1913. Previously, the orchestra was known as the Chicago Orchestra and, from 1905–1913, as the Theodore Thomas Orchestra.

Artur Rodzinski 1947–1948
Rafael Kubelik 1950–1953
Fritz Reiner 1953–1963
Jean Martinon 1963–1968
Irwin Hoffman (acting) 1968–1969
Georg Solti 1969–

The Chicago Symphony Orchestra keeps records of the number of seasons in which each work is performed, but not the total number of performances it receives. The following list, covering the orchestra's first 92 seasons, indicated in how many of those seasons each work has been included:

NINE BEETHOVEN SYMPHONIES

No. 7	67
No. 5	66
No. 3	62
No. 4	46
No. 8	44
No. 6	40
No. 1	34
No. 2	32
No. 9	25

BOSTON SYMPHONY ORCHESTRA

Founded: 1881
Home: Symphony Hall
(capacity 2,631)

MUSIC DIRECTORS:

George Henschel 1881–1884
Wilhelm Gericke 1884–1889; 1898–1906
Arthur Nikisch 1889–1893
Emil Paur 1893–1898
Karl Muck 1906–1908; 1912–1918
Max Fiedler 1908–1912
Henri Rabaud 1918–1919
Pierre Monteux 1919–1924
Serge Koussevitzky 1924–1949
Charles Munch 1949–1962
Erich Leinsdorf 1962–1969
William Steinberg 1969–1972
Seiji Ozawa 1972–

Totals in the following list are for all performances of each work, including tours and festivals, through 1983:

NINE BEETHOVEN SYMPHONIES

No. 3	403
No. 5	395
No. 7	389
No. 6	206
No. 4	188
No. 8	187
No. 2	150
No. 1	139
No. 9	113

BEETHOVEN IN LONDON

The Philharmonic Society of London was established in 1813 and was one of the first foreign orchestras to systematically play the music of Ludwig van Beethoven. This list shows the total of Beethoven symphony performances by the orchestra during its first 100 years as reported in 1913—offering the opportunity for comparison with the more recent totals compiled by U.S. orchestras:

No. 5	77
No. 6	69
No. 7	65
No. 4	54
No. 3	52
No. 8	47
No. 2	39
No. 1	19
No. 9	17

ORCHESTRAL PAY SCALES

The following list shows minimum annual pay scales for the 18 U.S. symphony orchestras that maintain 52-week contractual seasons. Also included is the Metropolitan Opera orchestra. The figures are based on information from the American Federation of Musicians. Some totals include guaranteed income from recordings, radio, television, etc. Not shown are fringe benefits, which vary from orchestra to orchestra, and guaranteed increases during the life of the contract. Figures are effective as of 1984:

ORCHESTRA	NUMBER OF PLAYERS	GUARANTEED ANNUAL WAGE
New York Philharmonic	106	$43,256
Philadelphia Orchestra	106	42,814
Los Angeles Philharmonic	105	41,220
Boston Symphony	105	40,560
Chicago Symphony	106	40,560
San Francisco Symphony	106	39,520
Cleveland Orchestra	106	39,410
Metropolitan Opera Orchestra	94	36,209
Pittsburgh Symphony	104	35,750
Minnesota Orchestra	95	35,698
Cincinnati Symphony	96	35,580
Detroit Symphony	104	34,060
National Symphony (Washington, D.C.)	104	32,720
Houston Symphony	97	31,330
Dallas Symphony	88	31,200
St. Louis Symphony	101	29,900
Baltimore Symphony	96	28,600
Atlanta Symphony	91	26,320
Utah Symphony	84	23,790

UNITED STATES AND CANADIAN OPERA COMPANIES

More than 1,000 opera companies are currently active in the United States and Canada, although about half are workshops rather than full-fledged operations. Following are 30 that have budgets of $1 million or more, that are independent of other companies, and that devote a major share of their efforts to staged performances of the serious rather than the light wing of the repertoire:

COMPANY	LOCATION
Baltimore Opera Company	Baltimore, Maryland
Canadian Opera Company	Toronto, Ontario
Cincinnati Opera Association	Cincinnati, Ohio
Cleveland Opera Company	Cleveland, Ohio
Connecticut Opera	Hartford, Connecticut
Dallas Opera	Dallas, Texas
Edmonton Opera Association	Edmonton, Alberta
Greater Miami Opera Association	Miami, Florida
Houston Grand Opera Association	Houston, Texas

COMPANY	LOCATION
L'Opéra de Montréal	Montreal, Quebec
Lyric Opera of Chicago	Chicago, Illinois
Lyric Opera of Kansas City	Kansas City, Missouri
Metropolitan Opera Association	New York, New York
Michigan Opera Theatre	Detroit, Michigan
Minnesota Opera Theatre	St. Paul, Minnesota
New York City Opera	New York, New York
Opera Colorado	Denver, Colorado
Opera Company of Boston	Boston, Massachusetts
Opera Company of Philadelphia	Philadelphia, Pennsylvania
Opera Theatre of St. Louis	St Louis, Missouri
Pittsburgh Opera Company	Pittsburgh, Pennsylvania
Portland Opera Association	Portland, Oregon
San Diego Opera Association	San Diego, California
San Francisco Opera	San Francisco, California
Santa Fe Opera	Santa Fe, New Mexico
Seattle Opera	Seattle, Washington
Tulsa Opera, Inc.	Tulsa, Oklahoma
Vancouver Opera	Vancouver, British Columbia
Virginia Opera Association	Norfolk, Virginia
Washington Opera	Washington, D.C.

OPERATIC REPERTORY

Although operatic repertory, like other musical programming, undergoes changes over the years, most opera houses in recent decades have displayed a striking similarity in the works they perform frequently. Undoubtedly, in response to audience demand, the so-called "A-B-C" operas (*Aida, La Bohème, Carmen*) show up at or near the top of all the lists. Sometimes certain operas become "house" specialties, such as the works of Mozart at the Vienna State Opera and Britten's *Peter Grimes* at Covent Garden in London. The following lists illustrate operatic popularity at four leading American companies and two European houses.

METROPOLITAN OPERA

The Metropolitan Opera in New York gave its first performance (of Gounod's *Faust*) on October 22, 1883. In the 101 years that have followed, it has given a total of 236 different operas. This is a list of every opera presented at the Met through its 1984–1985 season, in order of total times given, with the date of the first performance. Totals are for all performances in the house, including special festivals and student performances, but not tour or park performances. The 20 most frequently presented are numbered in sequence:

OPERA (COMPOSER)	TOTAL PERFORMANCES	FIRST PERFORMANCE
1. *Aida* (Verdi)	635	November 12, 1886
2. *La Bohème* (Puccini)	619	December 26, 1900
3. *Carmen* (Bizet)	509	January 9, 1884
4. *La Traviata* (Verdi)	495	November 5, 1883
5. *Tosca* (Puccini)	481	February 4, 1901
6. *Madama Butterfly* (Puccini)	445	February 11, 1907
7. *Rigoletto* (Verdi)	440	November 16, 1883
8. *Faust* (Gounod)	412	October 22, 1883
9. *Pagliacci* (Leoncavallo)	407	December 11, 1893
10. *Lohengrin* (Wagner)	385	November 7, 1883
11. *Cavalleria Rusticana* (Mascagni)	377	December 30, 1891
12. *Tristan und Isolde* (Wagner)	343	December 1, 1886
13. *Il Trovatore* (Verdi)	335	October 26, 1883
14. *Die Walküre* (Wagner)	329	January 30, 1885
15. *Lucia di Lammermoor* (Donizetti)	308	October 24, 1883
16. *Tannhäuser* (Wagner)	304	November 17, 1884
17. *Die Meistersinger* (Wagner)	291	January 4, 1886
18. *The Barber of Seville* (Rossini)	279	November 23, 1883
19. *Don Giovanni* (Mozart)	266	November 28, 1883
20. *Der Rosenkavalier* (R. Strauss)	228	December 9, 1913
Parsifal (Wagner)	205	December 24, 1903
The Magic Flute (Mozart)	202	March 30, 1900
La Gioconda (Ponchielli)	201	December 20, 1883
The Marriage of Figaro (Mozart)	187	January 31, 1894
Siegfried (Wagner)	181	November 9, 1887
Otello (Verdi)	174	January 11, 1892
Roméo et Juliette (Gounod)	174	December 14, 1891

OPERA (COMPOSER)	TOTAL PERFORMANCES	FIRST PERFORMANCE
Boris Godounov (Mussorgsky)	172	March 19, 1913
La Forza del Destino (Verdi)	166	November 15, 1918
Götterdämmerung (Wagner)	166	January 25, 1888
Hansel und Gretel (Humperdinck)	161	November 25, 1905
Manon Lescaut (Puccini)	157	January 18, 1907
A Masked Ball (Verdi)	156	December 11, 1889
Fidelio (Beethoven)	147	November 19, 1884
Manon (Massenet)	145	January 16, 1895
The Tales of Hoffmann (Offenbach)	139	January 11, 1913
L'elisir d'Amore (Donizetti)	123	January 23, 1904
Don Carlo (Verdi)	121	December 23, 1920
Andrea Chénier (Giordano)	110	March 7, 1921
Salomé (R. Strauss)	106	January 22, 1907
Samson et Dalila (Saint-Saëns)	105	February 8, 1895
The Flying Dutchman (Wagner)	101	November 27, 1889
Turandot (Puccini)	100	November 16, 1926
Gianni Schicchi (Puccini)	97	December 14, 1918
Das Rheingold (Wagner)	97	January 4, 1889
Norma (Bellini)	95	February 27, 1890
Falstaff (Verdi)	93	February 4, 1895
Così Fan Tutte (Mozart)	91	March 24, 1922
Don Pasquale (Donizetti)	87	January 8, 1900
Pelléas et Mélisande (Debussy)	77	March 21, 1925
Simon Boccanegra (Verdi)	77	January 28, 1932
Fledermaus (J. Strauss)	75	February 6, 1905
Le Prophète (Meyerbeer)	75	March 21, 1884
Martha (Flotow)	69	March 14, 1884
Orfeo ed Euridice (Gluck)	69	December 30, 1891
Les Huguenots (Meyerbeer)	66	March 19, 1884
Mignon (Thomas)	66	October 31, 1883

OPERA (COMPOSER)	TOTAL PERFORMANCES	FIRST PERFORMANCE
Elektra (R. Strauss)	64	December 3, 1932
Ernani (Verdi)	64	January 28, 1903
Eugene Onegin (Tchaikovsky)	64	March 24, 1920
La Fanciulla del West (Puccini)	64	December 10, 1910
L'Africaine (Meyerbeer)	55	December 7, 1888
Le Coq d'Or (Rimsky-Korsakov)	55	March 6, 1918
La Sonnambula (Bellini)	55	November 14, 1883
La Fille du Régiment (Donizetti)	53	January 6, 1902
Macbeth (Verdi)	53	February 5, 1959
The Bartered Bride (Smetana)	52	February 19, 1909
L'amore dei Tre Re (Montemezzi)	51	January 2, 1914
La Juive (Halévy)	48	January 3, 1885
Thaïs (Massenet)	48	February 16, 1917
Il Tabarro (Puccini)	46	December 14, 1918
Lakmé (Delibes)	45	February 22, 1894
Mefistofele (Boito)	45	December 5, 1883
Adriana Lecouvreur (Cilea)	44	November 18, 1907
L'oracolo (Leoni)	44	February 4, 1915
Suor Angelica (Puccini)	43	December 14, 1918
Luisa Miller (Verdi)	41	December 21, 1929
Peter Grimes (Britten)	41	February 12, 1948
Adriadne auf Naxos (R. Strauss)	40	December 29, 1962
Wozzeck (Berg)	39	March 5, 1959
Arabella (R. Strauss)	37	February 10, 1955
Louise (Charpentier)	37	January 15, 1921
La Perichole (Offenbach)	37	December 21, 1956
Werther (Massenet)	36	April 19, 1894
Die Frau Ohne Schatten (R. Strauss)	34	October 2, 1966
L'Italiana in Algeri (Rossini)	33	December 5, 1919

OPERA (COMPOSER)	TOTAL PERFORMANCES	FIRST PERFORMANCE
I Vespri Siciliani (Verdi)	31	January 31, 1974
The Abduction from the Seraglio (Mozart)	30	November 29, 1946
The Queen of Sheba (Goldmark)	29	December 2, 1886
The Queen of Spades (Tchaikovsky)	28	March 5, 1910
The Dialogues of the Carmelites (Poulenc)	26	February 5, 1977
Der Freischütz (Weber)	26	November 24, 1884
The Rise and Fall of the City of Mahagonny (Weill)	25	November 16, 1979
William Tell (Rossini)	24	November 28, 1884
Le Rossignol (Stravinsky)	23	March 6, 1926
Billy Budd (Britten)	22	September 19, 1978
Fedora (Giordano)	21	December 5, 1906
Les Troyens (Berlioz)	20	October 22, 1973
Zaza (Leoncavallo)	20	January 16, 1920
Lulu (Berg)	19	March 18, 1977
Alceste (Gluck)	17	January 24, 1941
La Favorita (Donizetti)	17	November 29, 1895
Francesca da Rimini (Zandonai)	17	December 22, 1916
L'enfant et les Sortilèges (Ravel)	16	February 20, 1981
Les Mamelles de Tirésias (Poulenc)	16	February 20, 1981
Oedipus Rex (Stravinsky)	16	December 3, 1981
Peter Ibbetson (Taylor)	16	February 7, 1931
Porgy and Bess (Gershwin)	16	February 6, 1985
Sadko (Rimsky-Korsakov)	16	January 25, 1930
I Puritani (Bellini)	15	October 29, 1883
Vanessa (Barber)	15	January 15, 1958
The Barber of Bagdad (Cornelius)	14	January 3, 1890
La Clemenza di Tito (Mozart)	14	October 18, 1984

OPERA (COMPOSER)	TOTAL PERFORMANCES	FIRST PERFORMANCE
The King's Henchman (Taylor)	14	February 17, 1927
Madame Sans-Gêne (Giordano)	14	January 25, 1915
Idomeneo (Mozart)	13	October 14, 1982
Iris (Mascagni)	13	April 1, 1915
Marouf (Rabaud)	13	December 19, 1917
Oberon (Weber)	13	December 28, 1918
Rienzi (Wagner)	13	February 5, 1886
La Rondine (Puccini)	13	March 10, 1928
The Siege of Corinth (Rossini)	13	April 7, 1975
Bluebeard's Castle (Bartók)	12	June 10, 1974
L'Oiseau Bleu (Wolff)	12	December 27, 1919
Jenufa (Janáček)	12	December 6, 1924
The Jewels of the Madonna (Wolf-Ferrari)	11	March 5, 1912
The Secret of Susanna (Wolf-Ferrari)	11	March 14, 1911
Der Trompeter von Säkkingen (Nessler)	11	November 23, 1888
The Emperor Jones (Gruenberg)	10	January 7, 1933
Esclarmonde (Massenet)	10	November 19, 1976
The Gypsy Baron (J. Strauss)	10	February 15, 1906
Königskinder (Humperdinck)	10	December 28, 1910
The Last Savage (Menotti)	10	January 23, 1964
Rinaldo (Handel)	10	January 19, 1984
Die Tote Stadt (Korngold)	10	November 19, 1921
Anima Allegra (Vittadini)	9	February 14, 1923
Death in Venice (Britten)	9	October 18, 1974
Euryanthe (Weber)	9	December 23, 1887
Nabucco (Verdi)	9	October 24, 1960
La Navarraise (Massenet)	9	December 11, 1895
Prince Igor (Borodin)	9	December 30, 1915

OPERA (COMPOSER)	TOTAL PERFORMANCES	FIRST PERFORMANCE
The Snow Maiden (Rimsky-Korsakov)	9	January 23, 1921
Boccaccio (Suppé)	8	January 2, 1931
La Cena delle Beffe (Giordano)	8	January 2, 1925
Le Donne Curiose (Wolf-Ferrari)	8	January 3, 1912
Lodoletta (Mascagni)	8	January 12, 1981
Loreley (Catalani)	8	February 13, 1919
Shanewis (Cadman)	8	March 23, 1918
La Vestale (Spontini)	8	November 12, 1925
Ariane et Barbe-Bleu (Dukas)	7	March 29, 1911
Armide (Gluck)	7	November 14, 1910
La Campana Sommersa (Respighi)	7	November 24, 1928
Le Cid (Massenet)	7	February 12, 1897
Cleopatra's Night (Hadley)	7	January 31, 1920
Germania (Franchetti)	7	January 22, 1910
Hamlet (Thomas)	7	February 10, 1893
Jonny Spielt Auf (Krenek)	7	January 19, 1929
Linda di Chamounix (Donizetti)	7	February 4, 1919
Philemon et Baucis (Gounod)	7	November 29, 1893
The Rake's Progress (Stravinsky)	7	February 14, 1953
Amelia Goes to the Ball (Menotti)	6	March 3, 1938
The Canterbury Pilgrims (De Koven)	6	March 8, 1917
Donna Juanita (Suppé)	6	January 2, 1932
Merry Mount (Hanson)	6	February 10, 1934
Mona Lisa (Schillings)	6	March 1, 1923
La Serva Padrona (Pergolesi)	6	February 23, 1935
L'amico Fritz (Mascagni)	5	January 10, 1893
Asrael (Franchetti)	5	November 26, 1890
Cyrano de Bergerac (Damrosch)	5	February 27, 1913

OPERA (COMPOSER)	TOTAL PERFORMANCES	FIRST PERFORMANCE
La Damnation de Faust (Berlioz)	5	December 7, 1906
Don Quichotte (Massenet)	5	February 3, 1914
The Egyptian Helen (R. Strauss)	5	November 6, 1928
The Fair at Sorochintzy (Mussorgsky)	5	November 29, 1930
Goyescas (Granados)	5	January 28, 1916
L'heure Espagnole (Ravel)	5	January 28, 1920
Iphigenia in Tauris (Gluck)	5	November 25, 1916
Julien (Charpentier)	5	February 27, 1914
Lobetanz (Thuille)	5	November 18, 1911
Madonna Imperia (Alfano)	5	February 8, 1928
Masaniello, or La Muette de Portici (Auber)	5	December 29, 1884
Merlin (Goldmark)	5	January 3, 1888
Le Roi de Lahore (Massenet)	5	February 29, 1924
Le Roi d'Ys (Lalo)	5	January 5, 1922
Saint Elizabeth (Liszt)	5	January 3, 1918
Schwanda the Bagpiper (Weinberger)	5	November 7, 1931
Semiramide (Rossini)	5	March 25, 1890
Le Villi (Puccini)	5	December 17, 1908
L'amore Medico (Wolf-Ferrari)	4	March 25, 1914
Fernand Cortez (Spontini)	4	January 6, 1889
Fra Gherardo (Pizzetti)	4	March 21, 1929
Giovanni Gallurese (Montemezzi)	4	February 19, 1925
Das Goldene Kreutz (Brüll)	4	November 19, 1886
Khovantchina (Mussorgsky)	4	February 16, 1950
Madeleine (Herbert)	4	January 24, 1914
Manru (Paderewski)	4	February 14, 1902
The Man Without a Country (Damrosch)	4	May 12, 1937
Mireille (Gounod)	4	February 28, 1919

OPERA (COMPOSER)	TOTAL PERFORMANCES	FIRST PERFORMANCE
Mona (Parker)	4	March 14, 1912
La Notte di Zoraïma (Monte-mezzi)	4	December 2, 1931
The Pearl Fishers (Bizet)	4	November 13, 1916
Le Prezioso Ridocole (Lattuada)	4	December 10, 1930
La Reine Fiammette (Leroux)	4	January 24, 1919
Il Signor Bruschino (Rossini)	4	December 9, 1932
Tiefland (D'Albert)	4	November 23, 1908
Der Vasall von Szigeth (Smareglia)	4	November 27, 1890
Versiegelt (Blech)	4	January 20, 1912
La Vida Breve (de Falla)	4	March 6, 1926
Violanta (Korngold)	4	November 5, 1927
La Wally (Catalani)	4	January 6, 1909
Alessandro Stradella (Flotow)	3	February 4, 1910
I Compagnacci (Riccitelli)	3	January 2, 1924
Crispino e la Comare (Ricci)	3	January 18, 1919
Dinorah (Meyerbeer)	3	January 26, 1892
Fra Diavolo (Auber)	3	February 5, 1910
La Habanera (Laparra)	3	January 2, 1924
In the Pasha's Garden (Seymour)	3	January 24, 1935
The Island God (Menotti)	3	January 20, 1942
The Legend (Breil)	3	March 12, 1919
Messaline (de Lara)	3	January 22, 1902
Phoebus and Pan (Bach)	3	January 15, 1942
The Polish Jew (Weis)	3	March 9, 1921
Robert de Diable (Meyerbeer)	3	November 19, 1883
Salammbo (Reyer)	3	March 20, 1901
The Temple Dancer (Hugo)	3	March 12, 1919
Caponsacchi (Hageman)	2	February 4, 1937
Diana of Solange (Ernest II, Duke of Saxe-Coburg)	2	January 9, 1891
Elaine (Bemberg)	2	December 17, 1894
Ero e Leandro (Mancinelli)	2	March 10, 1899

OPERA (COMPOSER)	TOTAL PERFORMANCES	FIRST PERFORMANCE
Il Matrimonio Segreto (Cimarosa)	2	February 25, 1937
The Pipe of Desire (Converse)	2	March 18, 1910
The Taming of the Shrew (Goetz)	2	March 15, 1916
Der Wald (Smyth)	2	March 11, 1903
The Warrior (Rogers)	2	January 11, 1947
La Dame Blanche (Boieldieu)	1	February 13, 1904
Lucrezia Borgia (Donizetti)	1	December 5, 1904
The Merry Wives of Windsor (Nicolai)	1	March 9, 1900

NEW YORK CITY OPERA

The New York City Opera gave its first performance at the New York City Center on February 21, 1944. Since then it has presented 191 different operas. Its present home is the New York State Theater at Lincoln Center, seating capacity 2,737. The 15 operas it has given most frequently in its first 40 years (through November 18, 1984), with the total number of performances of each, are:

OPERA (COMPOSER)	TOTAL PERFORMANCES
1. Carmen (Bizet)	299
2. La Bohème (Puccini)	285
Madama Butterfly (Puccini)	285
3. La Traviata (Verdi)	266
4. The Marriage of Figaro (Mozart)	152
5. Cavalleria Rusticana (Mascagni)	132
Pagliacci (Leoncavallo)	132
6. Tosca (Puccini)	127
7. Rigoletto (Verdi)	118
8. Die Fledermaus (J. Strauss)	95
9. Don Giovanni (Mozart)	92
10. Faust (Gounod)	87
11. Mefistofele (Boito)	76
12. The Barber of Seville (Rossini)	73
13. Manon (Massenet)	67
14. Lucia di Lammermoor (Donizetti)	64
15. The Tales of Hoffmann (Offenbach)	59

AMERICAN OPERAS AT THE NEW YORK CITY OPERA

During its first 40 years of existence, the New York City Opera performed 61 operas by American composers, more than any other company in history. Following is a complete list through the 1984 season in order of total performances of each work. Also included is the date of first performance by the company. World premieres are indicated by "WP" after the date. The list includes all works by Igor Stravinsky and Kurt Weill performed by the New York City Opera, even though some of these were composed prior to their arrival in the United States. For titles of such works, see note at end of list:

TITLE (COMPOSER)	TOTAL PERFORMANCES	DATE
1. *Oedipus Rex* (Igor Stravinsky)	38	September 24, 1959
2. *The Ballad of Baby Doe* (Douglas Moore)	35	April 3, 1958
3. *Street Scene* (Kurt Weill)	31	April 2, 1959
4. *Susannah* (Carlisle Floyd)	29	September 27, 1956
5. *The Consul* (Gian Carlo Menotti)	22	October 8, 1952
6. *Candide* (Leonard Bernstein)	21	October 13, 1982
7. *Naughty Marietta* (Victor Herbert)	20	August 31, 1978
The Old Maid and the Thief (Gian Carlo Menotti)	20	April 8, 1948
8. *The Student Prince* (Sigmund Romberg)	19	August 29, 1980
9. *Lost in the Stars* (Kurt Weill)	14	April 9, 1958
The Medium (Gian Carlo Menotti)	14	March 7, 1949
Song of Norway (Robert Wright/George Forrest, based on Grieg)	14	September 13, 1981
10. *Sweeney Todd* (Stephen Sondheim)	13	October 11, 1984

TITLE (COMPOSER)	TOTAL PERFORMANCES	DATE
11. *Porgy and Bess* (George Gershwin)	12	March 31, 1962
12. *Amahl and the Night Visitors* (Gian Carlo Menotti)	10	April 9, 1952
Regina (Marc Blitzstein)	10	April 2, 1953
The Saint of Bleecker Street (Gian Carlo Menotti)	10	March 15, 1965
Silverlake (Kurt Weill)	10	March 20, 1980
13. *The Crucible* (Robert Ward)	9	October 6, 1961 WP
14. *Amelia Goes to the Ball* (Gian Carlo Menotti)	8	October 8, 1948
The Dybbuk (David Tamkin)	8	October 4, 1951 WP
L'histoire du Soldat (Igor Stravinsky)	8	October 16, 1956
15. *Lizzie Borden* (Jack Beeson)	7	March 25, 1965 WP
16. *Die Dreigroschenoper* (Kurt Weill)	6	March 11, 1965
La Loca (Gian Carlo Menotti)	6	September 16, 1979
17. *Show Boat* (Jerome Kern)	5	April 8, 1954
The Wings of the Dove (Douglas Moore)	5	October 12, 1961 WP
18. *Akhnaten* (Philip Glass)	4	November 4, 1984
Before Breakfast (Thomas Pasatieri)	4	October 9, 1980 WP
The Cradle Will Rock (Marc Blitzstein)	4	February 11, 1960
The Golem (Abraham Ellstein)	4	March 12, 1962
Madame Adare (Stanley Silverman)	4	October 9, 1980 WP
Miss Havisham's Fire (Dominick Argento)	4	February 22, 1979 WP
The Most Important Man (Gian Carlo Menotti)	4	March 7, 1971
The Rake's Progress (Igor Stravinsky)	4	September 13, 1984

TITLE (COMPOSER)	TOTAL PERFORMANCES	DATE
The Student from Salamanca (Jan Bach)	4	October 9, 1980 WP
19. *Carrie Nation* (Douglas Moore)	3	March 28, 1968
The Devil and Daniel Webster (Douglas Moore)	3	April 5, 1959
Gentlemen, Be Seated (Jerome Moross)	3	October 10, 1963
The Good Soldier Schweik (Robert Kurka)	3	April 23, 1958
Help! Help! The Globolinks (Gian Carlo Menotti)	3	November 28, 1970
Lily (Leon Kirchner)	3	April 14, 1977 WP
Nine Rivers from Jordan (Hugo Weisgall)	3	October 9, 1968 WP
The Nightingale (Igor Stravinsky)	3	October 3, 1963
Of Mice and Men (Carlisle Floyd)	3	October 13, 1983
The Scarf (Lee Hoiby)	3	April 5, 1959
The Servant of Two Masters (Vittorio Giannini)	3	March 9, 1967 WP
Six Characters in Search of an Author (Hugo Weisgall)	3	April 26, 1959 WP
Summer and Smoke (Lee Hoiby)	3	March 19, 1972
Tale for a Deaf Ear (Mark Bucci)	3	April 6, 1958
The Taming of the Shrew (Vittorio Giannini)	3	April 13, 1958
Troubled Island (William Grant Still)	3	March 31, 1949 WP
Trouble in Tahiti (Leonard Bernstein)	3	April 6, 1958
Wuthering Heights (Carlisle Floyd)	3	April 9, 1959
20. *He Who Gets Slapped* (Robert Ward)	2	April 12, 1959
Maria Golovin (Gian Carlo Menotti)	2	March 30, 1959

Help! Help! The Globolinks was performed by the company in Los Angeles but not in New York.

TITLE (COMPOSER)	TOTAL PERFORMANCES	DATE
Miss Julie (Ned Rorem)	2	November 4, 1965
Natalia Petrovna (Lee Hoiby)	2	October 8, 1964 WP
The Passion of Jonathan Wade (Carlisle Floyd)	2	October 11, 1962 WP
The Tender Land (Aaron Copland)	2	April 1, 1954 WP
The Triumph of St. Joan (Norman Dello Joio)	2	April 16, 1959

Note: The following works were written before the composer's arrival in the United States. By Igor Stravinsky—*Oedipus Rex, L'histoire du Soldat, The Nightingale (Le Rossignol)*. By Kurt Weill—*Die Dreigroschenoper, Silverlake*.

SAN FRANCISCO OPERA

The San Francisco Opera gave its first performance on September 26, 1923, at the Civic Auditorium. Its home since 1932 has been the War Memorial Opera House, capacity 3,252. Including summer festival performance, it has staged 183 different operas. The following list gives its 15 most frequently performed operas through 1984. Unlike the lists of other opera companies, these totals include West Coast tour performances in such cities as Los Angeles, Seattle, and San Diego. Performances by the company's subsidiary groups such as Spring Opera and Western Opera Theater are not included:

OPERA (COMPOSER)	TOTAL PERFORMANCES
1. *La Bohème* (Puccini)	130
2. *Madama Butterfly* (Puccini)	106
3. *Aida* (Verdi)	103
Carmen (Bizet)	103
4. *Tosca* (Puccini)	93
5. *Rigoletto* (Verdi)	80
6. *La Traviata* (Verdi)	78
7. *Don Giovanni* (Mozart)	70
8. *Il Trovatore* (Verdi)	68
9. *The Barber of Seville* (Rossini)	67
10. *Lucia di Lammermoor* (Donizetti)	65
11. *Pagliacci* (Leoncavallo)	53
12. *La Forza del Destino* (Verdi)	52
13. *Faust* (Gounod)	51
Der Rosenkavalier (R. Strauss)	51

OPERA (COMPOSER)	TOTAL PERFORMANCES
14. *Otello* (Verdi)	50
15. *Tristan und Isolde* (Wagner)	49
Die Walküre (Wagner)	49

LYRIC OPERA OF CHICAGO

The Lyric Opera of Chicago was established in 1954 and makes its home in the Civic Opera House, capacity 3,563. Since its inception it has presented 109 different operas. Following are the 15 most frequently performed operas through its 30th season ending December 15, 1984:

OPERA (COMPOSER)	TOTAL PERFORMANCES
1. *La Bohème* (Puccini)	63
2. *Madama Butterfly* (Puccini)	54
3. *Tosca* (Puccini)	49
4. *The Barber of Seville* (Rossini)	46
5. *La Traviata* (Verdi)	38
6. *Rigoletto* (Verdi)	37
7. *A Masked Ball* (Verdi)	36
8. *Carmen* (Bizet)	33
9. *Don Giovanni* (Mozart)	27
10. *Don Pasquale* (Donizetti)	25
11. *Cenerentola* (Rossini)	23
L'elisir d'Amore (Donizetti)	23
12. *Aida* (Verdi)	22
Cavalleria Rusticana (Mascagni)	22
Simon Boccanegra (Verdi)	22
13. *Fidelio* (Beethoven)	21
Lucia di Lammermoor (Donizetti)	21
14. *Pagliacci* (Leoncavallo)	20
15. *Otello* (Verdi)	19
Salomé (R. Strauss)	19

ROYAL OPERA HOUSE (COVENT GARDEN)

The Covent Garden Opera Company was founded in 1946 as the resident company at the Royal Opera House in London. In 1968 it became the Royal Opera, sharing the theater with the Royal Ballet.

Seating capacity is 2,107, with space for 43 standees. Following are the 20 operas it has performed most frequently since its first production, Carmen, on January 14, 1947. The list is complete through the 1983–1984 season:

OPERA (COMPOSER)	TOTAL PERFORMANCES
1. *Aida* (Verdi)	253
2. *Carmen* (Bizet)	235
3. *La Bohème* (Puccini)	230
4. *Tosca* (Puccini)	184
5. *Rigoletto* (Verdi)	165
6. *The Marriage of Figaro* (Mozart)	162
7. *La Traviata* (Verdi)	159
8. *The Magic Flute* (Mozart)	154
9. *Madama Butterfly* (Puccini)	150
10. *Der Rosenkavalier* (R. Strauss)	140
11. *Il Trovatore* (Verdi)	117
12. *Fidelio* (Beethoven)	113
13. *Turandot* (Puccini)	107
14. *Otello* (Verdi)	103
15. *A Masked Ball* (Verdi)	101
16. *Don Giovanni* (Mozart)	96
17. *Cavalleria Rusticana* (Mascagni) *Pagliacci* (Leoncavallo)	94
18. *Peter Grimes* (Britten)	91
19. *Così Fan Tutte* (Mozart)	80
20. *Don Carlos* (Verdi)	76

VIENNA STATE OPERA

The Vienna State Opera (Staatsoper) opened in 1869, when it was known as the Court Opera. It has a capacity of 2,260. It was rebuilt following its destruction by bombs in World War II. Following are the 20 operas it has performed most frequently from its opening through the spring of 1984:

OPERA (COMPOSER)	TOTAL PERFORMANCES
1. *The Marriage of Figaro* (Mozart)	1,084
2. *The Magic Flute* (Mozart)	984
3. *Carmen* (Bizet)	939
4. *Aida* (Verdi)	919

OPERA (COMPOSER)	TOTAL PERFORMANCES
5. *La Bohème* (Puccini)	860
6. *Cavalleria Rusticana* (Mascagni)	848
7. *Fidelio* (Beethoven)	816
8. *Lohengrin* (Wagner)	799
9. *Pagliacci* (Leoncavallo)	792
10. *Der Rosenkavalier* (R. Strauss)	767
11. *Don Giovanni* (Mozart)	764
12. *Madama Butterfly* (Puccini)	756
13. *Tosca* (Puccini)	743
14. *The Flying Dutchman* (Wagner)	693
15. *Tannhäuser* (Wagner)	676
16. *Die Meistersinger* (Wagner)	641
17. *Faust* (Gounod)	622
18. *Die Fledermaus* (J. Strauss)	615
19. *The Abduction from the Seraglio* (Mozart)	610
20. *Rigoletto* (Verdi)	606

METROPOLITAN OPERA TICKET PRICES, 1883–1983

The impact of inflation on the arts has never been illustrated more dramatically than in the sharp rise of ticket prices at the Metropolitan Opera in New York over the last 20 years. For the first 80 years of the Met's 101–year history, prices in all areas of the house held fairly steady, but after that . . . The following chart shows ticket prices at 10-year intervals, starting with the first season, 1883–1884:

YEAR	ORCHESTRA SEAT	FAMILY CIRCLE SEAT	STANDING ROOM	
			ORCHESTRA	FAMILY CIRCLE
1883	$ 6.00	$ 2.00	$1.00	$1.00
1893	5.00	1.50 1.00	1.00	1.00
1903	5.00	1.50 1.00	1.00	1.00
1913	6.00	1.50 1.00	1.00	1.00
1923	6.50	2.00 1.50	1.00	1.00

YEAR	ORCHESTRA SEAT	FAMILY CIRCLE SEAT	STANDING ROOM	
			ORCHESTRA	FAMILY CIRCLE
1933	6.50	1.75	1.00	1.00
		1.50		
1943	6.05	1.65	1.00	1.00
		1.10		
1953	8.00	2.35	2.00	1.25
		1.50		
1963	11.00	3.00	2.00	1.25
	9.50	2.00		
1973	17.50	5.50	2.85	1.75
	16.50	4.00		
1983	65.00	13.00	7.00	5.00
	55.00	12.00		
	45.00			
	38.50			
	35.00			
	30.00			

COMPETITION WINNERS

Competition represents the traditional way of advancement in all fields, but nowhere is it more keen, continuous, and formalized than in the music profession. Competitions are held for musicians in all categories throughout the world, and many artists have made them their path to success. Following are the winners of some of the more prestigious American competitions over the years. The competitions are listed in the order of their year of establishment.

NAUMBURG COMPETITION

The Naumburg Competition was established in 1926 with the original aim of awarding the opportunity of a Town Hall recital to three young musicians. Over the years a number of procedural changes have been made, so that the number of winners varies, and the Town Hall recitals have been replaced by cash awards and other concerts. Naumburg Chamber Music Awards were added in 1965. The following is a list of Naumburg winners:

*1925	Catherine Wade Smith, violinist
	Adeline Masino, violinist
	Bernard Ocko, violinist
1926	Phyllis Kraeuter, cellist
	Margaret Hamilton, pianist
	Sonia Skalka, pianist
1927	Dorothy Kendrick, pianist
	William Sauber, pianist
	Sadah Stuchari, violinist
	Daniel Saidenberg, cellist
	Julian Kahn, cellist
	Sadie Schwartz, violinist
1928	Adele Marcus, pianist
	Helen Berlin, violinist
	Louis Kaufman, violinist
	Olga Zundel, cellist
	George Rasely, tenor
	August Werner, baritone
1930	Helen McGraw, pianist
	Ruth Culbertson, pianist
	Mila Wellerson, cellist
	Louise Bernhardt, contralto
1931	Lillian Rehberg Goodman, cellist
	Marguerite Hawkins, soprano
	Edwina Eustis, contralto
	Kurtis Brownell, tenor
1932	Milo Miloradovich, soprano
	Foster Miller, bass-baritone
	Dalies Frantz, pianist
	Huddie Johnson, violinist
	Inez Lauritano, violinist
1933	Catherine Carver, pianist
	Harry Katzman, violinist
1934	Joseph Knitzer, violinist
	Ruby Mercer, soprano
1935	Benjamin deLoache, baritone
	Judith Sidorsky, pianist
	Aniceta Shea, soprano

---

*The three winners in 1925 were selected after a series of special auditions; the actual formalized Competition started the following year. Where years are omitted, no award was made.

Harvey Shapiro, cellist
Florence Vickland, soprano
Marshall Moss, violinist

1936   Frederick Buldrini, violinist

1937   Jorge Bolet, pianist
Ida Krehm, pianist
Pauline Pierce, mezzo-soprano
Maurice Bialkin, cellist

1938   Carroll Glenn, violinist

1939   Mara Sebriansky, violinist
William Horne, tenor
Zadel Skolovsky, pianist
Gertrude Gibson, soprano

1940   Abbey Simon, pianist
Harry Cykman, violinist
Thomas Richner, pianist

1941   William Kapell, pianist
Robert Mann, violinist
Lura Stover, soprano

1942   Jane Rogers, contralto
Annette Elkanova, pianist
David Sarser, violinist

1943   Dolores Miller, violinist
Constance Keene, pianist
Ruth Geiger, pianist

1944   Jeanne Therrien, pianist
Jean Carlton, soprano
Carol Brice, contralto

1945   Jane Boedeker, mezzo-soprano
Paula Lenchner, soprano

1946   Leonid Hambro, pianist
Jeanne Rosenblum, pianist
Anahid Ajemian, violinist

1947   Berl Senofsky, violinist
Abba Bogin, pianist
Jane Carlson, pianist

1948   Sidney Harth, violinist
Paul Olefsky, cellist
Theodore Lettvin, pianist

1949   Lorne Munroe, cellist

1950	Angelene Collins, soprano Esther Glazer, violinist Betty Jean Hagen, violinist Margaret Barthel, pianist
1951	June Kovach, pianist Laurel Hurley, soprano Joyce Flissler, violinist
1952	Diana Steiner, violinist Yoko Matsuo, violinist Lois Marshall, soprano
1953	Gilda Muhlbauer, violinist Lee Cass, bass-baritone Georgia Laster, soprano
1954	William Doppmann, pianist Jean Wentworth, pianist Jules Eskin, cellist Martha Flowers, soprano
1955	Ronald Leonard, cellist Mary MacKenzie, contralto Nancy Cirillo, violinist
1956	Donald McCall, cellist Wayne Connor, tenor George Katz, pianist
1957	Regina Sarfaty, mezzo-soprano Angelica Lozada, soprano Michael Grebanier, cellist
1958	Joseph Schwartz, pianist Shirley Verrett, mezzo-soprano Elaine Lee, violinist
1959	Howard Aibel, pianist Sophia Steffan, voice Ralph Votapek, pianist
1960	Joseph Silverstein, violinist
1961	Werner Torkanowsky, conductor
1964	Elizabeth Mosher, soprano
1968	Jorge Mester, conductor
1971	Kun-Woo Paik, pianist Zola Shaulis, pianist
1972	Robert Davidovici, violinist

1973	Edmund LeRoy, baritone (First Prize) Barbara Hendricks, soprano Susan Davenny Wyner, soprano
1974	André-Michel Schub, pianist (First Prize) Edith Kraft, pianist Richard Atamian, pianist
1975–1976	50th Anniversary Competition) Dickran Atamian, pianist (First Prize) Santiago Rodriques, pianist Allen Weiss, pianist Clamma Dale, soprano (First Prize) Joy Simpson, soprano (First Prize) Elmar Oliveira, violinist (First Prize) Ani Kafavian, violinist Paul Tobias, cellist
1977	(for Cellists) Nathaniel Rosen (First Prize) Thomas Demenga Georg Faust
1978	(for Flutists) Carol Wincenc (First Prize) Marya Martin Gary Shocker
1979	Peter Orth, pianist
1980	(for Singers) Lucy Shelton, soprano (First Prize) Irene Gubrud, soprano (First Prize) Jan Opalach, bass-baritone (First Prize) Faith Esham, soprano (First Prize)
1981	(for Violinists) Nadja Salerno-Sonnenberg (First Prize)
1982	(for Violists) Thomas Riebl (First Prize) Paul Neubauer (Special Award)
1983	(for Pianists) Stephen Hough (First Prize) David Allen Wehr (Second Prize) William Wolfram (Second Prize)
1984	(for Violinists) (No first prize) Carmit Zori (Second Prize) Ian Swensen (Second Prize)

1985   (for Singers)
              Dawn Upshaw, soprano (First Prize)
              Christopher Trakas, baritone (First Prize)

              NAUMBURG CHAMBER MUSIC AWARDS

1965   Beaux Arts String Quartet

1971   The Contemporary Group (University of Washington)
              University of Michigan Contemporary Ensemble

1972   Speculum Musicae
              Concord String Quartet

1973   Cambridge Consort
              Da Capo Chamber Players

1974   American String Quartet
              Francesco Trio

1975   Calliope—A Renaissance Band

1976   Empire Brass Quintet
              Sequoia String Quartet

1977   Jubal Trio
              Primavera String Quartet

1978   Aulos Wind Quintet
              Emerson String Quartet

1979   New World String Quartet

1980   Liederkreis Ensemble
              New Arts Trio

1981   Muir String Quartet
              Emmanuel Wind Quintet

1983   Colorado String Quartet

1984   Lydian String Quartet
              Aspen Wind Quintet

1985   Meloria String Quartet

METROPOLITAN OPERA AUDITIONS WINNERS

In 1935 the Metropolitan Opera inaugurated a series of radio pro-
grams, under the sponsorship of the Sherwin-Williams Paint Company, called the "Metropolitan Opera Auditions of the Air." Among

the prizes offered was a contract with the company. After the Auditions went off the air, they were taken over by the Metropolitan Opera National Council. Although these public auditions have been held regularly since, their format, prizes, and system of operations have all undergone periodic changes. Winners no longer automatically receive Met contracts, and since 1979 all finalists (usually 11 in number) receive identical awards. The following list of Met Auditions winners is based on information provided by the Metropolitan Opera Archives and the National Council:

1935–1936	Anna Kaskas, Arthur Carron
1936–1937	Maxine Stellman, Thomas L. Thomas
1937–1938	Leonard Warren, John Carter
1938–1939	Annamary Dickey, Mack Harrell
1939–1940	Eleanor Steber, Arthur Kent, Emery Darcy
1940–1941	Mona Paulee, Mary Van Kirk, Lansing Hatfield
1941–1942	Margaret Harshaw, Frances Greer, Elwood Gary, Clifford Harvuot
1943–1944	William Hargrave, Morton Bowe, Hugh Thompson, Regina Resnik
1944–1945	Thomas Hayward, Robert Merrill, Pierrette Alarie (option)
1945–1946	(no awards)
1947–1948	Marilyn Cotlow, Frank Guarrera
1948–1949	Lois Hunt, Denis Harbour
1949–1950	(no awards)
1950–1951	Maria Leone, Paul Knowles, Fred Thomas
1951–1952	Charles Anthony, Arthur Budny
1952–1953	Heidi Krall, Maria Traficante, Robert McFerrin
1953–1954	Louis Sgarro, Albert DaCosta, Marjorie McClung, Christine Cardillo
1954–1955	Louis Quilico, Madelaine Chambers, William Lewis
1955–1956	Carlotta Ordassy, Maria Ferriero, Rose Byrum
1956–1957	Ezio Flagello, Saramae Endich, Charles O'Neill
1957–1958	Martina Arroyo, Lillian Messina, Grace Bumbry, Charles K. L. Davis, Lucille Kailer
1958–1959	Teresa Stratas, Roald Reitan
1959–1960	Mary MacKenzie
1960–1961	George Shirley, Francesca Roberto
1961–1962	Janis Martin
1962–1963	Justino Diaz, Junetta Jones, Russell Christopher
1963–1964	Robert Goodloe
1964–1965	Loretta Di Franco
1965–1966	Karan Armstrong

*1967	Costanza Cuccaro, Sakiko Kanamori, Paula Page
1968	Nancy Shade, Ruth Welting, Gwen Jones
1969	Gilda Cruz-Romo, James Johnson, Eugenie Chopin Watson, Elaine Cormany
1970	Jeannine Altmeyer, Philip Booth, Samuel Timberlake
1971	Barbara Pearson, Thomas McKinney
1972	Christine Weidinger, Jan Redick, Roger Patterson
1973	Douglas Ahlstedt, Cynthia Munzer, Kathryn Bouleyn, Nelda Nelson
1974	Alma Jean Smith, Katherine Ciesinski, Janice Felty
1975	Carmen Balthrop, Marianna Christos, Linda Kowalski
1976	John Carpenter, Ashley Putnam, Sunny Joy Langton
1977	Vinson Cole, Christine Donahue, Elizabeth Parcells
1978	Winifred Brown, Wendy White, Cheryl Studer
**1979	Michael Talley, Robert McFarland, Jane Bunnell, Susan St. John, Dianne Iaucco, Robert Overman, Delores Ziegler, Natalia Rom, Sandra McClain, Pamela Hicks, Jan Opalach
1980	Lauren Wagner, Thomas Woodman, Darren Nimnicht, Kevin Langan, Louise Deal-Pluymen, John Fowler, Leslie Richards, Margaret Vazquez, Lani Norskog, Marjo Carroll, Robin Reed
1981	Susan Dunn, Lawrence Bakst, Gail Dobish, Joyce Guyer-Hiller, Laurence Albert, Valerie Yova, Laura Rice, Gail Dubinbaum, Rebecca Cook, Thomas Hampson, Diane Kesling
1982	Nancy Gustafson, Lucille Beer, Hei Kyung Hong, Walter MacNeil, Katherine Ritz, Kathleen Segar, Pamela Coburn, Carla Cook, Sylvia McNair, Angela Blasi, Eduardo Villa
1983	Ellen Kerrigan, Alessandra Marc, Elizabeth Holleque, Herbert Mells Perry, Jo Ann Pickens, Stella Zambalis, Jean Marie Glennon, Joanne Kolomyjec, Harolyn Blackwell, Cecily Nall, Linda Caple
1984	Elaine Arandes de Celis, Philip Bologna, Richard Croft, Gerald Dolter, Marcus Haddock, Theresa Yvonne Hamm, Cynthia Lawrence, Emily Manhart, Lisa Saffer, Nova Thomas, Jonathan Welch
1985	Stephen Biggers, Maryte Bizinkauskas, Philip Cokorinos, Richard Cowan, Julia Faulkner, Anne Johnson, Victoria Livengood, Deborah Voight, Karen Williams, Margaret Jane Wray, Donna Zapola

---

*Format changed to single year designation.
**From this year on, all finalists divided the award equally, with no "winners" designated.

LEVENTRITT AWARDS

The Leventritt Foundation was established in 1939 with the intent of furthering the careers of exceptionally talented young artists. From 1940 to 1976 Gold Medal Awards were made through international competitions. Since then, the Awards have been made by a panel of musicians who have observed the young performers over a period of time. Winners are engaged for a concert with the New York Philharmonic. Following are the Leventritt Awards over the years (where a year is omitted, no Gold Medal Award was made):

1940	Sidney Foster, pianist
1941	Erno Valasek, violinist
1943	Eugene Istomin, pianist
1944	Jeanne Therrien, pianist
1945	Louise Meiszner, pianist
1946	David Nadien, violinist
1947	Alexis Weissenberg, pianist
1948	Jean Graham, pianist
1949	Gary Graffman, pianist
1954	Van Cliburn, pianist
1955	Betty Jean Hagen, violinist
	John Browning, pianist
1957	Anton Kuerti, pianist
1958	Arnold Steinhardt, violinist
1962	Michel Block, pianist
1964	Itzhak Perlman, violinist
1965	Tong Il Han, pianist
1967	Kyung Wha Chung, violinist
	Pinchas Zukerman, violinist
1969	Joseph Kalichstein, pianist
1981	Cecile Licad, pianist

VAN CLIBURN INTERNATIONAL PIANO COMPETITION

The Van Cliburn International Piano Competition, established in 1962, is normally held at four-year intervals in Fort Worth, Texas. A cash award of $12,000, plus recital and recording engagements, is given to the top contestant, with other prizes also offered. The winners have been:

1962 1. Ralph Votapek, United States of America
      2. Nikolai Petrov, Union of Soviet Socialist Republics

      3. Mikhail Voskresenski, Union of Soviet Socialist Republics
      4. Cécile Ousset, France
      5. Marilyn Neelēy, United States of America
      6. Sergio Varella-Cid, Portugal-England
      7. Arthur Fennimore, United States of America
      8. Takashi Hironaka, Japan

1966 1. Radu Lupu, Romania
      2. Barry Snyder, United States of America
      3. Blanca Uribe, Colombia
      4. Maria Luisa Lopez-Vito, Philippines
      5. Rudolf Buchbinder, Austria
      6. Benedikt Kohlen, Germany

1967 1. Cristina Ortiz, Brazil
      2. Minoru Nojima, Japan
      3. Mark Westcott, United States of America
      4. Gerald Robbins, United States of America
      5. Diana Walsh, United States of America
      6. Michiko Fujinuma, Japan

1973 1. Vladimir Viardo, Union of Soviet Socialist Republics
      2. Christian Zacharias, Germany
      3. Michael Houstoun, New Zealand
      4. Alberto Reyes, Uruguay
      5. Evgenii Korolev, Union of Soviet Socialist Republics
      6. Grassimir Gatev, Bulgaria

1977 1. Steven De Groote, South Africa
      2. Alexander Toradze, Union of Soviet Socialist Republics
      3. Jeffrey Swann, United States of America
   *4. Christian Blackshaw, England
       Michel Dalberto, France
   *5. Ian Hobson, England
       Alexander Mndoyants, Union of Soviet Socialist Republics

1981 1. André-Michel Schub, United States of America
   *2. Panayis Lyras, United States of America
       Santiago Rodriguez, United States of America
      3. Jeffrey Kahane, United States of America
      4. Christopher O'Riley, United States of America
      5. Zhu Da Ming, People's Republic of China

---

*Tie.

1985　1. José Feghali, Brazil
　　　2. Philippe Biaconi, France
　　　3. Barry Douglas, United Kingdom
　　　4. Emma Takhmizian, Bulgaria
　　　5. Károli Mocsári, Hungary
　　　6. Hans-Christian Wille, Germany

AVERY FISHER PRIZES

The Avery Fisher Artist Program, established in 1974, gives Prizes to artists of outstanding professional ability, consisting of a cash award of $10,000, major appearances, and other career assistance. (The Program also gives Career Grants to talented young instrumentalists at earlier stages of their career.) The Program is not a formal competition; recipients are selected by a recommendation panel of musicians. Until 1981, the top nominee sometimes received a Recital Award rather than a Prize, but this is no longer given. Following is a list of Prize and Recital Award winners:

1975　Lynn Harrell, cello (Prize)
1975　Murray Perahia, cello (Prize)
1976　Ani Kavafian, violin (Recital Award)
　　　Heidi Lehwalder, harp (Recital Award)
　　　Ursula Oppens, piano (Recital Award)
　　　Paul Schenly, piano (Recital Award)
1977　André-Michel Schub, piano (Recital Award)
　　　Richard Stoltzman, clarinet (Recital Award)
1978　Yo-Yo Ma, cello (Prize)
1979　Emanuel Ax, piano (Prize)
1980　Richard Goode, piano (Prize)
1981　(no award)
1982　Horacio Gutiérrez, piano (Prize)
1983　Elmar Oliveira, violin (Prize)
1984　(no award)
1985　(no award)

RICHARD TUCKER AWARD

The Richard Tucker Music Foundation, Inc., established in memory of the Metropolitan Opera tenor who died in 1975, gives an annual award of $20,000 to a promising young American singer. Winners since the inception of the Award have been:

1978   Rockwell Blake, tenor
1979   Diana Soviero, soprano
1980   Barry McCauley, tenor
1981   J. Patrick Raftery, baritone
1982   (no award)
1983   Susan Dunn, soprano
1984   Roger Roloff, baritone
1985   Aprile Millo, soprano

PULITZER PRIZES IN MUSIC

This is an award for a composition by an American (prior to 1977, by a composer resident in the United States) in the larger forms of chamber, orchestral, or choral music, or for an operatic work or a ballet score. The award originally $500, now is $1,000. It was established in music in 1943. The following list gives the winners since then, with the title of their prize-winning compositions:

1943   William Schuman: *Secular Cantata No. 2, A Free Song*
1944   Howard Hanson: *Symphony No. 4*
1945   Aaron Copland: *Appalachian Spring*
1946   Leo Sowerby: *The Canticle of the Sun*
1947   Charles Ives: *Symphony No. 3*
1948   Walter Piston: *Symphony No. 3*
1949   Virgil Thomson: *Louisiana Story*
1950   Gian Carlo Menotti: *The Consul*
1951   Douglas Moore: *Giants in the Earth*
1952   Gail Kubik: *Symphony Concertante*
1953   (no award)
1954   Quincy Porter: *Concerto for Two Pianos and Orchestra*
1955   Gian Carlo Menotti: *The Saint of Bleecker Street*
1956   Ernst Toch: *Symphony No. 3*
1957   Norman Dello Joio: *Meditations on Ecclesiastes*
1958   Samuel Barber: *Vanessa*
1959   John La Montaine: *Concerto for Piano and Orchestra*
1960   Elliott Carter: *String Quartet No. 2*
1961   Walter Piston: *Symphony No. 7*
1962   Robert Ward: *The Crucible*
1963   Samuel Barber: *Piano Concerto No. 1*
1964   (no award)
1965   (no award)
1966   Leslie Bassett: *Variations for Orchestra*
1967   Leon Kirchner: *Quartet No. 3*

1968 George Crumb: *Echoes of Time and the River*
1969 Karel Husa: *String Quartet No. 3*
1970 Charles Wuorinen: *Time's Encomium*
1971 Mario Davidovsky: *Synchronisms No. 6*
1972 Jacob Druckman: *Windows*
1973 Elliott Carter: *String Quartet No. 3*
1974 Donald Martino: *Notturno*
      (Special Citation to Roger Sessions)
1975 Dominick Argento: *From the Diary of Virginia Woolf*
1976 Ned Rorem: *Air Music*
      (Special posthumous award to Scott Joplin)
1977 Richard Wernick: *Visions of Terror and Wonder*
1978 Michael Colgrass: *Déja Vu for Percussion and Orchestra*
1979 Joseph Schwantner: *Aftertones of Infinity*
1980 David Del Tredici: *In Memory of a Summer's Day*
1981 (no award)
1982 Roger Sessions: *Concerto for Orchestra*
      (Special Citation to Milton Babbitt)
1983 Ellen Taaffe Zwilich: *Three Movements for Orchestra*
1984 Bernard Rands: *Canti del Sole*
1985 Stephen Albert: Symphony, RiverRun

Menotti, Piston, and Carter have each won it twice; no one has ever won it three times.

MUSICAL AMERICA'S MUSICIANS OF THE YEAR

Musical America, which is published by *High Fidelity* magazine, annually selects a Musician of the Year for "outstanding contribution to serious music on an international basis." Winners since the award's inception have been:

1960 Leonard Bernstein, conductor
1961 Leontyne Price, soprano
1962 Igor Stravinsky, composer
1963 Erich Leinsdorf, conductor
1964 Benjamin Britten, composer
1965 Vladimir Horowitz, pianist
1966 Yehudi Menuhin, violinist
1967 Leopold Stokowski, conductor
1968/9 Birgit Nilsson, soprano
1970 Beverly Sills, soprano
1971 Michael Tilson Thomas, conductor

1972   Pierre Boulez, conductor
1973   George Balanchine, choreographer
1974   Sarah Caldwell, conductor
1975   Eugene Ormandy, conductor
1976   Arthur Rubinstein, pianist
1977   Placido Domingo, tenor
1978   Alicia de Larrocha, pianist
1979   Rudolf Serkin, pianist
1980   Zubin Mehta, conductor
1981   Itzhak Perlman, violinist
1982   Jessye Norman, mezzo-soprano
1983   Nathan Milstein, violinist
1984   James Levine, conductor
1985   Philip Glass, composer

The 25 designees include 9 conductors, 5 singers, 4 pianists, 3 violinists, 3 composers, and 1 choreographer.

STEREO REVIEW'S CERTIFICATE OF MERIT WINNERS

Stereo Review magazine annually awards a Certificate of Merit for "outstanding contributions to the quality of American musical life." Winners usually alternate between the classical and popular fields. The following have received awards:

1975   Mabel Mercer, jazz singer
1976   Jascha Heifetz, violinist
1977   Arthur Fiedler, conductor
1978   Richard Rodgers, composer
1979   Beverly Sills, opera singer
1980   Earl Hines, jazz pianist
1981   Aaron Copland, composer
1982   Benny Goodman, clarinetist, band-leader
1983   Eugene Ormandy, conductor
1984   Frank Sinatra, pop singer
1985   Isaac Stern, violinist

The only names to appear on both magazines' (*High Fidelity* and *Stereo Review*) lists are Beverly Sills and the late Eugene Ormandy.

THE TWENTY MOST FREQUENTLY RECORDED MODERN SINGERS

This list, derived from the 1985 Artist Issue of the *Schwann Record & Tape Guide*, indicates the number of currently available LP records and albums for each singer:

Dietrich Fischer-Dieskau, baritone	119
Placido Domingo, tenor	84
Luciano Pavarotti, tenor	54
Christa Ludwig, mezzo-soprano	51
Joan Sutherland, soprano	51
Janet Baker, mezzo-soprano	49
Nicolai Gedda, tenor	48
Robert Tear, tenor	47
Kurt Equiluz, tenor	44
Sherrill Milnes, baritone	44
Peter Schreier, tenor	44
Elly Ameling, soprano	42
Maria Callas, soprano	42
Montserrat Caballé, soprano	41
Edith Mathis, soprano	40
José Carreras, tenor	39
Paul Esswood, counter-tenor	38
Lucia Popp, soprano	38
Jan de Gaetani, mezzo-soprano	37
Marilyn Horne, mezzo-soprano	37

Included are 6 sopranos, 6 mezzo-sopranos, 5 tenors, 2 baritones, and 1 counter-tenor.

GOLD RECORDS—-CLASSICAL

The Record Industry Association of America regularly presents Gold Record Awards for best-selling recordings. For certification a record must sell copies worth at least $1,000,000 at the wholesale level.

Since the program started in 1958, nearly 2,400 Gold Album Awards have been made to 33-⅓ rpm long-playing records. Of these, only a few have been connected with classical music—and some of the connections have been pretty remote. Following is a list of Gold Record winners that use classical music or artists, along with their labels and year of issuance:

Tchaikovsky: *Piano Concerto No. 1 in B-flat*, Van Cliburn, pianist	RCA	1961
Tchaikovsky: *1812 Overture*, Antal Dorati, Minneapolis Symphony	Mercury	1963
Eugene Ormandy with the Philadelphia Orchestra and Mormon Tabernacle Choir in *The Lord's Prayer*	CBS	1963
Eugene Ormandy with the Philadelphia Orchestra and the Temple University Choir in *The Glorious Sound of Christmas*	CBS	1963
Handel: *Messiah*, Eugene Ormandy with the Philadelphia Orchestra and the Mormon Tabernacle Choir	CBS	1963
Gershwin: *Porgy and Bess* (sound track)	CBS	1963
Switched-On Bach (Walter Carlos—Moog Synthesizer)	CBS	1969
Jean-Pierre Rampal and Claude Bolling performing *Suite for Flute and Jazz Piano*	CBS	1980
Placido Domingo and John Denver, *Perhaps Love*	CBS	1982
Royal Philharmonic in *Hooked on Classics*, Vol. I	RCA	1982
Royal Philharmonic in *Hooked on Classics*, Vol. II	RCA	1982

A PRACTICAL LIST OF REFERENCE BOOKS

"Practical" means that these books are currently in print and accessible. All—along with many others—have been useful in the preparation of this book:

HARDCOVER

Baker's Biographical Dictionary of Musicians, 7th ed. Nicolas Slonimsky. Schirmer Books, 1985. 2,600 pages. $95. Authoritative, complete; the indispensable work on composers and performers.

International Cyclopedia of Music and Musicians. Oscar Thompson, Nicolas Slonimsky, eds. Dodd, Mead and Company. 11th rev. ed., Bruce Bohle, ed. 2,511 pages. $69.95. 1985. The most comprehensive and useful one-volume general reference work.

Music in Western Civilization. Paul Henry Lang. W. W. Norton & Company. 1941. 1,107 pages. $34.95. The best general history of music; a classic.

The New Grove's Dictionary of Music and Musicians. Stanley Sadie. Grove's Music Dictionaries, Inc. 1980. 20 volumes, approximately $2,000. The most extensive as well as expensive of all musical reference works. Get your local library to order a set.

The New Kobbé's Complete Opera Book. The Earl of Harewood. G. P. Putnam's Sons. 1922 rev. 1972. 1,694 pages. $25. Excellent for plot and background of standard operas.

The Simon & Schuster Book of the Opera. 1979. 512 pages. $32.50. Looks like a coffee-table book, but is actually an informative guide, including many unusual and obscure works.

PAPERBACK

Dictionary of Music. Theodore Karp. Northwestern University Press. 1983. 448 pages. $4.95. Comprehensive, concise, and useful.

Harvard Concise Dictionary of Music. Don Michael Randel. Belknap Press. 1978. 577 pages. $6.95. Extensive in coverage, especially on 20th century.

New College Encyclopedia of Music. J. A. Westrup and F. L. Harrison. Revised by Conrad Wilson. W. W. Norton & Company. 1960. 608 pages. $12.95. Authoritative and complete, often from a British perspective.

Schwann Record & Tape Guide. ABC Schwann Publications. $1.95. Issued monthly. Useful not only for record listings but for dates, spellings, and panoramic view of the current recording picture.

LIST OF ACKNOWLEDGMENTS

To the author, at least, no list is more important than this one, for it acknowledges the many institutions, organizations, and individuals that have contributed information, assistance, advice, and suggestions to the making of this book. I wish to offer them, as well as to any whose names I may have inadvertently omitted, my heartfelt thanks:

INSTITUTIONS AND ORGANIZATIONS

American Federation of Musicians, Local 802
American Symphony Orchestra League
Boston Symphony Orchestra
Chicago Symphony Orchestra
Cleveland Orchestra
Van Cliburn International Piano Competition
Avery Fisher Artist Program

J. B. Keller Associates
Keynote Magazine
Leventritt Foundation
Lyric Opera of Chicago
Metropolitan Opera
Metropolitan Opera Archives
Metropolitan Opera National Council
Walter W. Naumburg Foundation
New York City Opera
New York Philharmonic
New York Public Library
   Library of the Performing Arts
   Cathedral Branch
Philadelphia Orchestra
Queensborough Public Library
   Forest Hills Branch
   Jamaica Main Library
Royal Opera Company, Covent Garden, London
San Francisco Opera Company
Richard Tucker Music Foundation
Vienna State Opera
Edgar Vincent-Cynthia Robbins Associates

INDIVIDUALS

Helen Atlas
Christie Barter
Lisa Battersby
T. Roland Berner
Terry Blackburn
Richard Blackham
Dr. Richard Bletschacher
Sara Brzowsky
Shirley Burke
Robert Carver
Sedgwick Clark
Kevin Copps
Kensington Davison
M. L. Falcone
Lois Farber
Shirley Fleming
Francesca Franchi
Anita Goss
H. W. Heinsheimer
Joyce Idema

Gida Ingrassia
Judith Karp
Chester Lane
Francis Little
Koraljka Lockhart
Sybil Mailman
George Martin
Audrey Michaels
John Molleson
Karen Kriendler Nelson
Danny Newman
Guy Olson
John Orr
Sheila Porter
Mrs. William L. Porter
David Reuben
Klaus G. Roy
Robert Tuggle
Dorothy Waage
Susan Woelzl
Thayer Woodcock

INDEX of
COMPOSERS

INDEX of
COMPOSITIONS

233

BOSTON PUBLIC LIBRARY

3 9999 02284 475 5

WITHDRAWN
No longer the property of the
Boston Public Library.
Sale of this material

Boston Public Library

COPLEY SQ
GENERAL LI

ML63
.K88
1985

The Date Due Card in the pocket indicates the date on or before which this
book should be returned to the Library.

Please do not remove cards from this
pocket.